Economics for Management and the Professions

Also by Graham Donnelly: The Firm in Society,
Longmans 1981.

ECONOMICS FOR MANAGEMENT AND THE PROFESSIONS

Graham Donnelly

Longman
London and New York

Longman Group Limited
Longman House, Burnt Mill, Harlow
Essex CM20 2JE, England
Associated companies throughout the world

Published in the United States of America
by Longman Inc., New York

First published 1985

British Library Cataloguing in Publication Data
Donnelly, Graham
  Economics for management and the professions.
  1. Managerial economics
  I. Title
  330'.024658   HD30.22
ISBN 0-582-29644-7

Library of Congress Cataloging in Publication Data
Donnelly, Graham.
  Economics for management and the professions.

  Bibliography: p.
  Includes index.
  1. Economics. I. Title.
HB171.5.D614   1985   330   84-19416
ISBN 0-582-29644-7

Set in Linotron 202 10/12pt Palatino
Produced by Longman Singapore Publishers (Pte) Ltd.
Printed in Singapore

CONTENTS

21 *The financial structure of international trade*

The gold standard – Floating and fixed exchange rates – The International Monetary Fund – International liquidity

22 *International economic organisations*

GATT – Customs unions and free trade areas – The European Economic Community and its institutions – Achievements of the EEC – Multinational companies – Economic impact of the multinationals – Control over the multinationals

PREFACE

In introducing this text I am aware of the need to explain why yet another introductory book on economics is thought necessary. For some time I have felt that the needs of two groups of students were not adequately recognised and I have referred to them in the title. Both groups have a number of common elements to their studies. Firstly they are required to study economics as part of their examination programme even though they may have little interest in the subject and often see it as peripheral to their vocational employment. Secondly they are often studying on a day-release or evening basis and therefore have little time to spend on reading. Thirdly they are frequently maturer in years than many other groups reading the subject for the first time, and may find many introductory texts a little patronising. Finally they are more likely to approach the subject from a practical perspective rather than seeing it as an academic discipline to be studied out of interest alone. It is hoped that this text, with its questioning approach and emphasis on the relationship of economic problems to practical business situations, will appeal to these two groups. All the main areas of economics are examined and, while not every element of all professional and management syllabuses is guaranteed to be included, the book should be suitable for all the principal examining bodies' Foundation examinations, and beyond in some cases. In addition it is hoped that some topics will be of interest to 'A' Level and other students seeking an alternative approach to their primary text.

Where, in the text, reference is made to either manager or professional these terms are not intended to be mutually exclusive since it is anticipated that most able professional students will eventually be performing managerial functions while good management requires, by definition, a professional attitude. The case studies and questions at the end of each chapter are not intended to be representative of the sort of questions to be encountered by students in their examinations but to provide a variety of exercises to provoke thought, comment and argument. Individual groups of students will, no doubt, obtain guidance from tutors on their own examination requirements.

Finally a word of thanks for all those people who made helpful comments and suggestions in the preparation of the manuscript and especially to Stuart Wall who read the manuscript in its entirety and pointed to a number of improvements. Special thanks, too, for the typing, proof-reading and other support I was lucky to receive from a very able assistant.

Graham Donnelly, 1985.

ACKNOWLEDGEMENTS

We are grateful to the following for permission to reproduce copyright material:

Bank of England for table 9.1 from table C p 236 *Bank of England Quarterly Bulletin* (June 1983); European Community Statistics Office for figs 22.1, 22.2 *Statistical panorama of Europe*; The Controller of Her Majesty's Stationery Office for table 13.2 *Department of Employment Gazette* (1984), table 19.2, 14.1 & figs 13.2, 18.3, 18.4 *Economic Progress Report*, tables 7.1, 20.5 *Annual Abstract of Statistics* (1984), figs 15.4 *Economic Trends* (April 1983), 20.1 *Economic Trends* (Jan 1984), 10.1, 17.1 *Economic Trends* (April 1984); National Institute of Economic and Social Research for table 19.3 *National Institute Economic Review*.

Chapter 1

THE SCOPE OF ECONOMICS

It is customary when introducing an academic discipline to begin by examining the scope and nature of the discipline. In the case of economics this is especially necessary; not because of the reader's ignorance of the existence of the major economic problems but rather the reverse. All but the very young are aware of the major economic problems which confront society and the effect these have on their own lives and it is this awareness, coupled with the frequent failures of society to deal with these problems, which has contributed to the formation of attitudes towards the study and application of economics which are often hostile or cynical. These attitudes themselves discourage people engaged in practical business situations from studying economics. It is the aim of this opening chapter, therefore, to examine the nature and purpose of economics and the extent to which it can be useful to the manager, either as a tool of management or as an indicator of the framework within which he takes his decisions.

Economics as a social science

Economics is one of a group of disciplines, which also includes Sociology and Political Science, which used the scientific methods of observation, experimentation and research in studying the behaviour of society. While the social sciences may to some extent be able to predict behaviour and the results of various courses of action there are limitations on this ability far greater than those imposed on the natural sciences like physics and chemistry where a given experiment will always yield similar results provided the conditions are identical each time. This is because the social sciences do not work within situations where the conditions are identical each time but instead are engaged in the field of human behaviour where circumstances are constantly changing and behaviour patterns are never entirely predictable. Thus the social sciences are concerned more with predicting trends and likelihoods rather than exact results and even these predictions may have to be altered over time with evolving circumstances.

The area of social activity with which economics is concerned is the allocation of scarce resources between the various demands made upon them. How individuals or societies decide on the allocative process will clearly depend on the nature of the individual and of society, the influence of cultural, historical and sociological factors and the nature of the prevailing political system. This interrelationship of economics with other fields of human behaviour and attitudes not only makes the study of economics in isolation a fruitless task, it also gives a clue to the sources of the critical attitudes encountered by economists. Economists are frequently accused of being unable to agree among themselves. In fact all economists are agreed as to the basic issues and problems of economics; where they differ is in the matter of solutions, priorities and methods. Such differences are inevitable given that economists, like the society from which they have emerged, are subject to political, historical and cultural influences in the formation of their own attitudes. Because he is concerned with an area of study directly related to the quality of human existence it is difficult to envisage an economist achieving the same degree of detached observation exhibited by the geologist or astronomer dealing with natural phenomena. The second major criticism levelled at economists is their inability to provide solutions to the problems they encounter. In fact it is more likely to be the implementation of a solution that presents the bigger difficulty. If an economist by research or observation were able to provide a potential solution to a particular economic problem this solution would not be adopted if it were found to be politically or socially unacceptable. In the final analysis only society itself can solve its economic problems.

Economics as a study of the problems of resource allocation

Every economic society is confronted with the fundamental problem of how to allocate the scarce resources available to it in the face of unlimited demands for those resources. Scarcity in the economic sense means that however plentiful the resource in question it is sufficiently limited in supply that, if it were free, total demand could not be satisfied, and thus the resource is able to command a price. In this sense all resources, whether human, capital or natural, are scarce, with the exception of air. In allocating its scarce resources society must solve three fundamental problems:

1. What shall be produced – what goods and services and in what quantity shall society choose to produce with the limited resources at its disposal?
2. How shall these goods be produced – what combinations of the available resources and what technological processes shall be employed in producing these goods and services?
3. For whom shall they be produced – how is society to allocate the goods and services produced when the supply can never satisfy the demand?

These problems are common to all economic decision-takers whether they be the individual deciding his own pattern of consumption, the firm planning and executing its production activities or the government taking collective decisions for society as a whole. Each decision taken involves a choice and in making a choice in favour of one alternative another is lost. The individual may choose to buy a refrigerator and abandon plans for a new television, the firm may opt for the installation of new machinery and cut back on its advertising budget, the government may increase expenditure on defence and reduce its funding of local authorities. In each case a choice made results in a cost – the cost of the alternative next best use to which the resources so used could have been put. This cost is known as *opportunity cost* and all economic decisions must contain an element of this cost. Because the economist assumes that human behaviour is rational (however strong the evidence to the contrary) a particular economic decision is regarded as being at the time when it is made the decision entailing the least opportunity cost. If an individual buys a refrigerator instead of a new television it must be assumed that at the time this choice involved a smaller opportunity cost and therefore greater satisfaction than if he had decided in favour of the television. While at times the behaviour patterns of individuals, firms or governments may seem to the observer quite irrational it must be assumed that the decisions taken were in fact rational, partly because different individuals and groups have different views of what constitutes the best use of their resources and partly because to attempt to base any study of human behaviour on its irrationalities would be impossible.

Collectively individuals, firms and the government make up the economic society which is moulded in its aims and ambitions by the other values and goals of society with which it comes into contact. Thus the prevailing economic system in any society is the result of the mixture of the social, political and ethical values of that society in addition to the customary practices through which economic decisions as to the use of resources are made. Comparisons between different economic systems, therefore, must be made not only in terms of their relative efficiency but also in terms of the costs incurred in relation to the other aims of society. The proponent of a particular economic system may argue that within that system the economic benefits more than compensate for any detrimental effects on society or even that the system actually increases the likelihood that other aims in society will be met. Attempts to identify particular economic systems encounter the familiar problem of distinguishing between the economic as opposed to the political system. All the great political theorists have recognised that political power rests with those groups in society which possess economic power. So the economic system may be the foundation on which the political system rests or it may be manipulated to produce a distribution of economic resources appropriate to the balance of political power, rather than be regarded as the means by which society's resources may be used most effectively. In the Middle Ages the feudal system consciously aimed to harmonise economic, political and social objectives to ensure the maintenance of the status quo and tried to achieve this through a formalised social structure and established patterns of economic behaviour. Ultimately the feudal system could no longer restrain the development of new economic practices and the growth of the merchant classes and it gradually fell apart to be replaced by the rudimentary capitalist ethic of Mercantilism in the sixteenth and seventeenth centuries. The decline of state control over economic activity from this period on opened the way for the political economists of the late eighteenth century and after to adopt new approaches to evaluating the economic system. This culminated in the formulation of 'ideal' economic societies which, though much altered since then, remain the main forms of economic society recognised in modern times.

Economic systems

'Laissez-faire' or free enterprise system

Within a pure *laissez-faire* or free enterprise economic system the problems of resource allocation are solved by the price mechanism. Thus resources go to those who can afford to pay for them, whether they want them for use in production or for consumption. Those early political economists who saw the *laissez-faire* system as an ideal, notably the French physiocrats and also Adam Smith, believed that such an economic system represented a return to a system of natural harmonies and that each man, by pursuing his own best interest, unconsciously worked for the good of all. Therefore there was no role whatever for the state in the economy since government regulations directed the economy from its natural course and inhibited economic growth and encouraged the self-interest of privileged groups to the detriment of society as a whole. Left to itself the natural economic order would promote an environment to stimulate competition and counter the natural tendency of businessmen to act against the public interest.

The events of the nineteenth century in which the faith of the early economists in the natural harmony of the *laissez-faire* system was shown to be unfounded led to a more cynical reappraisal of the worth of the system. Confronted by the poverty and misery endured by the economically weak under a system of virtually unbridled free enterprise, later liberal economists had to admit that the *laissez-faire* system did not guarantee a better economic condition for the whole of society. They maintained, however, that its worth in terms of the promotion of economic growth justified its existence. Indeed the economically weak were held to be partly to blame for their own suffering since the fruits of economic growth were bound to go to those, like the capitalist and the entrepreneur, who contributed the most to economic growth, and thus those who could not or would not take a decisive economic role had inevitably to enjoy a return on their labours commensurate with their contribution. This later *laissez-faire* liberalism with its acceptance of economic hardship as a fact of life still represents the modern, if muted, view of those who support minimal interference by government in the economic affairs of the nation.

The centrally-controlled economy

The modern centrally-planned economy is loosely based on the Marxist reaction to the evils of nineteenth-century *laissez-faire* economies. The view of Marx that the state acting as the will of the people could achieve a just and prosperous economic society and then itself become unnecessary has been distorted to justify the rise of all-powerful state economies which determine the allocation of resources ostensibly on behalf of the people but frequently without reference to their views. The questions of What, How and For Whom are settled by the Central Planning Committee with reference to the current National Plan and its stated priorities. The individual retains some control over his expenditure patterns but is subject to the availability of the goods he wishes to purchase. The inevitable problem of excess demand is not solved by market forces acting through the price mechanism but by rationing and waiting lists. By extolling the virtues of co-operation against the wasteful tendencies of competition the centrally-planned economy aims at self-sufficiency and is suspicious of foreign trade where overseas competition may pose a threat to its own industries.

The mixed economy

The mixed economy differs from the *laissez-faire* and centrally-planned economies in that it is not based on a theoretical model devised as a perfect economic system and it cannot therefore be compared against a theoretical ideal. Furthermore the absence of an absolute standard means that it is possible for the mixed economy to take many different forms. Thus while all mixed economies contain elements, substantial elements, of both individual and collective decision-making, the precise balance between the two sectors may vary substantially from one country to another and, over a period, may vary considerably within one country. In practice all economies have elements of both free enterprise and state direction. There is no evidence that there has ever been a pure free-enterprise society and even during the peak period of *laissez-faire* economics in the middle of the nineteenth century the state still exerted considerable influence over certain sectors of economic activity and found itself intervening, albeit unwillingly, in those areas where there were acute resource allocation problems. Similarly all modern state-directed economies tolerate a degree of private enterprise on a small scale and much more occurs unofficially. What distinguishes the mixed economy from the other types of economic system is that it is the only one in which the presence of private enterprise alongside a substantial public sector is regarded as both necessary and desirable. The nature of the mixed economy will be examined further in the next chapter when the British mixed economy will be discussed.

Economics as a managerial tool

So far economics has been examined both as a social science and as a study of the problems of resource allocation. These two areas expose economics as a discipline which can neither give exact answers concerning human behaviour in the allocation of scarce resources nor predict without error the exact response of society to a given economic occurrence. Furthermore the interrelationship of economics with politics and other social phenomena means that no economic event is capable of repeating exactly previous similar events. Thus in any given economic problem a number of possible solutions will present themselves and all will have some validity. The precise solution proposed by an economist will depend on his own personal views as to the optimum least-cost alternative taking into account the society within which the problem has presented itself, the political and social conditions impinging on any solution offered and his own informed estimate as to the likely outcome of adopting that solution. Clearly there will be many different interpretations to be placed on any given evidence and when this is combined with variations as to attitude and the precise goal to be achieved there will be a whole range of possible solutions. What therefore is the use of economics to the business manager or professional consultant when it can produce a bewildering range of problems and solutions any, or none of which, may be relevant to the success of his business?

Economics is capable of being a valuable aid to the manager on three levels. Firstly, the manager who understands how the economy works will be better placed to interpret the information he receives as to economic trends and forecasts and how this will affect his company and its activities. Secondly, on an active level he will be able to adapt his company's overall policy with all that this entails for the changing economic climate. Thirdly, within the company he can use economics as a tool in helping to make the best use of its resources. On each of these levels economics impinges on the decision-making of the manager because all firms are concerned directly with the three basic economic questions of what to produce, how to produce it and for whom to produce. Thus economics interrelates with such areas as the production function, costing, accounting and marketing and provides at the same time an overview of the economic environment within which decisions in these areas must be taken.

Case for discussion

Your company is a manufacturer of high-technology engineering equipment which has had a successful sales record over the past five years though as yet your markets have been limited to Western Europe and the United States. The director responsible for overseas marketing is keen to enter the East European market and initial contacts with two East European embassies have shown evidence of interest on their part. All future discussions must be conducted via the appropriate ministry in each country through whom the purchasing of overseas engineering goods is made. Before proceeding further the director has asked you to discuss the project with him and to consider in particular the following points:

1. What special problems arise for a Western manufacturing company attempting to establish a market in a communist country compared to an untried Western market?
2. Given that normal marketing techniques are of little use in a communist country what steps are open to you to increase the attractiveness of your products to the potential market and make possible users aware of them?
3. What advantages are there to a firm from a capitalist country trading in a communist country compared to attempting to establish itself in new free-enterprise markets?

Chapter 2

THE BRITISH ECONOMIC SYSTEM

In the last chapter the various economic systems were classified as three main types; *laissez-faire*, planned and mixed economies. When applying these broad classifications to real economies throughout the world certain qualifications are necessary. In order for any economic system to survive it must also evolve so that the modern mixed economy is different both in balance and in emphasis to that of thirty years ago. Furthermore the economic system in a particular society is the unique result of the historical, social, political and legal factors which have moulded its development as well as the economic evolution which has taken place. Thus the planned economies of the Soviet Union and China exhibit many differences despite their origins in Marxist–Leninist economic thought.

Like all other economies that of the United Kingdom has evolved from one form to another over the centuries. However, just as there was no one year or decade when feudalism can be said to have disappeared or was abolished the modern mixed economy was beginning to take shape even before it was recognised as a separate form of economic system. It has its roots in the reaction to the worst excesses of the *laissez-faire* economic system which held ideological sway in the early nineteenth century but which yielded unacceptable consequences in practice. The idealisation of the freedom of the individual and his ability to control his own economic destiny was meaningless cant when applied to the typical factory worker or agricultural labourer who were not only subject to economic laws outside their control but still suffered the consequences of the agricultural protectionism which the landed classes refused to relax. By the time that the Corn Laws were repealed in 1846 in the name of free trade the state had already become heavily involved in legislation aimed at remedying the abuses resulting from unbridled free enterprise in industry. While social reformers pleaded for change on humanitarian grounds the great movements for factory, education, poor law and public health changes gained ground both because the working classes gradually increased their effectiveness in combined action and because powerful interests became converted to the economic advantages to be gained from reform. While early reforms were often motivated by fear of social unrest their results did not signal lower profits or a weakening of economic progress and opposition to reform subsided. Economists realised that national income depended in part on the efficiency of labour and that whatever increased this efficiency ultimately increased the wealth available for distribution. Thus they gave their support to reforms which improved the working environment and so the quality of labour. Furthermore, reforming employers, like Cadbury, Lever and Salt, found that productivity was improved when their employees were given better living and working conditions. In consequence, often unwillingly, the state was increasingly drawn into regulation of the economy, a process accelerated in the present century by two world wars and a great depression. Indeed, in the twentieth century the nature of the British mixed economy has undergone fundamental changes. Before the First World War the role of the government was seen as primarily regulatory with minimum direct involvement in the economy but from 1914 to the outbreak of the Second World War the government found itself both directing and aiding industry and unable to disentangle itself from a key responsibility for economic matters. After 1939 the government gradually assumed the role of primary responsibility for the well-being of the economy and accepted a direct influence over the conduct of industry, the achievement of economic growth and the maintenance of living standards.

The evolutionary path followed by the British mixed economy is not, however, linked solely to economic development. In order for it to survive it must, like other economic forms, be accompanied by a compatible political structure which accepts, reinforces and manipulates the prevailing economic system. Unless these two are in some degree of harmony the resultant friction will lead to conflict and the eventual decline of one or the other. As to the question which of these, the political or the economic sphere, controls the form of the other it would appear that in most cases economic conditions change first and then the new economically powerful groups are able to control the political system, if necessary after a revolution. The new political elite then holds on to power even when economic forces are moving against it until it too is eventually forced to give way. If, however, a political revolution occurs during a period of social and economic turmoil, as in Russia in 1917, the new political rulers may be able to impose a new economic order in line with their political order.

The modern politico-economic environment

While Britain can be said to have had the rudiments of a mixed economy in the 1930s, when the government tried to counter the hardships of the depression through assistance to industry and various social welfare programmes, the mixed economy in its modern form began with the major shift in emphasis initiated by the first majority Labour government, elected in 1945. The relative failure of government attempts to deal with the problems of the 1930s had led the Labour Party to adopt a policy of greater state intervention in the economy to avoid a repeat of the problems of mass unemployment and economic stagnation while at the same time establishing a welfare state to remove the problems of individual economic hardship. Basing much of its policy on the Beveridge Report on Social Welfare and the Keynes White Paper on Full Employment the new government established the National Health Service, a comprehensive system of social welfare and state ownership of many of the country's key industries and also accepted a principal role in the management of the economy.

Such had been the change in attitude towards the proper role of government in the mixed economy in the previous decade that when the Conservatives were returned to office in 1951 they continued to accept the principle of government management of the economy and made only minor attempts to reverse the national isation programme which had been carried out by Labour. Indeed there was so little difference between the two major parties on economic matters at this time that the phrase 'Butskellism' was coined to describe the similar economic policies of R. A. Butler, the Chancellor of the Exchequer, and Hugh Gaitskell, his Labour predecessor and later Shadow Chancellor. The overlap between the two parties was so great that there was little room for a centre party and in the 1950s the Liberal Party all but disappeared, gaining only around 2 per cent of the vote at the 1955 General Election. During the thirteen years of Conservative government after 1951 there was sustained economic growth and rising living standards, although a series of balance of payments and sterling crises led to regular interruptions of growth by the government to restore international confidence, necessitating the dampening of the domestic economy. The government of Harold Macmillan readily identified itself with the economic progress of the late 1950s and early 1960s but in claiming the credit for economic success it lay itself open to the blame for failure and the Labour government elected in 1964 came to power as a moderate party claiming to have a better set of managers for an economy showing signs of strain. During the late 1960s, however, this strain became more apparent with growth slowing and both inflation and unemployment rising to post-war heights. In the 1970s the consensus between the parties on economic policy was breaking down. The Conservatives, first under the leadership of Edward Heath and later, more emphatically, under Margaret Thatcher, aimed to halt the increasing involvement of the government in the economy and to achieve a decisive shift back towards a more free-market oriented system. In the Labour Party, meanwhile, the defeat at the General Election of 1970 was blamed by those on the left of the party on the fact that the government had not been socialist enough in its policies. While the right-wing of the party retained control in the 1974 government many of its policies were evidence of a movement in the party's centre of gravity to the left. After the electoral defeat in 1979 the divisions within the party became even more apparent with many MPs of the social democrat tradition leaving the party or failing to be reselected for their constituencies while more radical economic policies were adopted by the party, notably with regard to the extension of public ownership and withdrawal from the Common Market.

In the 1980s the political situation in Britain has become more uncertain than at any time since the Second World War. The failure of the British economy to solve its problems in the previous two decades has led to both the major parties seeking new solutions, though with limited success. The fact that Britain has a mixed economy means that any government must take into account the views of powerful pressure groups in the formulation of its economic policies. The alternative is to follow the path of confrontation with all that implies for the well-being of the economy and thus its own economic aims. Unless a government is prepared to adopt measures which would go beyond the limits of acceptable behaviour in a parliamentary democracy it can only tinker with the mixed economy, it cannot alter its fundamental nature. Thus while the Conservative government elected in 1979 and 1983 has certainly shifted the balance of the economy by its policy of privatisation there are limits on the extent to which it could privatise the welfare state before it encountered concerted and powerful opposition. Furthermore modern governments are more than ever confronted by pressures outside their control such as world economic conditions or decisions taken by supra-national organisations of which they are members, such as the Common Market. Yet despite the many constraints on the freedom of action of governments, not least the attitudes of the society in which they operate, they are none the less increasingly held to blame for national economic failure. This has resulted both in a greater willingness on the part of the electorate to throw out governments after one term of office and also a weakening of traditional voting patterns leading to massive swings against governments at by-elections and a steady increase in protest voting. This latter trend contributed to the resurgence of the Liberal Party in the 1960s and 1970s and the growth of nationalism in Scotland and Wales.

The mixed economy and private enterprise

The greater emphasis placed by the present Conservative government on the solution of economic problems through a reliance on market forces reflects to some extent the view that the mixed economy is itself the source of many modern economic problems. This particular view stems from the recognition that the mixed economy is based on a number of conflicting ideas. On the one hand there is an acceptance of the profit motive as the main incentive for economic activity while at the same time there is an insistence on the restraint of free enterprise to protect the interests of the community in general and the weaker members of society in particular. Furthermore it gives the government a key role in economic affairs, both directly through the public sector and indirectly through its management of the economy and this leads to another paradox. While the government is expected to act decisively in dealing with major economic problems the mixed economy is closely identified with democratic political institutions so that action requires lengthy consultations with interested parties to attempt to reach agreement, perhaps through compromise. Where a government does intervene in the economic environment it may arouse suspicion and some antipathy in the private sector if such activity appears counter to business interests. Thus free enterprise may seem to be under attack from an ever-growing barrage of government regulations, inspired both by the objectives of national and EEC authorities and the aims of the various pressure groups seeking to influence the government. Such a view of private business initiative weighed down by government legislation is not new; in the 1940s Joseph Schumpeter advanced the argument that capitalism would eventually destroy itself by introducing so much welfare legislation to counter the problems created by free market forces. This would cause entre-preneurial activity to both diminish and become less effectual as the potential profit ceased to be adequate compensation for the risk-taking involved. In the post-war period the growth in size of the public sector has itself seemed to pose problems for the success of private enterprise. Firstly, the government, by taking a greater share of total national expenditure, has naturally increased its in-fluence over the availability and allocation of resources. Secondly, governments have used their own activities in the industrial sector to influence the policies of firms in the private sector, as in the case of prices and incomes policies. Thirdly, public sector monopolies could use their power to compete unfairly or charge excessive prices to their private sector customers. Finally the availability of safe investment opportunities in the public sector may deter inves-tors from taking up riskier capital opportunities in the private sector despite the fact that these may represent a more efficient use of resources.

Criticisms of the impact of government economic activity on the private sector in a mixed economy must, however, be tempered by the undoubted advantages which have accrued to British industry through the development of the mixed economy, particularly where government intervention has acted to stimulate economic growth and where it has been directed at assisting specific indus-tries or firms. In fact direct government involvement in the econ-omy has arisen initially usually because of the failures of free market forces to deal with the problems and crises they had cre-ated. Social legislation in the nineteenth century was a reaction to the inability of the *laissez-faire* system to enable every individual to control his own economic circumstances; government management of the economy in the present century was shown to be necessary by the failure of market forces to cure the depression of the 1930s; many of the industries nationalised after 1945 had shown them-selves incapable of raising the capital necessary for their long-term survival, notably coal and the railways. Industry and commerce in general have benefited from an economic environment in which government management of demand has promoted stability and market growth to a degree unlikely to occur under the conditions produced by free market forces. Furthermore however successful an individual firm or industry it has undoubtedly benefited from the assistance given to weaker sectors of the economy if these have made patterns of economic activity less volatile and ensured the maintenance of a healthy economic infrastructure in terms of transport, communications, primary products and the provision of funds for research and development. In any case while industry may resent the interference of government in its activities it has not been slow in seeking government regulation of trade where this would be of benefit nor of seeking financial support when required. It would be unrealistic to expect that the benefits of government support of the economy could be gained without paying the price of greater government direction of the ways in which enterprise is conducted. Thus in the modern mixed economy the reduced scope for unrestricted profit-making is in part a counterweight to the reduced risks encountered by much of modern private enterprise in an economy partly sheltered by government activity from the full impact of economic forces.

Although the private sector is regulated to a degree far greater than that in the past it need not take a purely passive stance when confronted by government supervision of its activities. In the mixed economy the government must win the support of some of the key interests represented in society and its policies will reflect this. Furthermore the government can be expected to respond to economic events which could affect its record and thus its chances of re-election. In this context firms and industries can, like trade unions and other economic pressure groups, coax, cajole and coerce the government into responding positively to their wishes if failure to do so could seriously harm an important part of the economy and so reflect adversely on the government. Unfortunately government support may be dependent on the potential dangers of not taking action rather than on the merit of a particular request for help; an industry employing large numbers of the workforce and backed by a strong trade union is more likely to receive help than a small industry. The government is not merely responsive to economic power, however, since it will also respond to changing social attitudes in the electorate–though these may have economic implications as in the case of legislation to give equal employment opportunities. On the other hand social pressures must have some electoral force if they are to achieve major successes; in West Germany environmentalist groups have had much more success in curbing industrial pollution than have their British counterparts because of the greater influence of the environmental lobby in politics, particularly because of the electoral success of the Green Party.

The mixed economy and the role of the entrepreneur

In the idealised theory of *laissez-faire* capitalism the entrepreneur is an heroic figure. His contribution to economic society is the organisation of the other factors of production; Land, Labour and Capital. Yet in performing this function the entrepreneur is not purely a manager or administrator carrying out tried and trusted policies since the entrepreneurial function possesses other characteristics too. Firstly the entrepreneur is an innovator introducing new products or services or new methods of supplying existing products or services. Secondly the entrepreneur is a risk-taker, willing to back his own ideas with capital and effort without the guarantee of financial reward. Thirdly the entrepreneur receives no wage or salary but a profit after all costs have been met. During the heyday of the Industrial Revolution the facts appeared to support the theory and the great 'Captains of Industry' were seen as justifying the profits they made on the basis of their contribution to the economy, and therefore to society as a whole. Yet as the nineteenth century wore on the less seemly side of entrepreneurial activity became more difficult to ignore; rash ventures using other people's funds, unscrupulous dealings with rivals, profits increasingly earned through monopoly power rather than entrepreneurial skill, the exploitation of workers and a lack of concern for ethics in dealings with customers. Legislation was now enacted to deal with the economic problems created by unrestrained free enterprise as well as with the unpleasant social side-effects which had long been recognised. In addition by the end of the century many successful companies were into the third generation of the original founder and the current owners were thus not entrepreneurs but the inheritors of wealth, indistinguishable in outlook and attitude from their contemporaries from much older wealthy families. In short the role of the entrepreneur, always treated with some contempt by the upper classes, was now regarded by the middle classes too as less attractive than the professions or mere idleness.

In the twentieth century the development of the modern mixed economy has weakened still further the attractions of entrepreneurial activity, not only because of economic developments but also because of social change. The development of a system of universal free education has made it increasingly less likely that an intellectually able individual will receive virtually no education and will leave school with no choice but to become a self-made man or woman, a likelihood further reduced by the growth of the welfare state. For the most able in our society the choice of careers is much greater than it was fifty years ago and the attractions of a prestigious and rewarding career in the professions may be expected to push into the background such entrepreneurial instincts as most people possess. Even those who do go into industry will tend to join a large company where the scope for individual initiative is muted and where the role of the entrepreneur is diffused among a number of departments. Thus the modern industrialist is more likely to be a manager working within a bureaucratic organisation and subject to an array of government regulations rather than being able to make quick decisions based on his own judgement or knowledge. Furthermore the mixed economy's suspicion of the entrepreneur may lead the manager to take a subdued line on his entrepreneurial talents and instead emphasise the social role his company performs in order to maintain a good public image.

Yet despite the less favourable economic, social and legal conditions confronting the modern entrepreneur such individuals still exist and presumably always will provided that potential profits provide a sufficient incentive for risk-taking. Indeed to talk of the entrepreneurial spirit withering away is as illogical as saying that the urge to gamble can be removed from society – and gambling has in the past been subject to far more legislative and social condemnation than has enterprise. The continued survival and formation of small firms is the strongest evidence that there is a permanent stream of new entrepreneurial talent.

The main forms of economic enterprise in the mixed economy

The majority of economic production units in the British economy remain small private firms. In this category, however, three distinct forms of organisations exist.

(a) *The sole proprietor.*   Here ownership is vested in one person who is alone responsible for all decision-making and the raising of capital, though there may be several other people working in the business. It is in this type of organisation that the entrepreneur can be most easily identified as all the functions of the entrepreneur are united in one person. Not all sole proprietors are innovators, many take over established businesses, but they all risk their own capital and take the profits or losses which result from their efforts. Though the sole proprietor enjoys the unity of purpose and flexibility of a small organisation the price of failure can be very high since the sole proprietor bears unlimited liability for the debts of the business and may lose his personal property and possessions if the business fails. Failure is quite common as many sole proprietorships are established by people with little or no commercial experience who lack the expertise necessary for success. In consequence most sole proprietorships have difficulty in raising capital to get started or even to expand a successful operation because they are not attractive propositions to the potential backer. Sooner or later the sole proprietorship which wishes to expand must consider going into partnership or forming a limited company.

(b) *The partnership.* Prior to the advent of limited liability in the middle of the last century the partnership was the normal step-up from the growing sole proprietorship. The advantages of partnership were that in addition to increased funds the firm would gain by each partner contributing a particular expertise or area of goodwill. Unfortunately partnerships also suffered from unlimited liability, a problem magnified when each partner was responsible for the debts incurred in the business by the others. Although the institution of limited partnerships has largely removed this particular problem there is little to recommend the partnership as a business form when compared to the limited liability company and it survives now mainly in the professions where the expertise of the firm, rather than its capital resources, are of paramount importance.

(c) *The limited company.* In a joint-stock company the shareholders contribute capital jointly for the purpose of carrying on the business. Except in the rare case of the unlimited company the shareholders enjoy limited liability and are thus only responsible for the debts of the company to the extent of their individual shareholdings. Limited liability is an attractive inducement to potential investors, therefore, but is a disadvantage to creditors of the company who may already experience difficulty in realising their assets should something go wrong with the company. The potential abuses arising out of limited liability delayed its being generally permitted until modern times but it has now been adopted by the vast majority of larger enterprises and there are now over 600,000 limited liability companies registered in the United Kingdom.

Unfortunately there are limits on the amount of new capital which can be raised by the small private limited company since new shares cannot be offered for sale to the public and the transfer of existing shares is hampered by the lack of a market in the shares. The largest firms, therefore, tend to be public limited companies (Plcs) which have access to larger injections of capital through their ability to offer for sale new share issues to the public. There are over 50,000 public limited companies registered in the United Kingdom though many of these are subsidiaries of larger companies and the top 200 or so are the companies which dominate British trade and industry.

Despite the importance of the main forms of business organisation in the mixed economy there are of course many sections of the economy dominated by other forms of enterprise, most notably the various public corporations and other bodies which make up the public sector and dominate such areas as energy, transport (public) and communications. The public corporations attempt to combine commercial viability with public accountability and to counter the need to be profitable with that of providing a service based on social needs. In a sense they sum up the dilemma of the mixed economy–how to maintain the profit motive while at the same time balancing this with social and ethical responsibility. The nationalised industries represent one way in which economic society has attempted to resolve the problems of industrial organisation thrown up by the evolution of the market economy but there also remain vestiges of the many alternative ways of economic organisation attempted as a counter to the growth of big business in the past hundred years or so. Thus there are the building societies and friendly societies, mostly associated with life assurance, where profits are not distributed to shareholders but are ploughed back into the business for the benefit of members of the society, or policy-holders. The co-operative movement with its distribution of profits on the basis of expenditure with the society rather than shareholdings grew up out of a desire to protect the interests of the consumers in their dealings with wholesalers and retailers though today it is barely distinguishable from other High Street shops. The relative lack of development of the co-operative movement, especially into manufacturing, leads inevitably to the public corporation being the only option available for industrial development in the mixed economy other than through the capitalist private sector. A number of firms, however, most notably the John Lewis Partnership, do operate schemes involving part-ownership of the company by the workforce – though frequently such schemes are a token gesture rather than a serious attempt at shared ownership.

Question for discussion

Consider to what extent the role of the entrepreneur is assisted or hindered in the British economy by the existence of the following 'pillars' of British society:

1. Strong Parliamentary majorities for governing parties.
2. The public school system.
3. The welfare state.
4. Special relationships with the Commonwealth and the EEC.
5. The perceived importance of tradition and evolution in society.
   Why might the entrepreneur fare better in both the United States and a communist country like Hungary?

Chapter 3

THE NATURE OF MARKETS

It has frequently been asserted that economics is capable of being summed up in the phrase 'Supply and Demand' and there is some truth in this since the concepts of supply and demand are at the heart of economics. The fundamental problem of economics is that of scarcity and the supply of and demand for scarce resources interact in the market to decide the problem of allocation. These economic terms; 'the market', 'supply and demand', 'market forces', are used in everyday speech to describe patterns of resource allocation but very often the same terms are used to describe very different economic phenomena. Thus the market may be freely accessible or subject to barriers to entry, demand and supply may be static or volatile, market forces may be the result of independent decisions by producers and consumers or may be manipulated by strong individuals or groups acting within the market. In addition to the internal pressures of the market there are also the external constraints imposed by the behaviour of other related markets and, especially in a mixed economy, the impact of the government and its agencies, whether as a consumer or a supplier or through its economic and legal regulation of the market. If, therefore, an attempt is to be made to formulate some basic truths about the behaviour of markets in general it is necessary to begin by examining a market in which there are no external influences and in which the forces of supply and demand operate as freely as possible and are not manipulated by powerful interests acting within the market. Such a market is, by its nature, unlikely to exist in the real world since it would be a perfect market in an imperfect world; so the perfect market is used as a convenient hypothesis.

For a perfect market to exist the following conditions would apply:

1. All goods produced in the market would be homogeneous. They would therefore be unbranded and identically packaged.
2. All buyers and sellers would have perfect knowledge of what is happening in the market so that no individual producer could charge higher prices than another due to the ignorance of a consumer that he could obtain the product more cheaply elsewhere.
3. Neither buyers nor sellers would be able individually to influence the market price by their activities. Each producer would contribute only a very small part of total production and each consumer take up only a very small part of that production so that any change in the activity of any one producer or consumer would have too small an impact to affect the prevailing market price. There would also be no co-operation between either groups of buyers or groups of sellers.
4. There would be perfect mobility of those resources used in production, i.e. the factors of production, so that entrepreneurs could move from one sphere of operations to another without difficulty. Similarly buyers would have perfect mobility within the market so that choosing to go to one seller rather than another would involve no cost, either in monetary terms or in time. Unless all the producers are in one place this would involve the ability to transport oneself from one place to another instantaneously.

Were it possible to obtain the conditions for a perfect market the allocation of resources would be determined solely by the interaction of supply and demand via the working of the price mechanism.

Demand

In economic terms demand is meaningless without reference to price. Demand refers to the willingness or ability of the consumer to purchase a certain quantity of a product at a given price rather than a vague desire for the product. As price changes the quantity demanded will also change for obvious reasons. Firstly, as the price falls more potential consumers will be able to afford the product and thus come into the market. Secondly a lower price means that existing consumers will be able to buy more of the product without any increase in expenditure. Thirdly, a lower price will lead to some consumers switching expenditure from other products to the now more attractive product. If the price of a product rises the re-

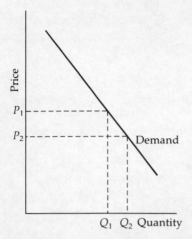

Fig. 3.1

verse will happen. Thus, other things being equal, demand will vary inversely with price and this results in the downward-sloping demand curve (Fig. 3.1).

In Fig. 3.1 a fall in the price from P_1 to P_2 leads to an increase in the quantity demanded from Q_1 to Q_2. At each point on the demand curve the quantity demanded can be found for a particular price. Since only one price can prevail in a perfect market at any one time the demand curve is a projection of quantity demanded at all other prices and therefore assumes that other things are equal, i.e. that there is no change in any other factor which might affect demand. If there were to be a change in some other influence on demand it would not be possible to show this on the existing demand curve since demand would change without any accompanying change in price. To take an example a fall in the price of a product could be expected to lead to an increase in the quantity demanded and a movement along the existing demand curve but a rise in incomes, an increase in the population, a change in fashion or taste towards the product or a rise in the price of a substitute for the product can also be expected to increase demand with price remaining constant. The effect of a change in one of these conditions of demand will result in a new demand curve showing more being demanded at all prices and to the right of the old curve. Similarly if there were a change in one of the conditions of demand leading to a fall in demand at all prices there would be a new demand curve to the left of the old curve. These are shown in Fig. 3.2.

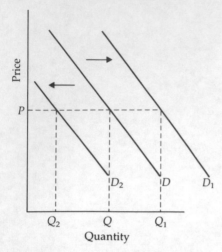

Fig. 3.2

While the demand curve indicates the quantity that will be demanded at different prices it cannot, on its own, determine the price that will prevail in the market. This only becomes apparent with a knowledge of the market supply curve.

Supply

The supply of a product is influenced by fewer variables than is demand. The most important factor is again the price of the product. The higher the price the greater the quantity supplied as producers see the opportunity to make higher profits. A market supply curve will therefore slope upwards and to the right to illustrate the quantity supplied at each price (Fig. 3.3).

However, there are circumstances in which a producer would find it possible to increase supply without any rise in price. Thus a fall in the cost of production, an improvement in the state of technology and a fall in the price of other goods which the producer could supply may lead him to increase production with price remaining constant. This would result in a rightward shift of the supply curve with more being supplied at whatever price prevails in the market. Similarly, a deterioration in the conditions of supply would lead to a leftward shift in the supply curve. Both these circumstances are shown in Fig. 3.4.

A comparison of the demand and supply curves reveals that if

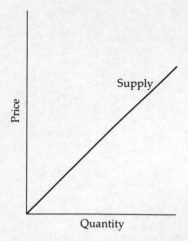

Fig. 3.3

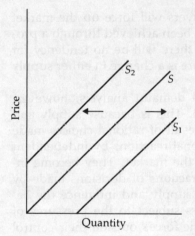

Fig. 3.4

they are plotted on the same graph the two curves will intersect. If they did not there would be no price at which both suppliers and buyers would enter the market and therefore no market in that product. The point at which the two curves intersect is the equilibrium price for the product and is the only maintainable price because it is the only one at which the quantities supplied and demanded are equal. In Fig. 3.5 at any price above P there will be an excess of quantity supplied over quantity demanded and the market price will fall as suppliers try to dispose of stocks. At any price below P there will be an excess of quantity demanded over quantity

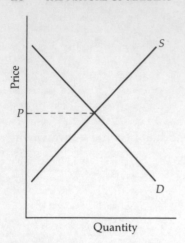

Fig. 3.5

supplied and competition among buyers will force up the market price. Once the equilibrium price has been achieved through a process of trial and error in the market there will be no tendency for the market price to change unless there is a change in either supply or demand conditions.

Difficulties arise with supply and demand analysis, however, when it is applied to the real world. This is because supply and demand conditions cease to be the result of rational choices made by independent consumers and rational reactions by independent suppliers in response to changes in the market. They become instead the result of the complex interactions of decisions made by suppliers with the ability to control supply and influence the behaviour of consumers, by consumers subject to the pressures of suppliers, governments and economic forces outside their control and by the government itself which as supplier and consumer and as regulator of economic forces can strongly influence the nature of supply and demand. It is not the case that supply and demand analysis have no place in the real world – rather that market forces are complicated and are frequently the result of supply and demand conditions acting simultaneously either in the same or in opposite directions. The practical use of supply and demand analysis can be seen on occasion, however, in a sequence of relatively straightforward interactions of supply and demand. For example, automatic calculators were highly expensive in the early 1970s and barely portable so that ownership was confined to a small minority, primarily for commercial use. The impact of micro-technology enabled both a reduction in price and of size so that far more people could afford to buy them and they became truly pocket calculators. This new availability of electronic calculators was accompanied by a change in social custom so that people who ten years previously would not have considered ownership of one now possessed them by the late 1970s – they being often accompanied by other gadgets. By 1980 the pocket calculator was so cheap both to produce and to buy that it had ceased to be a luxury and had become a throwaway item performing a social convenience. This sequence of events could be shown graphically, as in Fig. 3.6.

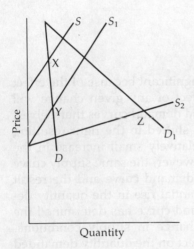

Fig. 3.6

The original demand and supply curves for small electronic cal-culators are D and S which intersect at the equilibrium point X. New technology enables more calculators to be supplied at each price leading to a new supply curve S_1 and the equilibrium is now where S_1 intersects D, i.e. at Y where a greater quantity is de-manded at a lower price. The tremendous growth in popularity of the new cheap calculators is represented by a new demand curve D_1 but while this could be expected to cause the price to rise this did not happen since at the same time ever-improving technology together with the reduced costs following from mass production enabled supply to shift further to the right to S_2, resulting in a new equilibrium of Z. This example illustrates what is perhaps the crucial point in understanding supply and demand analysis – the actual sequence of events. Thus when price rises we would quite reasonably expect that the quantity demanded will fall; yet if de-

mand rises so that there is a rightward shift in the demand curve
price will rise so that the price and quantity demanded actually
move in the same direction. In the first case demand was responding to a change in price while in the second, demand was the cause
of the change in price. Similarly, if supply responds to a price
change it is to be expected that the quantity supplied will move in
the same direction as price whereas if supply itself shifts price itself
will respond to the change in supply. The reader might find it
worthwhile to see if supply and demand analysis can be used to
explain how it is that with a world glut of oil, petrol prices in the
UK have gone up in the early 1980s.

Elasticity of demand

Changes in supply and demand are significant because of the effect
they have on the market but the effect of any given change will
depend on the shape of the supply and demand curves themselves.

In Fig. 3.7(a) the supply curve has shifted to the right resulting
in a substantial fall in price but a relatively small increase in the
quantity demanded. In Fig. 3.7(b), however, the same supply curve
is shifted to the right on a different demand curve and the result
is a marginal fall in price but a substantial rise in the quantity demanded. Thus the shape of the demand curve has determined the
impact on the market of a given change in supply conditions.
Furthermore it has determined the effect on the quantity demanded

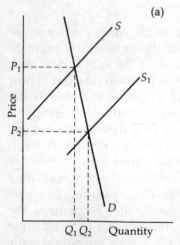

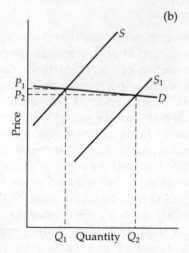

Fig. 3.7(a) & (b)

of the price change resulting from a shift in supply. The responsiveness of the quantity demanded to a given price change is known as the **price elasticity of demand** and can be given an approximate mathematic value by the formula:

$$\text{Price elasticity of demand} = \frac{\% \text{ Change in quantity demanded}}{\% \text{ Change in price}}$$

If this ratio yields an answer greater than one demand is elastic and a fall in price will lead to a rise in the revenue received by the supplier, e.g. if a cut in price of 20 per cent led to a rise in quantity demanded of 40 per cent the price elasticity of demand would be 2 and total revenue would rise, while if with the same price cut the quantity demanded rose by only 10 per cent the price elasticity of demand would be only $\frac{1}{2}$ and revenue would fall. Normally the elasticity of demand will vary at each price except in the extreme theoretical cases where demand is perfectly elastic (an infinite horizontal demand curve), perfectly inelastic (an infinite vertical demand curve) or possesses an elasticity of exactly one along the whole length of the demand curve – in this last case any change in price will have no effect on the revenue received by the supplier.

The price elasticity of demand for a product will depend on three main factors:

1. The availability of close substitutes. The closer the substitute available the more elastic will be demand. Thus while the demand for cigarettes as a whole is inelastic that for most brands is elastic.
2. The proportion of the consumer's income spent on the product. The smaller the proportion of income spent on a product the more inelastic the demand, e.g. the doubling of the price of a box of matches would have very little impact on the demand.
3. The time during which a price change has its effect. The longer the time period after a change in price the greater the opportunity for substitution to occur and thus the more elastic the response to the price change. A sudden rise in petrol prices may initially have little effect on the demand for petrol but after a few weeks consumers may have had time to reorganise their travel through greater use of car-sharing or public transport.

Using these criteria one would normally expect cheap goods and necessities to be inelastic in demand and luxury items and goods differentiated only by their brand names to be elastic in demand. However, elasticity in this context is price elasticity of demand and it is possible that demand may also vary in intensity to changes other than price such as changes in income or changes in the price of other goods; in short to changes in the conditions of demand.

Cross-elasticity of demand measures the responsiveness of demand to a change in the price of a complementary or substitute product; the closer the relationship of the two products in question the greater will be the cross-elasticity of demand. Thus if two products are merely different brands of the same product and are therefore close substitutes a cut in the price of one brand could normally be expected to lead to a shift towards that brand from its rival so that the demand of the latter could fall dramatically as the result of a price cut in the former. An obvious example is petrol where few consumers care about which brand they buy but are on the whole extremely price-conscious so that the prices charged by the main petrol distributors are never out of line for more than a few days since the cross-elasticity of demand between them is so high. On the other hand there are those products which are substitutes to some extent but have a much lower cross-elasticity such as petrol and gas as alternative means of driving an internal combustion engine. With regard to complementary goods the higher the cross-elasticity of demand the stronger the relationship between the two products. Thus a substantial rise in the price of petrol could have an effect on the demand for cars in general, large cars in particular and even some impact on the demand for tyres.

$$\text{Cross elasticity of demand} = \frac{\%\text{ Change in quantity demanded of product X}}{\%\text{ Change in price of product Y}}$$

In theory it is possible to hypothesise an elasticity of demand related to many of the conditions of demand such as changes in population or changes in the distribution of income or in the national income itself. In practice the most important of these is **income elasticity of demand**. This measures the responsiveness of demand to a change in income and is found by the formula:

$$\text{Income elasticity of demand} = \frac{\%\text{ Change in quantity demanded}}{\%\text{ Change in money income}}$$

Clearly some allowance must be made for the problem of inflation or else a doubling of money income is a meaningless increase if prices have also doubled. On the whole an increase in real income can be expected to increase the demand for luxury goods and to reduce the demand for very inferior goods. When this principle is applied to elasticity this results in there being a number of different positions of income elasticity of demand for the same product as income changes (Fig. 3.8).

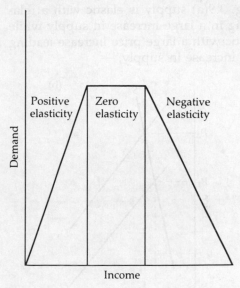

Fig. 3.8

In Fig. 3.8 as income rises consumption rises from zero and income elasticity is positive (it may be either positively elastic or positively inelastic). As income rises further demand becomes static and elasticity reverts to zero. Eventually further income rises may result in a fall in demand and income elasticity becomes negative (again this may be elastic or inelastic). In theory it is possible for all products to proceed through this cycle as with technological progress and rising incomes yesterday's luxuries may become today's necessities and tomorrow's inferior goods. In practice as income rises there will be a tendency for the demand for goods to reach a plateau once income has risen sufficiently to permit desired demand to be achieved, with further increases in income being allotted to those other goods for which desired demand remains greater. Demand will only decline for those goods which are bought because income does not allow the purchase of anything better until income rises.

Elasticity of supply

Supply is also subject to the principle of elasticity so that a given increase in demand may result in either a proportionately large or proportionately small increase in quantity supplied as a result of the ensuing price rise. In Fig. 3.9(a) supply is elastic with a relatively small price rise resulting in a large increase in supply while in Fig. 3.9(b) supply is inelastic with a large price increase leading to only a relatively moderate increase in supply.

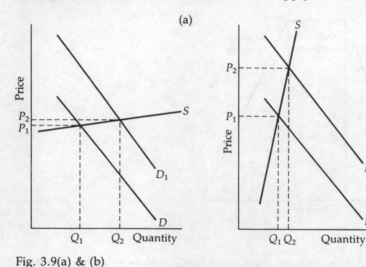

Fig. 3.9(a) & (b)

Price elasticity of supply can be quantified by the formula:

$$\text{Price elasticity of supply} = \frac{\% \text{ Change in quantity supplied}}{\% \text{ Change in price}}$$

The elasticity of supply will depend on the ability or willingness of suppliers to respond to a change in price, which itself depends on the following factors:

1. The rate at which costs rise when output increases. Higher prices will only stimulate additional output if the extra revenue so earned exceeds the extra costs incurred in increasing output. If a firm is already enjoying economies of scale and is producing at its optimum output level any increase in production will inevitably involve higher costs per unit for the extra output. This is because the firm will have to attract factors of production

away from other industries and in so doing will push up the prices of these factors and therefore of its own costs. The faster that costs rise with each extra unit of output the less elastic will be supply.

2. The length of time under consideration. If there is a sudden or sharp rise in demand it may be impossible for supply to respond for a time and during this period it will be totally inelastic. Thus a sudden series of power cuts would lead to a rise in the demand for candles but even if higher prices were offered manufacturers could not instantaneously increase output. Within a fairly short time, however, candle manufacturers could, through overtime working and greater use of existing machinery, push up output in response to higher prices. If market demand were now to be sustained at a higher level over a long period manufacturers could consider increasing the scale of output with new plant and machinery to bring down unit cost and thus offer the prospect of higher profits. In the long term supply would become more elastic so that the longer the time period in question the greater the elasticity of supply.

The issues raised by supply and demand analysis and the concept of elasticity are of economic significance both to firms and to government and in the next chapter the theory so far outlined is applied to the activities of these two sectors.

Revision test

1. What are the main conditions necessary for a perfect market?
2. Explain the phrase 'the working of the price mechanism'.
3. What are the main factors influencing demand other than price?
4. The statement 'An increase in demand causes an increase in supply' is not correct, though often stated. Explain the sequence of events to which the statement refers.
5. What are the main factors affecting elasticity of demand?
6. Why is the supply elasticity of cassette tapes higher than that of wheat?
7. Why are supply conditions more predictable than demand conditions?
8. Consider the different advantages of being producers of necessity and luxury goods.
9. Use demand and supply analysis to explain why in the present

century the demand for blacksmiths' services has fallen yet
their prices have risen sharply in real terms.

10. | Price | Demand |
|---|---|
| 10 | 0 |
| 8 | 1 |
| 6 | 2 |
| 4 | 6 |
| 2 | 12 |

Using the above table calculate the price elasticities of demand for
each price change, both when prices fall and when they rise. What
doubts do your answers raise concerning the usefulness of arith-
metical calculations of elasticity? What alternative methods are
available?

Chapter 4

THE APPLICATION OF SUPPLY AND DEMAND ANALYSIS

In the artificial world of perfect competition there is little that the manager can do to counter the pressure of market forces let alone manipulate them to his own advantage. The dominant role in the market belongs to the consumer who decides his wants and then allocates his expenditure to his chosen preferences. The role of the producer is a passive one and consists of responding to the desires of consumers via the price mechanism. Any attempt by an individual producer to produce what he, rather than what the consumer, wants will lead to him losing out to those producers who continue to obey the instructions of consumers. In the real world, however, markets are imperfect and are subject to the influence of powerful consumers and producers. Producers are able to influence the tastes of consumers through the various marketing techniques available, notably advertising. They, rather than consumers, tend to dictate fashion and they initiate the development of new products and thus control the range of choice open to consumers. This does not mean that consumers have no control over events at all. They can still refuse to buy products which do not approximate to the intended purchase; they can inform themselves about the choices available through consumer guides and they can adopt a cynical approach to advertising to increase their resistance to sales pressure. Ultimately there must be some balance between the influence of producer and consumer – if only because competition between producers will lead them to attempt to satisfy more closely the wants of consumers and thus gain a larger share of the market. None the less the producer does possess one unassailable advantage over the consumer in that suppliers have the resources and knowledge at their disposal to both manipulate and respond to changes in demand as well as controlling supply while the individual consumer is too insignificant to influence the market on his own and co-operation between consumers is both rare and difficult to achieve.

The formation of demand

It is difficult to separate out the precise roles of consumer and supplier in the formation of demand. The consumer's own preferences are the result of the many influences to which he or she is subject; those of other consumers, the press and television as well as the consumer's own personal tastes and beliefs, however misguided or ill-informed these may be. Indeed while the consumer must be regarded as rational in the exercise of choice if consumer behaviour is to have any meaning at all what appears rational to one person may seem to be quite illogical behaviour to another. In addition to the influences outlined above the consumer is also subject to the pressure arising from modern marketing methods but even here there is room for speculation as to the precise impact of marketing on the behaviour of consumers. A supplier may stress the most important qualities of the product, as he sees them, in his advertising material and then find that it is other qualities entirely which attract consumers to the product. There have been many instances in the past where, despite mounting an impressive selling campaign, a company has failed to gain public support for a particular brand or product; unpredictability and perversity remain the two great qualities which enable the consumer to escape domination by suppliers. If the supplier is to successfully play a role in the formation of demand he must maintain a dialogue with the consumer in which information is both disseminated and received. Important to this process is **market research**. In launching a product the firm will find it easier to sell this new product if it meets little resistance and obtains a passive, if not an enthusiastic response. The firm therefore has a vested interest in assessing consumer reaction before the heavy costs of launching a new product are undertaken. It is the role of market research to enable the firm to test market reaction and evaluate the attitudes of consumers to its products. This does not mean, however, that market research aims to find out what consumers want since few consumers are either able or willing to take such a pro-active role and those that are will not be representative of consumers as a whole. Instead consumers confine themselves to expressing approval or disapproval of what is on offer. Thus market research tends to consist of testing the acceptability of proposed or even existing products coupled with a willingness to respond to revealed consumer preferences where this does not constitute too big a problem in terms of increased production costs or redesign. In 1983 the failure of the Ford Sierra to achieve the general acclaim of its predecessor, the Cortina, resulted in changes being made to the wheel trim and the bumpers but the shape of the car had to stay as it was in the hope that it would 'grow on' the less enthusiastic potential market.

Despite the undoubted benefits of market research in attempting to achieve a closer harmonisation of the expressed needs of consumers and the products and services on offer and thus aiding in the process of achieving economic efficiency, the fact that it is often undertaken *after* the firm has committed itself to a particular product means that market research probably contains an element of self-delusion in that the questions asked and the inferences drawn from the answers given may tend to reinforce the firm's preconceived beliefs rather than challenge them. This danger does, of course, arise in all research, however scientific it claims to be. Market research is also concerned with the projection of future demand patterns and this topic will be referred to again later in the chapter.

The principal method for disseminating information to consumers is advertising. The aim of advertising is clearly to bring a product or service to the attention of consumers to maintain or increase sales. Economists have traditionally tried to distinguish between informative and persuasive advertising – the former being regarded as beneficial to the consumer and the latter as not. In practice all advertising contains elements of both since an advertiser is hardly likely to include in an advertisement any information detrimental to the product, while however full of information an advertisement might be the purpose so far as the advertiser is concerned must surely be to persuade the public to buy the product. The irony of advertising is that it constitutes a cost to be borne by the producer who then passes the cost on to the consumer in the form of higher prices so that the consumer pays to be persuaded to buy something he may not even want! On the other hand the growth of advertising is inevitable, given the continued raising of real incomes in the long term so that more and more income is available for expenditure on goods and services other than necessities and producers have to compete for the expenditure of consumers available for luxury goods and services. Furthermore it is unlikely that the balance of power between advertiser and the public has changed much over the years; consumers have become more sophisticated and are fully aware of the purpose of advertising so that they have become adept at the selection of information. Indeed an advertisement that is appreciated by the public as intellectually or artistically or humorously pleasing is not necessarily going to increase sales – a good advert is like a good joke; it can be appreciated without being believed.

However well a firm responds to the changing patterns of consumer behaviour, acts on information gleaned from market research and attempts to influence demand through its marketing operations it will still be subject to market pressures arising from the nature of the product and the supply and demand conditions pertinent to the situation. The firm must therefore be prepared to modify its policies to accommodate or offset conditions in the market.

The impact of government intervention

Governments influence supply and demand in several ways as they pursue their political aims. Firstly a government may ban the sale of a product completely, as in the case of hard drugs, so that supply is very restricted and an equilibrium price is established through the underground market in the product. Secondly the government may attempt to encourage the expansion of a particular market through the granting of subsidies to either producers or consumers. Thirdly it may impose taxes on products either to raise revenue or to cut demand for the product. Fourthly it may attempt to deal with the problem of wildly fluctuating prices in a market by the imposition of price controls or the establishment of some form of buffer stock scheme. Finally it may insist that the public buys certain goods or services such as seat-belts in cars or motor insurance. Apart from the first of these cases, which does not concern the typical manager in this country, all of them have implications for market conditions and thus for the activities of firms in the industry concerned.

SUBSIDIES

A subsidy can be paid either to a consumer or to a producer and in both cases the effect is to expand the market in the product in question.

In Fig. 4.1(a) the government has granted a subsidy to consumers, for example in house-buying by granting tax relief on mortgage interest, and the effect is to shift demand to the right as more people can afford to take out a mortgage than if there were no such relief while existing houseowners could afford to take out a bigger mortgage. The effect is to increase the quantity supplied though at

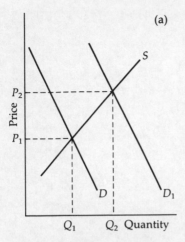
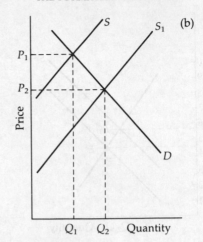

Fig. 4.1(a) & (b)

a higher real price, as opposed to the price paid by consumers. In Fig. 4.1(b) the subsidy has been granted to suppliers so that they can now supply more at the true equilibrium price or the same amount as before at a lower price. The effect will be to stimulate supply to shift to the right and lead to an increase in the quantity demanded due to the lower prices charged. While beneficial to the producer in whatever form they take, subsidies depend for their effectiveness on there being a favourable elasticity of supply and demand. Where the subsidy is granted to consumers, and supply is highly inelastic, the subsidy may be virtually absorbed by higher costs as firms attempt to increase output to meet the extra demand. Similarly, if the subsidy is granted to producers and demand is inelastic, the result will be that existing consumers will benefit without a significant growth in the number of people actually buying the product; though of course it is possible that the government's aim was indeed to subsidise a relatively small market, as with the theatre, for cultural or other reasons rather than to expand the market.

TAXES

Whether the tax is levied directly on to the consumer or on the producer the *incidence* of the tax, i.e. the way the burden of the tax is ultimately borne, depends on the elasticity of demand for the product being taxed. In Fig. 4.2 the imposition of a tax of two pounds per unit leads to supply shifting to the left as producers attempt to pass on this tax to their customers – for the producers

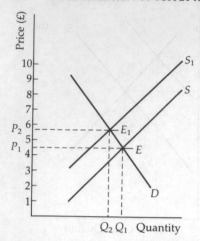

Fig. 4.2

the effect of the tax is the same as if their costs had risen by the same amount. As far as the consumer is concerned, however, the tax represents a price increase and the quantity demanded will fall accordingly. At the new equilibrium price of E_1 (£5.70) the price is higher than it was before the tax was imposed but not as high as it would be if the entire tax had been passed on to the consumer. The more elastic the demand the greater the proportion of tax that will have to be borne by the producer with virtually no effect on price while the more inelastic the demand the greater will be the proportion of the tax which can be passed on to the consumer. This is shown in Fig. 4.3(a, b) where in (a) the fact that demand is perfectly elastic means that the producer must absorb the whole tax increase himself or lose his entire market while in (b) perfectly inelastic demand results in producers being able to pass on the whole amount of the tax to their customers.

The taxation of goods and services by the government depends in its value on the aim of imposing the tax and the elasticity of demand for the good or service. Thus if the aim of imposing the tax is to raise revenue there is little point in levying the tax on goods with elastic demand since the market in the product will contract. Most of the tax is absorbed by the producer resulting in a relatively small increase in tax revenue at the cost of a substantial reduction in demand and the income of manufacturers and distributors of the product. When taxes are imposed on goods with elastic demand the aim of the government is to reduce demand in the

(a)

(b)

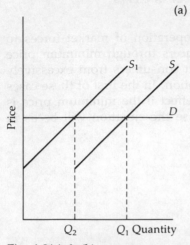
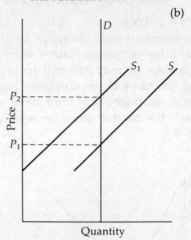

Fig. 4.3(a) & (b)

economy by making spending on luxury goods less attractive. While the aim of such a measure is to reduce consumer spending and thus counter inflationary pressures in the economy there is the disadvantage attached to it that the manufacturers and other industries dependent on the product will suffer reduced income and profits – imposing strains on the long-term viability of the firms unless they can find new markets, perhaps abroad. If the government wishes to raise revenue it should tax those goods which have inelastic demand. There is a problem here in that many of these goods are necessities and as such, food etc., are politically unsuitable items for taxation. However, there are some goods which are not necessities but do have inelastic demand such as tobacco, alcoholic drink and petrol and all these have been popular items for taxation over the years. However, it is important for the government to remember that no product will enjoy inelastic demand whatever the price and in recent years regular increases in the tax on drink and tobacco have proved less remunerative than previously as consumers have reduced their consumption in response to higher taxes, a process stimulated by the health hazards associated with excessive smoking and drinking. Thus in the 1980s governments have not increased taxes on these goods in line with inflation as they did in the past. Similarly, the high taxation increases on petrol in the early 1970s induced car manufacturers to improve greatly the fuel economy of all ranges of car and make petrol consumption less inelastic than it was in the past.

PRICE CONTROLS

Governments may interfere in the operation of market forces to guarantee minimum prices to producers through minimum price legislation or may attempt to protect consumers from excessively high prices by maximum price legislation. In the first of these cases minimum prices will only have an effect if the minimum price is above the market price in which case the situation will be as in Fig. 4.4.

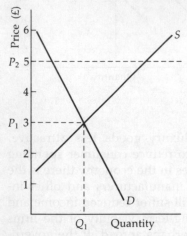

Fig. 4.4

In Fig. 4.4 the imposition of a minimum price P_2 of £5 is £2 above the market equilibrium price of £3. The effect of this is to reduce the quantity demanded and increase the quantity supplied so that the available supply exceeds the effective demand at the minimum price and stocks build up. Faced with this situation producers may be inclined to unofficially cut prices to try to get rid of their excess production. Indeed most suppliers will be happy to sell their stocks at any price over £3 which is what they were prepared to receive for their produce before the minimum price was introduced; though since the available supply will only match effective demand if the price drops to £2 some stock will be sold at prices below the equilibrium. The effect of the government's action is therefore to lead to disequilibrium in the market. It could alternatively ensure that all supply is sold at the higher price if it controlled distribution itself and paid the producers a guaranteed price. This would result in enthusiastic suppliers increasing production while demand contracts and excess stocks build up. The reason for such action by the government would obviously be to stimulate production and perhaps enable the build up of buffer stocks which could be released on to the market if production fell, e.g. in the case of agricultural products a bad harvest. Thus prices could be stabilised rather than allowed to fluctuate through market forces. The danger of this system, as has been seen in the operation of the Common Agricultural Policy of the EEC, is that supply continually outpaces demand and stocks consistently build up into wine lakes and butter mountains without ever being offset by periods of under-production.

The imposition of a maximum price is an attempt to protect consumers from the hardship resulting from excessively high prices. Such legislation will have no practical effect unless the maximum price is below the equilibrium price. In Fig. 4.5 the government has imposed a maximum price of £3 in a market where the natural equilibrium price would be £5. The result is that the quantity demanded expands to Q_2 while the quantity that suppliers are willing to provide falls to Q_3 and there is now excess demand in the market.

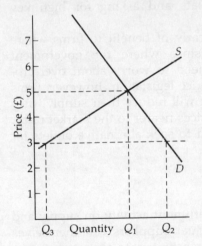

Fig. 4.5

In Fig. 4.5 the excess demand represented by $Q_2 - Q_3$ cannot be satisfied and there will be a number of possible ways in which the available supply is distributed. Firstly there may be some form of rationing. This could be regulated by the producers or distributors themselves either on a first-come first-served basis or favoured customers may be given preferential treatment. Alternatively the government could itself supervise some form of rationing through the issue of coupons. In the absence of rationing a black market is bound to develop since those consumers willing to pay the market price will also be prepared to pay above the artificial price imposed by the government. As a result the actual price paid by buyers in the market could be anywhere between the legal maximum price and the highest price which any one consumer is willing to pay. Even if rationing has been introduced some consumers may be tempted to sell their coupons so that a black market develops in the coupons. Once again stability in the market breaks down and while some consumers will have benefited from the introduction of artificially low prices many will be forced to pay much higher prices or be among those forced to go without. While rationing and price controls may be appropriate under emergency conditions brought about by a temporary shortage they can have harmful side-effects if kept in operation over a long period. Thus the various attempts which have been made at controlling rents since the last war have succeeded in keeping down the price of rented accommodation but have also helped to reduce substantially the stock of such accommodation and led to landlords avoiding controls through switching to furnished flats and asking for high key deposits.

Artificial price intervention is clearly of benefit to firms where this involves minimum pricing, since where the government guarantees the price there is no need to worry about over-production. In the case of maximum price legislation, however, firms can only benefit if, given that most will reduce their supply, they can avoid the controls and sell at prices nearer to the market price. In some cases they may be tempted to seek alternative outlets for their production, perhaps overseas.

Elasticity and the producer

In the last section the effect of government activity on supply and demand was examined but individual suppliers can themselves take the initiative in adapting their activities to the market conditions of their product. Reference has already been made, in the section on taxation, to the fact that where demand is elastic higher prices will lead to a reduction in revenue whereas if demand is inelastic higher prices will tend to increase revenue. This is illustrated by Table 4.1.

The producer of Product X would benefit by cutting prices since sales would increase faster than prices fell. However, as output increases certain costs of production will also increase so that the profit on each unit produced will get squeezed between a falling

Table 4.1

Price	Demand (X)	Revenue (X)	Demand (Y)	Revenue (Y)
10	60	600	60	600
9	80	720	65	585
8	100	800	70	560
7	120	840	72	504

price and rising costs of production. Thus the producer can only capitalise on elastic demand if elasticity of supply is also relatively high and costs do not rise rapidly as output expands. The producer of Product Y, on the other hand, has no such dilemma. The higher the price the higher will be the revenue received and so there is little to be gained from lower prices while with higher prices the fall in sales will be more than compensated for by higher revenue and falling costs per unit. So the fewer the units produced and sold the higher the likely profits.

While in general firms benefit from price inelasticity of demand other elasticities tend to be more complex. In the case of substitutes high cross-elasticity means that demand for the two products is highly interchangeable and that attempts to raise prices in isolation will result in a decline in revenue. In the case of complementary products a high degree of elasticity means that the producer of one of the goods is highly dependent on demand for the other and if the price of the latter rises there is little he can do to stop a substantial fall in his own sales and revenue. It does not necessarily work both ways; a rise in the price of petrol could seriously affect the demand for larger cars but a rise in the price of these cars will have little effect on the demand for petrol.

The most complex problems of all arise out of income elasticity of demand. As real incomes rise it is to be expected that the demand for inferior goods will decline and this will be reflected in negative income elasticity so that industries producing these inferior goods could find themselves in decline while industry as a whole is expanding. Even where the goods are not inferior but demand is limited, as in the case of light bulbs or tea, the supplier may find himself in a market where expansion is difficult to achieve. The situation is complicated by the fact that real incomes rise at a much steadier rate than do money incomes and money prices so that consumers can convince themselves that they cannot afford a particular product because of sudden sharp rises in prices even when prices relative to real incomes have actually fallen; such self-delusion affected consumers with regard to meat in the 1970s.

In a sense all the problems of any supplier arise out of elasticity. If the producer could be sure that he could charge any price he liked without seriously affecting demand and without attracting rival suppliers into the market he would hardly need to concern himself with becoming more efficient, reducing costs or attracting new customers – he could just keep pushing up his prices. In the absence of this ideal position the aim of any firm must surely be to make its products as indispensable as possible to the consumer. While there may be considerable merit in the statement that the purpose of marketing is to ascertain the needs of consumers and to seek to satisfy these needs the aim of marketing in purely economic terms is surely to reduce the elasticity of demand for a firm's products. The more distinctive that marketing can make a particular product, whether it be its brand image, design, packaging or whatever, the less will be the substitutability between it and other products and the less will be the effect of a change in price on demand. Common sense dictates that when two virtually identical articles of similar quality are on offer the consumer should take the cheaper of the two. However, consumers are liable to take the view that if something is dearer than an apparently identical alternative it must be of superior quality. If marketing can exploit this human behavioural characteristic the producer will be able to evade, to some extent, the handicaps placed on his pricing policy by the constraints of elasticity. The greater the individuality of a product the less damaging, also, will be the problem of high cross-elasticity of substitutes. Income elasticity poses different problems and a new challenge to marketing techniques in the face of changing patterns of consumer demand. In the last twenty years many of the chain retailers, especially Woolworths and the Co-operative Societies, have had to shift the emphasis of their stores from cheap functional goods to a more up-market image in response to the changing demand conditions resulting from higher real incomes. Other producers have survived by altering the basis of the appeal of their products – margarine was bought thirty years ago by those who could not afford butter while now it is just as likely to be bought by those afraid of what butter might do to them. Other products have reasserted themselves as the fashion has swung away from the synthetic products and materials developed in the 1960s; the resurgence of cotton, linen and wool and the growth in interest of natural and health foods all reflect in part the successful use of marketing to enable more expensive products to gain in popularity. A successful marketing strategy may be made all the more necessary where the goods produced are subject to supply conditions outside the producers' immediate control, e.g. where raw material costs are prone to large price fluctuations or where the product is required as a complement to another.

In the long term supply and demand conditions clearly have a bearing on the viability of firms and of whole industries and there is a need to be able to predict these long-term trends if the firm is to plan rather than merely react to the pressures to which it is subjected. There is a wealth of information available to firms, both from government sources and from trade and financial journals, to enable them to anticipate future demand patterns and plan output decisions accordingly. For those industries where future demand is likely to decline due to population, income or taste changes diversification may be the only solution, as with the movement of the Imperial Group away from tobacco into food products. Alternatively the solution may be the development of new products to meet changing needs or the development of new production or distribution processes where supplies of labour or materials may present problems. Of course the most successful companies are those which can anticipate or even manipulate demand changes while even the largest company is not safe from decline if it sees its future solely in terms of past demand and supply patterns.

Problems for analysis

1. Consider the different effects and effectiveness of the use of rent controls and rent subsidies in dealing with the problem of the high rents charged for private accommodation.
2. A major car manufacturer decides to introduce a new range of medium-sized saloon in the hope of making a breakthrough in the lucrative but competitive company-car market. To what extent could the company make use of the various demand elasticities in both the design and the pricing of its products? Are there any demand factors it might wish to consider that have nothing to do with elasticity?

Chapter 5

THE ORGANISATION OF PRODUCTION: I

In the discussion of demand and supply conditions of the previous two chapters it was seen that the supplier would attempt to increase demand, but only if the revenue so earned would more than cover the extra costs incurred. Clearly there is no point whatever, if a firm is aiming to increase its profits, in selling more of its goods or services at a cost higher than the revenue earned. Costs are thus a fundamental element in the company's policy-making since they will dictate the company's supply conditions.

Costs

The costs incurred by a firm in the production of a given output represent the payments it must make for the various factors of production used in the manufacturing process. These costs include not only purchased costs such as raw materials and hired costs such as labour, but also the intangible costs of depreciation, of the use of the owner's capital and of the need to compensate for risk-taking. These intangible costs repesent the foregone choices to which the assets of the enterprise could have been put. Costs can be further broken down into *fixed costs* and *variable costs*. Fixed costs are those which do not vary with output and include such items as rent, rates, interest charges, depreciation, etc. Variable costs are those which do vary with output and include the costs of labour, raw materials and power. Together fixed and variable costs add up to *total costs*.

In Fig. 5.1 as total costs (TC) = total fixed cost (TFC) + total variable cost (TVC), TC will be parallel to VC but will commence from the level of FC, not from zero. At first sight fixed costs would ap-

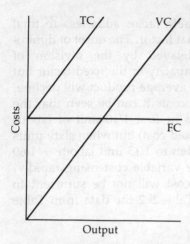

Fig. 5.1

pear to be advantageous to the firm since they become relatively less important as the enterprise expands its output but fixed costs imply that some of the factors of production are also fixed – depreciation implies that there is a fixed stock of machinery and plant available to the enterprise, rent implies that the working premises are also limited, etc. As the enterprise increases output, therefore, it is the variable factors which must bear the onus of increasing output and this becomes an increasingly less productive exercise so that the variable costs steadily increase per unit of output. This problem is illustrated in Table 5.1 where taking on more and more labour to expand output will become steadily less efficient as the extra (or marginal) unit of labour has to work with the same capital resources. The extra output contributed by each unit of labour will eventually decrease giving rise to **diminishing marginal returns**

Table 5.1

Quantity of capital	Quantity of labour	Total product	Average product	Marginal product (TP_n-TP_{n-1})
1	1	10	10	—
1	2	30	15	20
1	3	48	16	18
1	4	60	15	12
1	5	65	13	5
1	6	66	11	1

whereby the marginal unit of a variable factor adds less to total production than the previous unit of that factor. The onset of diminishing marginal returns may be delayed by the division of labour and by the using up of slack capacity in the fixed factor but eventually both marginal product and average product will decline.

Relating the figures in Table 5.1 to costs it can be seen that the average cost of one unit produced is at first 1/10 unit of labour (variable cost) + 1/10 unit of capital (fixed cost) but when sixty units are produced the average cost has fallen to 1/15 unit labour + 1/60 unit capital. Eventually, with average variable cost rising rapidly, the continuing fall in average fixed cost will not be sufficient to prevent average total cost rising. In Table 5.2 the data from Table 5.1 are revamped to illustrate costs.

Table 5.2   The short-run costs of the firm

Cap. (£390) (per unit)	Lab. (£39) Output	Fixed cost (capital) (£)	Variable cost (labour) (£)	Total cost (FC + VC) (£)	£ Average fixed $\frac{FC}{O}$	£ Average variable $\frac{VC}{O}$	£ Average total $\frac{TC}{O}$	£ Marginal cost $(TC_n - TC_{n-1})$
1	1	10	390	39	429	39	3.9	42.9	—
1	2	30	390	78	468	13	2.6	15.6	1.95
1	3	48	390	117	507	8¼	2.4	10.5	2.01
1	4	60	390	156	546	6½	2.6	9.1	3.25
1	5	65	390	195	585	6	3.0	9.0	7.80
1	6	66	390	234	624	5.9	3.5	9.5	39.00

The table differentiates fixed and variable costs and, what is of great importance to a producer, *average* fixed and variable costs since it is average costs which determine the efficiency of production rather than the cost of producing any one unit. Also in the table is *marginal cost* which is the addition to total cost of producing one extra unit. The relationship between the various types of cost can also be shown graphically, as in Fig. 5.2. Here average fixed costs fall continuously as total fixed cost is spread over a rising number of units of output. Although average variable costs also fall at first as the enterprise is able to use its variable factors to their best advantage they subsequently rise as diminishing marginal returns set in. The onset of diminishing marginal returns is shown by the path followed by the marginal cost curve which, as it represents the cost of producing one extra unit, is effectively the marginal variable cost curve. If the marginal cost is below the average variable cost, the average variable cost will fall as the extra cost of

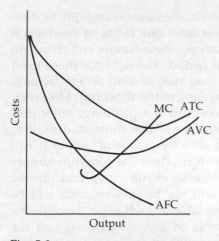

Fig. 5.2

each unit of output brings the average down (e.g. if the average is six and marginal cost is five then average variable cost must fall below six). When marginal cost is above average variable cost the latter will rise on the same principle so that the rising marginal cost curve must cut the average variable cost curve at its lowest point. Similarly the marginal cost curve will cut the average total cost curve at its lowest point.

Short run and long run

Thus far attempts to increase output have encountered the problem of diminishing marginal returns so that each successive unit produced becomes more and more costly in terms of resources used and therefore less efficient. The situation corresponds to the upward sloping supply curve since given rising costs producers will only be willing to increase output if price goes up. It also corresponds to the situation which prevails in many parts of Africa and Asia where each baby born represents both a mouth to feed and a pair of hands to work but as the numbers of pairs of hands increases (the variable factor) while the land to be worked is constant (the fixed factor) the problem of diminishing marginal returns sets in and the marginal output of the last pair of hands is not sufficient to feed the extra mouth that comes with it, resulting in malnutrition. Clearly there must be a solution to this problem otherwise Britain, which frequently suffered itself from an excessive number of people tied to the land in the past, could not now sup-

port a population of over 50 million. Given the inevitability of diminishing marginal returns where at least one factor of production
is fixed the solution must lie in varying these factors and changing
the scale of production. The time period necessary for these fixed
factors to become variable is the long run; as long as one factor is
still fixed the enterprise is still operating in the short-run. However,
it is important to note that the long run is a planning, not a production, period, since once the enterprise has committed itself to
its long-run plans and embarked on a new scale of output it will
be producing within a new short-run. Thus the long-run supply
curve will be more elastic than the short-run curve and, as the
problem of diminishing returns will not be present costs will be
lower and more supply will be available at each price. Since in the
long run all factors become variable so also do all costs and the
average variable cost curve becomes the average total cost curve,
though retaining its relationship with marginal costs. Because the
long run is a planning period any combination of factors of production is possible provided that the combination is technically appropriate and the chosen combination should reflect the lowest-cost
combination and the most efficient means of producing the target
level of output. The long run is not, however, necessarily a period
in which the scale of operations is expanded. If a producer finds
that the market is declining he may choose to cut back production
or even close down in the long run.

Increasing returns to scale

It might be expected that in the long run the doubling-up of all
factors of production would enable output to be doubled and thus
avoid the problems associated with diminishing returns to scale.
In practice the doubling-up of factors may enable output to more
than double and give rise to increasing returns to scale, i.e. **economies of scale**.

In Table 5.3 an increase in all factors of production to scale leads
to proportionately greater increases in output. As the average product continues to increase over most of the total product range the
average cost falls. Increasing returns to scale arise out of the fact
that as the scale of operations is enlarged the opportunities for
specialisation of the different factors also grow so that both labour
and capital can be used in different functions. The main areas in
which economies of scale can be achieved include:

1. *Technical economies.*   As production grows it becomes possible

Table 5.3   Increasing returns to scale

Units capital	Units labour	Total product	Average product	Marginal product
1	1	10	10	—
2	2	24	12	14
3	3	39	13	15
4	4	56	14	17
5	5	70	14	14
6	6	82	13⅔	12

to use specialisation and the division of labour to increase labour productivity. As workers specialise in different functions better use can be made of their individual talents and strengths and proficiency in different areas of expertise developed. Large-scale production also permits more efficient use of capital equipment especially as some capital cannot be used efficiently unless it is operating above a certain level of output. Modern mass production and conveyor belt systems, for example, are impracticable at low levels of output.

2. *Financial economies.* The larger the firm the easier and the cheaper it becomes to raise finance for capital projects and the cost of expansion thus becomes cheaper than the initial establishment of the business.

3. *Marketing economies.* The larger the scale of production the more the enterprise will benefit from the bulk-buying of materials and favourable purchasing terms. The selling of products becomes cheaper as advertising costs are spread over a greater level of sales and sales offices will be able to get larger orders per salesman.

4. *Management economies.* A larger enterprise can afford specialist staff at managerial level and so improve the efficiency of its management functions in areas such as accounting, marketing, production and industrial relations.

In theory there is no reason why increasing returns to scale should not go on indefinitely as the size of the enterprise grows. In practice this is not so as the last two lines of Table 5.3 indicate. After a certain point marginal output begins to decrease as additional factors of production fail to add as much to output as previous ones. This is due to the fact that the advantages associated with large-scale output begin to be overtaken by the disadvantages experienced by large scale organisations – **diseconomies or decreasing returns to scale**. As the functions of the workforce become increasingly more specialised two problems develop. Firstly increasing compartmentalisation of function requires increased channels of communication and this can lead to a bureaucratic structure in which management is unable to cope effectively with the demands being made upon it. Secondly the workforce as a whole suffers from the monotony and frustration associated with over-specialisation which can result in falling efficiency and a deterioration in industrial relations as individuals within the organisation become detached from the overall aims and interests of the firm. Theoretically the organisation should plan to achieve maximum economies of scale in its long-run operations within the existing establishment and then replicate it, i.e. begin a similarly constituted establishment elsewhere.

In the long run the enterprise will aim to produce a particular level of output in line with conditions prevailing in the market. Fig. 5.3 represents the long-run average cost curve and, as such, the lowest cost of producing any given output since all factors of production are variable in the long run and the enterprise can therefore choose that combination of factors which will prove most efficient for any given output. When long-run average cost is falling, output will be produced under conditions of increasing returns to scale. If, however, the enterprise chooses to produce where average cost is rising it will be experiencing decreasing returns to scale and ought to consider instead the option of replication. But

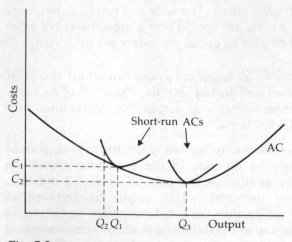

Fig. 5.3

the long run is, in any case, a planning and not a production period. Once a commitment has been made to a particular scale of output (e.g. Q_1), the enterprise will be producing under short-run conditions as it will once again have fixed factors of production and the fixed costs attached to these. Thus if the optimum long-run output is Q_1 the average cost will be C_1 since this is the lowest average cost attainable for the chosen output in both the long-run and the new short-run conditions which will obtain. Only if actual production deviates from the predicted output, e.g. at Q_2, will average cost rise above the long-run minimum. If predicted market conditions allow the planned long-run output to be Q_3, greater economies of scale will be realisable and minimum average cost will be reduced to C_2. The enterprise will then operate along a different short-run average cost curve, though with similar restraints on maintaining this optimum cost level if output deviates from Q_3.

Optimum resource allocation: theory and constraints

The theory of cost points also to a theory of optimum resource allocation within the economy. Supply and demand theory predicts that within a perfect market price will be determined by market forces and only those producers able to sell their output at the prevailing price and still cover the costs of production with the revenue so earned can continue to operate in the market. It follows that if further output is contemplated it can only be achieved by producers in general if either they are operating under conditions of falling average costs or if price rises to compensate for rising average cost. Clearly producers in the first category are in a stronger position to bid for the factors of production necessary for an increase in production since they can offer higher rewards to these factors. A producer entering a phase of long-run expansion and expecting to enjoy economies of scale will be able to employ extra units of labour more effectively than one operating under short-run conditions of diminishing marginal returns and will thus be able to offer higher wage rates. Furthermore resources will tend to gravitate towards those producers with the lowest average cost curves since these can both offer the highest rewards to factors of production when output is expanding and best cope with the difficulties arising from a contraction in the market and the falling prices which follow. If perfect market conditions prevail throughout the economy resources will ultimately be allocated to those producers who can use them most efficiently so that even if temporarily producers experience diminishing returns in the short run, long run production will be carried out under conditions of increasing returns to scale and with average cost at a minimum.

The fact that production is not carried out under conditions associated with a perfect market is one of the two key constraints on optimum resource allocation. The other is the working of the price mechanism itself which does not guarantee that those who can bid the most for resources are those who will use them most efficiently; it only guarantees that they have the greatest bargaining power. Thus even if production did take place under perfect market conditions producers willing to forego profitability for the satisfaction derived from running their own businesses might still outbid more efficient producers demanding some net income from their activities. The fact that production does not take place under perfect market conditions means that market conditions may cushion inefficient producers against market forces and the theoretical pre-eminence of their competitors. Imperfections in the market may prevent consumers from knowing that they could obtain an identical product elsewhere much more cheaply and enable an inefficient producer to remain commercially viable. Similarly the costs to the consumer imposed by considerations of travel and time may prevent him from going to that part of the market where prices are lowest; there is no gain from using fifty penceworth of petrol to travel to a supermarket to save sixpence on a packet of cigarettes when there is a local tobacconist within walking distance. Nor do lower prices guarantee that production is taking place more efficiently. A producer may be operating under decreasing returns to scale but still enjoy sufficient scale advantages to enable him to have lower costs than a small producer unable to benefit from economies of scale and unable to be price-competitive. Other unpredictable factors such as customer loyalty, a successful brand image or tradition may also enable the inefficient producer to function profitably.

In addition to the problems of resource allocation posed by the type of market and the relative power of the firms within an industry there is also the question of the internal structure of the firm and its ability to respond to dynamic market conditions. The question of replication may be quite straightforward for the producer who has reached optimum size in his existing establishment in theory but may pose many problems in practice. It is assumed, for example, that a firm can predict future cost and output levels to a degree of accuracy unlikely to be attained in reality. A lack of certainty that replication is a viable proposition leads most businesses to expand on existing sites with over-utilisation of existing resources even if this means encountering diseconomies of scale. Indeed the fact that the enterprise is suffering from such diseconomies of scale as a bureaucratic management structure, directors operating beyond their level of competence and poor industrial relations make it less likely that it will be able to take the steps necessary to maximise resource utilisation.

Finally there is the constraint imposed by the economic environment. Optimum resource allocation requires that resources can be moved easily from one enterprise to another and from one industry to another. In practice the more complex the economic society the less mobile the factors of production become so that machinery built for a specific use cannot be transferred to another occupation while lack of training, qualifications or experience may prevent workers moving from one industry to another. During a recession industries are often loath to unload resources in the hope that an upturn will soon materialise while trade unions will be at their most vociferous in support of jobs during a recession however underutilised the workforce may be. The government, too, in support of its policies may help industries in difficulty because they are large employers or because they play a strategic role in the economy as a whole. Thus the state of the economy has a major bearing on the attainment of optimum resource allocation. When the economy is booming producers are able to make high profits and not worry too much about some inefficiencies within the business while during a recession circumstances may prevent rationalisation taking place as inertia and pride lead firms to stay in business long after the point has been reached where they should close down. This issue raises serious questions as to the effectiveness of deflationary measures in promoting efficiency through shaking the weak firms out of industry by a tight control of credit and so on. Ultimately, though, the failure of resource optimisation to be realised in the real world stems from the fact that without a perfect market the decision as to whether or not to continue in business depends on the extent to which revenue can be pushed up to cover costs.

Revenue

The total revenue received by a producer from the sale of output consists of the number of units sold multiplied by the price. Since average revenue is equal to total revenue divided by the number of units sold it must be equal to price as long as all units are sold at the same price. Marginal revenue is the addition to total revenue obtained from the sale of one extra unit of output. Where, as in a perfect market, the individual producer is unable to influence price by his behaviour both price and average revenue will be constant, whatever the output, and will be represented by a horizontal straight line. Furthermore as each extra unit sold will also equal price marginal revenue will be equal to average revenue as in Fig, 5.4(a). Where, however, the market is imperfect and individual producers can only attract more buyers by lowering their price average revenue will be represented by a downward-sloping line as the price charged when twenty units are sold will be lower than when ten are sold. In this case marginal revenue will slope downwards even more steeply since when the seller lowers the price to sell one extra unit the price is cut to existing consumers too and the sale of the extra unit adds less to total revenue than the price charged for it, as in Fig. 5.4(b). Marginal revenue is effectively the gain to the producer when sales are increased but as this must also cover any rise in costs resulting from the extra output the effect on marginal revenue of an expansion of output is critical in determining whether such expansion is profitable for the producer.

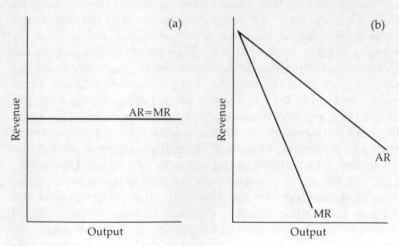

Fig. 5.4(a) & (b)

Profit

The aim of an enterprise is normally to make a profit and if total revenue is greater than total cost a profit will result. At first sight, then, it seems fairly simple to ascertain whether or not a particular firm is making a profit or a loss. However, the section on costs referred to such intangible costs as the use of the owner's capital and labour and the pressure borne by the entrepreneur in taking risks and surely such costs should be taken into account in arriving at a true profit figure. If an entrepreneur starts up in business with his own capital of £20,000 and gives up a salaried occupation of £14,000 to end his first year in business with the Trading and Profit & Loss Account shown in Table 5.4 has he made a profit?

Table 5.4

	(£)		(£)
Materials	40,000	Sales	70,000
Labour	8,000		
Depreciation	2,000		
Other operating costs	5,000		
Cost price of goods	55,000		
Less closing stock	5,000		
Cost price of goods sold	50,000		
Gross profit	20,000		
	70,000		70,000
Selling & admin. costs	4,000	Gross profit	20,000
Fixed interest charges and taxes	6,000		
	10,000		
Net profit	10,000		
	20,000		20,000

In accounting terms he has made a profit of £10,000 but if account is taken of the labour he has himself put into the business which elsewhere could earn £14,000 and the fact that his capital could earn another £1,600 or so per year the entrepreneur is probably worse off if some need to compensate the cost of running his own business is included. If his sole purpose for going into business was to receive higher earnings he should close down in the long run, unless things improve, and ask for his old job back. On the other hand the aim of this particular entrepreneur may have been to be his own boss and enjoy greater freedom while still earning enough to live on and in this case a profit of £10,000 a year may well be acceptable. Seen in this light profits must be related to expectations and while in one case an accounting profit of £20,000 is insufficient to keep a business going in another a profit of £10,000 will be. The term used to describe this expected profit is **normal profit** which can be defined as the profit necessary to keep an entrepreneur in the industry. Normal profit must be counted as a cost in assessing

Table 5.5

	Company X		Company Y
Revenue	£20,000	Revenue	£20,000
− Costs	£ 7,000	− Costs	£ 7,000
	£13,000		£13,000
− Normal profit	£13,000	− Normal profit	£ 5,000
Profit	Nil	Profit	£ 8,000

whether or not an enterprise has made, in economic terms, a profit, as Table 5.5 illustrates.

While Company X has merely broken even on the basis of expected profits Company Y has exceeded its normal or expected profits and has therefore achieved **super profits**. The larger and more complex the structure of an enterprise the more difficult it becomes to evaluate normal profit as those who run the business, the directors and the managers, are rarely the sole or even major owners of the business and are therefore concerned more with their salary than with their direct benefit out of the profits of the company.

Profit maximisation

Where profit is the sole preoccupation of the enterprise it may reasonably be assumed that the entrepreneur will seek to maximise profits. Within a perfect market consisting of small independent producers such an assumption is consistent with the theory of supply and demand and also that of costs since producers will aim to sell their products at the highest price the market will bear and also strive to keep costs to a minimum. Indeed the producer within a perfect market is subject to such intense price competition that anything less than maximisation of profits may well mean no profits at all. Even where the producer aims to maximise profits it may well be the case that total revenue is not sufficient to cover total costs and then the aim will be to minimise losses. Under normal circumstances this would appear to point to closure but again it is necessary to differentiate between short and long runs. In the short run the firm will incur fixed costs and these will have to be met whether the firm produces or not so they can be discounted in deciding whether or not to carry on production. If, therefore, total revenue more than covers total variable cost it will pay the firm to produce in the short run since this surplus of revenue over variable costs will help defray some of the losses which are inevitable because of the existence of fixed costs. If total revenue does not exceed total variable costs, however, there would be no gain in producing even in the short run since losses will be greater if production is undertaken than if it is not. Thus when TR = TVC the enterprise should shut down, even in the short run. In the long run all costs are variable and thus the enterprise must be able to more than cover total costs with revenue otherwise it should shut down.

Given that it is worthwhile for the firm to produce at all it will maximise profits (or minimise losses) when marginal revenue is equal to marginal cost, i.e. MR = MC. If MR > MC profits will be increased if output rises since the extra revenue gained from selling one more unit will be greater than the extra cost incurred in producing that unit. If MR < MC profits will be increased by reducing output since the lost revenue will be less than the reduction in costs.

In Fig. 5.5 a firm operating under conditions of perfect competition can sell any output at the prevailing market price and thus MR is constant over the whole output range. The MR line is cut by the MC curve at two points, Q_1 and Q_2. At point Q_1 MR=MC but profits are not maximised because if output is increased MR will be greater than MC and profits will also therefore increase. In order for profits to be maximised MR must not only equal MC, the MR line must be cut by the MC line from below, as is the case with an output of Q_2. The principle illustrated by Fig. 5.5 applies whether the firm is striving to maximise profits or minimise losses, but to

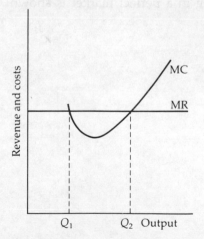

Fig. 5.5

determine whether it is profits or losses which are made reference must be made to average costs and average revenue. At the profit-maximising output the difference between AR and AC represents the average profit per unit produced and this average profit multiplied by output is the total profit because (AR − AC) × output = (AR × output) − (AC × output) = TR − TC. It would of course be possible to calculate the profit or loss on each unit and calculate profit from those figures.

In Fig. 5.6 the optimum output is at Q where MC = MR. At that point profits can be measured by multiplying the difference between AR and AC by output, i.e. the rectangle $axyb$. Since normal profits are included in costs the profits thus made must be super profits; an enterprise whose total revenue just covered costs plus normal profits would be breaking even, as was Company X in Table 5.5. In the short run an enterprise producing where MR = MC could be incurring losses, breaking even or making super profits but in the long run perfect competition ensures that all producers will break even. Thus in the long run those firms making losses will leave the market causing supply to fall and price to rise so that the individual's AR line will be forced up until the most efficient firms are able to break even. Where producers are making super profits in the short run new producers will enter the market in the long run and increase market supply, reducing price and the AR received by existing firms in the market until all producers earn only normal profits. Only where all the existing producers earn normal profits in the short run will there be no tendency for producers either to enter or leave the market in the long run. The long-run equilibrium of a producer operating in a perfect market is shown

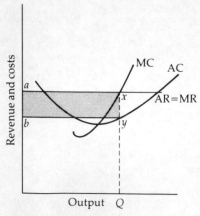

Fig. 5.6

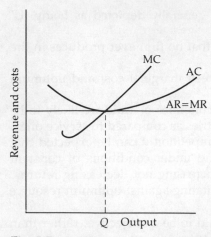

Fig. 5.7

in Fig. 5.7 where at output Q MR = MC = AC = AR so that the firm earns only normal profit. Since at point Q MC = AC the producer is also operating at the minimum cost output, he is both maximising his profits and operating at maximum efficiency.

Profit maximisation and, with it, the maximisation of efficiency, are inevitable features of the perfect market since producers have no alternative to striving for efficiency and profitability in a harsh world where they have no control over the market, little influence over the consumer and fierce competition from their co-producers. Fortunately for the vast majority of enterprises they do not operate in such a harshly competitive environment since the conditions necessary for perfect competition never pertain. Even if they did how long would they last if the producers just once sat down together and realised that by co-operating they could restrict supply and force up prices? Furthermore, since in the long run only the efficient will survive there will be a tendency for the number of producers in the market to fall over a long period and this in itself will increase the chances of some producers becoming big enough to influence by their activities what happens in the market.

Revision test

1. Explain the relationship between variable cost and marginal cost.
2. Why is it that the law of diminishing returns is inevitable while decreasing returns to scale are not?

3. Why are average cost curves generally depicted as being 'U' shaped?
4. In what sense is it true to say that no firm ever produces in the long run?
5. What is the relationship between marginal cost and optimum output?
6. Contrast the ways in which economies of scale are likely to be found in manufacturing industries as compared to service ones.
7. Explain why under perfect competition it can be expected that all producers will be operating under conditions of constant returns to scale, i.e. neither increasing nor decreasing returns.
8. What are the main factors militating against optimum resource allocation in the economy?
9. In what sense can profit be said to be a subjective, rather than an objective, term?
10. Analyse the difference between short-run and long-run shut-down points.

Question for analysis

Table 5.6 details the costs and revenues relating to the possible outputs of a firm during a month.

Table 5.6

Output	Total costs (£ 000s)	Total revenue (£ 000s)
8,000	94	152
10,000	114	180
12,000	132	204
14,000	148	224
16,000	160	240
18,000	170	252
20,000	182	260
22,000	198	264
24,000	220	264

(a) What is the most profitable monthly output?
(b) If fixed costs increased by £15,000 what would be the effect on the profit maximising output, and why?
(c) Costs and market demand remain as above. A large retailer places an order of 10,000 units per month at a price of £30 per unit. Consider the proposition and explain if it should be accepted.

Chapter 6

THE ORGANISATION OF PRODUCTION: II

If production takes place other than in a perfect market a wide range of possible market forms is feasible. Each of these market forms is imperfect in the sense that the individual producer has some influence, however slight, over the market by his activities and thus possesses an element of monopoly power. On the other hand monopoly power is never absolute; even where a producer is the monopolist or sole supplier of a particular product or service it must still compete with the producers of other goods and services for the finite incomes of consumers. The three main forms of imperfect competition are monopolistic competition, oligopoly and monopoly.

Monopolistic competition

Monopolistic competition closely resembles perfect competition in that there are many sellers in the market all producing goods or services similar to that of their rivals and each subject to market forces which as individuals they cannot control. The monopolistic competitor does, however, have some influence over the market since consumers are able to differentiate between his product and those of his competitors. Thus the decision to buy one firm's product is based not purely on price, as is the case under perfect competition, but is also influenced by taste, fashion and image, too. While the perfect competitor cannot raise his price without losing all his customers to cheaper identical alternatives the monopolistic competitor can expect to retain some share of the market if he raises his price and gain more customers if he lowers his price. Product or service differentiation is not, of course, limited to physical or tangible qualities such as size, shape, colour, design, etc.; it may also take the form of accessibility, geographical location, standard of service or a traditional arrangement between buyer and seller. There are countless examples of customers preferring to pay a little more to get personal rather than self-service or to obtain something a little out of the ordinary while prices can vary from area to area for obvious reasons. The effect of all these factors is to face the monopolistic competitor with a downward-sloping demand curve since price changes will affect his share of the market but neither make it disappear altogether nor allow him to capture the entire market as rivals will also have some customer loyalty and monopoly power of their own. Not only does the demand curve slope downwards and with it the average revenue curve (since they are the same thing) but so does the marginal revenue curve. This is because the sale of an extra unit adds less to total revenue than its own price, as shown in Table 6.1.

Table 6.1

Price (£)	Output	TR	AR	MR
10	10	100	10	—
9	12	108	9	4 (8 ÷ 2)
8	14	112	8	2 (4 ÷ 2)
7	16	112	7	0
6	18	108	6	−2 (−4 ÷ 2)

In Table 6.1 the increased revenue resulting from the price cut from £10 to £9 is £8 but this must be spread over the two extra units sold so that the marginal revenue from selling one extra unit is only £4. By the time the price is cut from £8 to £7 marginal revenue has become zero as the extra revenue gained from selling two more units is cancelled out by the lost revenue on the fourteen units already sold. At this point the MR line meets the output axis and price elasticity is now unity. Any further price cut will lead to a reduction in total revenue as elasticity becomes less than one and marginal revenue becomes negative.

Like the perfect competitor the monopolistic competitor faces different equilibrium positions in the short and long runs, since as no one seller is large enough to dominate the market existing producers will be unable to prevent new firms entering the market if the profits are attractive enough.

In Fig. 6.1(a) the AC and MC curves follow a similar path to those experienced by the firm under perfect competition while the AR and MR lines slope downwards. If the firm maximises profits

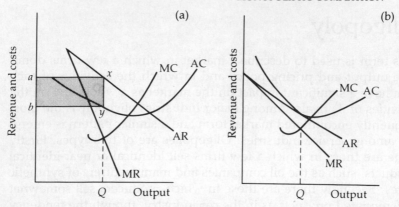

Fig. 6.1(a) & (b)

it will produce at output Q and receive the super profits illustrated by the shaded rectangle *axyb*. In the long run the possibility of making super profits attracts new firms into the market and these new producers will take customers away from existing producers who will now sell less than before at all prices. Thus the AR line of an existing producer shifts leftwards and becomes more elastic as with a greater number of choices available substitution between the various products becomes closer. Eventually with firms having to cut prices to try to maintain their share of the market the AR line lies tangent to the AC line so that all firms now break even and make only normal profits, as shown in Fig. 6.1(b). In both the short and the long run the firm is likely to produce at a level less than that where MC = AC so that it is producing at less than its most efficient output and suffers from excess capacity. However, there will be no incentive for firms to leave the market while normal profits are being made.

The typical monopolistic competitor is a small producer or distributor who can maximise profits without the need to minimise costs due to monopoly control of one corner of the market. Given that the firm can never hope to dominate the market the only real incentive will be to concentrate on reducing the elasticity of demand for his product. He will then be able to raise prices, earning supernormal profits in the short run, and normal profit (with a higher price) in the long run. There is thus a strong inducement to strengthen the brand image if a producer and the service given if a retailer; the corner grocery shop can still survive by being open when supermarkets are closed, possessing a localised monopoly and giving credit to a known clientele.

Oligopoly

This term is used to describe a market in which a few firms dominate output and pricing policy and in which the activities of each firm have a significant impact on the market as a whole and on the activities of its rivals. Among major industries oligopoly is the most frequently encountered market form and a similar pattern is emerging among service industries. Oligopolies are of two types. Firstly there are those in which a few firms sell identical or near-identical products, such as the oil companies and manufacturers of synthetic fibres. Secondly there are those in which producers sell somewhat differentiated products as in the car industry, though the tendency is for such industries to move towards very similar products. In isolation the oligopolist's equilibrium could be expected to resemble that of the monopolistic competitor in the short run but oligopolists do not operate in isolation since each firm is large enough to influence the behaviour of its rivals by what it does. In such circumstances it might be postulated that each firm will seek to adopt patterns of behaviour least likely to bring it into conflict with its competitors. This arises from the effect that conflict would have on each of the firms in the industry. Suppose, for example, that three firms are all producing very similar products and one cuts prices to capture its rivals' market share. Before it can benefit the other firms will retaliate and set off a disastrous price war in which all three would lose as they all end up with the same share of the market as before but with lower revenue and consequently lower profits. Conversely an individual producer who raises prices will lose because the others will hold their prices steady to attract their customers. The effect is to push oligopolies towards stable prices and the so-called kinked demand curve shown in Fig. 6.2.

THE KINKED DEMAND CURVE

The line DD represents the demand curve of one firm when all sellers move their prices together while dd is the demand curve when the firm changes its prices independently of its rivals. Point K is the equilibrium price which the oligopolists think will be the most profitable in the long run and firms will tend to stick to this price. If one firm cuts its prices the others will follow and curve DD operates while if it raises prices above K the others will leave prices as they are and the firm will then be operating with the highly elastic demand curve dd and greatly reduced demand. Since MR is also kinked and is a straight line between point C and point F there are a number of possible MC curves all of which would cut the MR

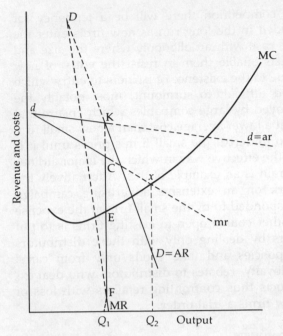

Fig. 6.2

line at an output of Q_1 and thus maintain maximisation of profits, so that both price and output are relatively resistant to a change in marginal cost.

The empirical evidence to support the kinked demand curve is rather thin. None the less there is considerable evidence to support the view that, given the opportunity, oligopolistic firms will attempt to avoid price wars and instead move prices up together to enable them to increase revenue without disturbing their relative shares of the market. This leads the members of an oligopoly to form a cartel or make a price-fixing agreement either tacitly through following a price-leader or formally through regular meetings to discuss output and pricing policies. The price fixed by a cartel is certain to be above that which would prevail under a competitive system and as it is geared to providing some profit for the weakest producer it will enable strong efficient firms to earn substantial super profits. The stronger the cartel the closer it will become to being a joint monopoly with joint profit maximisation, while if the cartel goes so far as to allocate an output quota to each member or arranges for the distribution of the total output of the cartel centrally the industry will have even the external appearance of a monopoly.

Under monopolistic competition there will be a tendency for super profits to be eroded in the long run as new firms enter the market. This is not the case with an oligopoly where the size and power of the oligopolists enable them to resist the entry of new firms. This is largely due to the existence of barriers to entry which small firms would find difficult to surmount, most notably the economies of scale enjoyed by large companies which ensure that they will be operating at a lower average cost than a new small firm and will thus be able to undercut the small firm's prices until it is forced out of business; the effective way in which the major airlines saw off the Laker Skytrain is an example of this. Alternatively the oligopolists can embark on an extensive advertising campaign which could only be responded to by the small firm at the expense of its profitability. Another course open to existing firms is to put pressure on distributors by dealing only with those distributors who abide by cartel policies and take goods only from cartel members, or offering 'loyalty' rebates to distributors who deal exclusively in their products thus confronting retailers with loss of income if they give new firms a trial order.

COMPETITION BETWEEN OLIGOPOLISTS

Even in the absence of legislation to control cartels (see Chapter 11) there are strains on their long-term viability because of the natural desire of the cartel members to evade agreements where they can and thus gain an advantage over their rivals. From Fig. 6.2 it can be seen that if any member of the oligopoly can lower prices without retaliation it will enjoy the benefits of the demand curve dd below K and thus be able to attract customers away from its competitors with MC now cutting the mr line at point x and an output of Q_2. Thus firms will be tempted to avoid price-fixing agreements by giving 'under-the-counter' discounts and rebates, particularly if they are the firms with low costs based on an efficient scale of operations. Firms with overseas subsidiaries or with interests in other industries will wish to negotiate exemptions for these companies, thereby causing further friction between cartel members. In a declining industry excess capacity will cause a scramble among members to hold onto their existing market share and under these circumstances price-fixing may well break down entirely. Thus in the mid-1970s the battle for the shrinking mass-produced bread market led to a major price war among the three biggest bakeries and led to Spillers French being forced out of the market. Price wars also break out from time to time among the airlines, tobacco firms and petrol companies while the activities of the international oil cartel OPEC have, over the years, shown all the characteristics of the cartel.

Far less dangerous to all the members of an oligopoly than price competition is non-price competition based on the various marketing techniques at their disposal. With little difference in prices firms must aim to accentuate the other differences of their products to reduce the degree of substitution between them and with it the elasticity of demand. Thus advertising is a very strong feature of oligopolistic competition and it is interesting that the more similar the different car manufacturers models become the more the advertising concentrates on comparisons between them. Branding is another key area of competition both because a strong brand name can dominate the market and because the more brands one company sells the greater the chance of it taking a large share of the market, especially where consumers switch brands frequently. Other options include sponsorship of sport and the arts (particularly important to industries like tobacco and whisky where they are unable to advertise on television), competitions, free offers and joint-marketing promotions such as the offer of coupons as part-payment towards an article.

Monopoly

The true monopoly where one supplier has total control of a market is rare. This is partly due to the stability of oligopolies which prevent any one member of the industry becoming powerful enough to squeeze out the others and partly due to the antipathy towards monopoly which has persisted over the centuries. This attitude towards monopoly is not surprising when one considers the immense power the monopolist possesses as the sole supplier, particularly if the product or service in question is a necessity. In fact this power can be exaggerated since it is by no means absolute. The perfect monopoly would be a situation in which the monopolist could dictate both price and output – so offering the prospect of infinite profits. Such a position is not possible since however necessary the product demand must inevitably become elastic once the price has become so high that consumers can no longer afford to buy it – even if they cannot live without it. The monopolist can decide either price or output but not both; if he wishes to sell more of his product he must cut his price while if he raises the price he must accept that demand, and therefore output, will fall. For this reason the equilibrium position of a monopolist is similar to that of the monopolistic competitor. The essential difference is that there will in this case be no tendency for super profits to disappear in the long run since no new firms can enter the industry. Potential long-run entrants into the market will be confronted by barriers to entry even greater than those erected by oligopolists. In addition to the barriers to entry discussed under oligopoly the newcomer will be confronted by competition from a firm whose name is well-established and synonymous with the industry in the public mind and whose position may well be protected by patent.

Price discrimination

The monopolist can only increase demand for his product by cutting his price and this means cutting the price even to those who are prepared to pay the higher price, these consumers enjoying a 'consumer surplus' or cheap prices. If, however, the monopolist could charge each consumer the maximum price that particular consumer is prepared to pay the consumer surplus would be eliminated and both revenue and profits increased. The practice of charging different prices to different buyers is known as price discrimination and its effect can be seen in Table 6.2.

Table 6.2

Price	Marginal quantity sold	TR	AR	MR
10	10	100	10	—
9	3	127	9.7	9 (27 ÷ 3)
8	2	143	9.5	8 (16 ÷ 2)
7	2	157	9.2	7 (14 ÷ 2)

In the absence of price discrimination the highest total revenue which can be earned is 120 with 15 units being sold at eight each. Under price discrimination, however, ten units can be sold at the price ten, three more at nine, two at eight and so on with total revenue rising with each price change. Profits will continue to rise too as long as MR remains greater than MC. Under price discrimination the MR line replaces the AR line as the demand curve while the AR line shifts to a higher position than before. Thus a discriminating monopoly will produce more and receive a higher total revenue than a single-price monopoly. Unfortunately price discrimination is not always possible as the supplier must be able to control what is offered to each buyer and be able to prevent resale from one buyer to another. Therefore discrimination is possible on a regional basis or in international markets, when selling services rather than goods and when selling relatively immobile goods like capital equipment. Price discrimination is not confined to monopolies since any producer with monopolistic power such as an oligopolistic firm can also use price discrimination effectively. Common examples are the different prices charged by car manufacturers in Britain as compared to the Continent or the cheaper prices charged by hairdressers to children and old-age pensioners.

Price discrimination clearly benefits the seller but the impact on the consumer is more debatable. On the face of it discrimination appears bad as the seller is manipulating the market to squeeze the highest price possible from each buyer. However, discrimination is desirable in the sense that buyers who would not otherwise have been able to afford the product can now do so while those paying the higher prices would have done so anyway. Furthermore resources are being used more efficiently than under a single-price monopoly as output more closely equates to what it would have been under perfect competition.

The question mark over profit maximisation

The theory of profit maximisation indicates that there is an optimum output for any producer, whether operating under perfect or imperfect competition. As perfect competition is a hypothetical situation the importance of the profit-maximising output revolves around its applicability to imperfect markets. For a producer to maximise profits as a monopolist, an oligopolist or a monopolistic competitor output must be at the point where marginal revenue is equal to marginal cost. The producer must therefore accept that price which equates market demand with that output. The theory also implies that the producer is able to project the price which will be received at all possible outputs otherwise it is not possible to calculate the marginal revenue curve and thus the optimum output. The theory of profit maximisation is based on two important assumptions. Firstly that the producer is able to determine the profit-maximising output and secondly that it is the aim of all suppliers to maximise their profits. The first of these assumptions is open to question because of the complexities of cost structures in most industries so that it is often impossible to separate out the contributions of the various factors of production and the proportion of costs attributable to each. Thus while it is possible to cost a particular output in terms of total and average cost it may be extremely difficult to calculate marginal cost over a range of outputs.

The marginal revenue curve is also difficult to estimate since it assumes that demand is static and therefore predictable over various price ranges. Even if the producer were able to describe with any accuracy the shapes of the marginal cost and revenue curves, traditional patterns of behaviour in price and output policies cannot be dismissed by the emergence of a relatively recent economic theory. Thus most firms have long been used to the cost-plus method of pricing based on an estimate of likely demand, the expected average total cost for this level of output and a percentage added to this as profit margin. The emphasis has thus been in the past on fixing prices rather than fixing output and it must be remembered that the theory of profit maximisation was based not on observed behaviour but on an assessment of how firms might be expected to behave if they wished to maximise profits.

Apart from the difficulty of actually achieving the profit-maximising position there is also the question of whether this is the firm's objective. The perfect competitor has no choice since unless it maximises profits it will not survive but imperfect competition allows a firm to make substantial profits without profit maximisation. Nor can it be assumed that profit is the sole driving force of an enterprise, especially in the mixed economy where excessive profits are viewed with such suspicion and antagonism and where large firms are rarely managed by people with a major shareholding in the company. An extreme example of where profit maximisation is never considered is the Football League club where profits are rarely made and profits are less important than the winning of honours, even for the directors and shareholders who own the club. It is also rare for a football manager to be dismissed through financial incompetence – rather his career depends almost entirely on the team's record; though this will, of course, affect the club's financial position. Other examples of where profit is not the sole objective of the enterprise are not difficult to find; many of the early car and aeroplane manufacturers wanted to make the most prestigious car or plane in the world, not the most profitable. On a less grand scale there is no shortage of people wanting to run their own restaurant or bookshop despite the statistical evidence to show that they are high-risk, low-profit ventures. Just as it is nonsensical to see the consumer as being driven solely by considerations of price it must be recognised that the individual entrepreneur is influenced by power, fame, public recognition and personal satisfaction as well as by the desire to make a profit. When the entrepreneurial motives are further confused by the dividing of the function between managers and shareholders even more complex aims may be formulated. In many large organisations personal or inter-departmental rivalries, traditional targets of achievement and the pattern of individual progression within the organisation all militate against profit-maximisation being the sole, or even chief aim of the organisation. It is also possible that a firm whose long-term objective is profit-maximisation will take short-term measures contrary to this aim, as, for example, an oligopolist cutting prices to force a competitor out of the market or the monopolist who cuts prices temporarily to assuage fears of excessive profits among public or government circles.

SALES MAXIMISATION

A firm concerned with growth and prestige rather than with the maximisation of profits may well seek to achieve some form of sales maximisation. Clearly this would not entail the sale of unlimited quantities of the firm's product but the maximisation of sales commensurate with a laid down level of minimum profits. *Pure* sales maximisation is achieved when the firm can maximise revenue while still achieving its minimum profit requirement so that total revenue is at its maximum and marginal revenue is zero. If sales maximisation leads to profits being below the minimum acceptable level output must be reduced until that level of profit is attained so that the firm operates under conditions of *constrained* sales maximisation. A comparison of the output of a firm under profit maximisation and both forms of sales maximisation is illustrated in Fig. 6.3 where Q_1 represents the output under profit maximisation, Q_2 the constrained sales mazimisation output with a minimum profit requirement of P_2 and Q_3 the pure sales maximisation output with a profit requirement of P_1. Thus output is higher

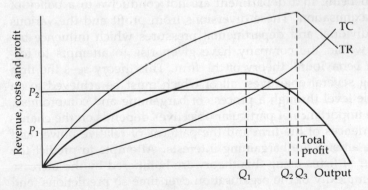

Fig. 6.3

under sales maximisation than under profit maximisation while price is lower as the higher output can only be sold at a lower price.

In practice pure sales maximisation is as unlikely as pure profit maximisation since a firm could expand sales indefinitely by increasing advertising expenditure until the higher costs incurred lead the firm to reach its profit constraint output; constrained sales maximisation is the more likely proposition. Nevertheless the existence of sales maximisation as the objective of the firm is likely to increase the emphasis on marketing and advertising in the firm's operational strategy.

BEHAVIOURAL THEORIES

The proposition of sales maximisation arises from the tendency in large organisations for the decision-making managers to be a different group from the profit-earning shareholders and thus to have goals other than making profits. However, it is important not to overstress the differences between the objectives of the two groups. In large companies the directors frequently own relatively large blocks of shares – not large perhaps as a proportion of the total share issue but large enough to represent an important slice of their wealth – and are therefore concerned with profit. In addition both managers and shareholders are more likely to have a common view as to what constitutes an acceptable level of profits rather than the former being concerned with sales maximisation and the latter with profit maximisation. If managers can maintain an adequate level of profits they will be free to pursue other objectives like high sales and the growth of the firm, especially if such objectives are likely to bring them higher salaries and greater power. In many companies the fact that bonuses are linked to higher sales rather than higher profits and that salary scales rise with more, rather than less, staff being in a department are not conducive to a policy of profit maximisation. These diversions from profit and the various other individual and departmental pressures which influence behaviour within the company have given rise to attempts to formulate a behavioural theory of the firm. This theory sees the firm as having several objectives, all of which must be achieved to an acceptable level through a process of bargaining and compromise. Thus the importance of particular objectives depends on the changing experiences of the firm and the patterns of relative power and influence among the bargaining interests. Attempts to predict the behaviour of firms using this theory are hampered by the increase in the complexity of the organisation over time so predictions tend to be based only on expected performance in the short run.

Furthermore it is extremely difficult to build into a behavioural model the various external influences on the firm's behaviour so that while behavioural theory attempts to stress the multi-dimensional character of the objectives of the firm it is unable to predict with any certainty what these objectives will be and how far they are likely to be realised.

Cases for discussion

I. THE LANCASHIRE COTTON INDUSTRY

At least until the 1950s the industry was highly compartmentalised. Different parts of the county concentrated on the various sectors of the industry and each firm specialised in one particular function, such as spinning, weaving, dyeing or printing. Most of the firms were small and had remained family businesses. They had suffered decline throughout the inter-war period, firstly because of cheap overseas competition and later because of the slump of the 1930s. Capital replacement had been almost non-existent in some areas with profits too small to provide sufficient internal investment funds. The workforce was highly skilled, tradition-conscious and paid on piece-rate. The numbers in the industry declined between the wars but picked up in the Second World War and the boom which followed it. Despite the profits made in the 1940s very little recapitalisation took place and the industry went into its last slow but inevitable decline in the mid-1950s.

1. What characteristics of monopolistic competition did the cotton industry display in the 1940s, both in the short and long term?
2. What various interests and motivations would you have to bring together to provide some sort of behavioural theory for the cotton firm?
3. Why might it be said that the industry illustrated how profit-maximisation can be in conflict with long-term efficiency?

II. THE PETROL COMPANIES

Until the 1960s the petrol manufacturing companies mounted extensive advertising campaigns to promote the relative merits of their products in terms of quality and performance. Market research then revealed that consumers paid little attention to brand names and were concerned only with relative prices. Mindful of the dangers to an oligopoly of a price-war the companies have attempted to avoid price competition but in the 1970s and 1980s the

oil price rises and world glut of oil have resulted in constant pressures on prices with occasional price-cutting attempts.

1. Discuss the validity of the statement by a petrol company
   spokesman that 'The public are better off without price wars
   because they mean higher prices in the long run'.
2. What main marketing methods have the different companies
   adopted in the 1980s?
3. If the demand for petrol is inelastic how can prices be low
   enough for companies to claim that they lose money on the
   petrol section of the business?

Chapter 7

THE SIZE OF FIRMS

In the last chapter stress was laid on the importance of control over the market in determining the profitability of the enterprise. In itself the size of the firm does not indicate the extent of its control over the market since it is monopolistic power which is the determining factor. However, where there is weak product differentiation or where control of the market depends on the possession of large resources, large firms will enjoy a substantial advantage and this gives firms in those industries an incentive to grow.

FACTORS LEADING TO GROWTH

1. *Profitability.* If the firm is to grow it must be able to raise funds for new investment and whether these funds are raised from internal or external sources the rate of profit will affect the ability to raise these funds. On the other hand profitability may itself be hindered by growth since in a competitive environment new demand can only be obtained by attracting customers through lower prices or by increasing advertising costs. Thus sustained growth is more likely to be achieved by the efficient, high-profit firm rather than the inefficient firm since the former will be able to bear the costs of growth and take over the market share of the latter.

2. *Innovation.* Since efficient low-cost firms have an edge within the market, less efficient firms can only grow through innovation and technological change which will enable them to restore their competitiveness and so innovation is an important source of growth.

3. *Management enterprise.* The more competent the management the greater the likelihood that opportunities for growth will be rec-

ognised and seized upon. These new opportunities occur through the existence within the firm of unused productive resources and as the firm takes up these opportunities and expands, new opportunities are recognised. As growth occurs the management team becomes more experienced at handling growth opportunities and itself expands through the infusion of new expertise so that management itself provides a further pool of under-used resources. In theory there should be no limit to the potential for management to handle new growth opportunities but in practice this is unlikely to be the case since it is doubtful if managerial expertise can grow indefinitely in the face of increasingly more complex management structures and a growing diversity of operations.

4. *Economies of scale.* While growth may represent the only means whereby economies of scale can be achieved they are themselves likely to be a direct source of growth since they tend to make the firm more competitive, widen its market and thus increase its sales and profits. The ability of economies of scale to promote growth depends, however, on the potential size of the market being large enough to justify new technical processes or other economies being introduced.

5. *Diversification.* If there are limits to the growth of the firm imposed by the size of its market further expansion might be sought in other markets. In theory there should be no limit on the ultimate size of the firm since it could continue to grow indefinitely by finding new markets in which to diversify. Large firms, especially those in the research-based industries, are more easily able to diversify since they possess the resources of capital and skilled manpower required. Furthermore since new industries both present the best prospects for growth and are also increasingly likely to be research-based such industries are more likely to be better placed for growth through diversification. The main limit posed on growth through diversification is the fierce competition likely to be encountered from existing firms within the industry who may have an edge on specialist knowledge and familiarity with market conditions.

Integration

As a firm grows it is increasingly likely to be confronted by a situation in which further growth is difficult. If it stays within its existing market it will come up against the growth aspirations of its competitors and if it diversifies it may enter areas where it is inadequately equipped to rival existing firms. A solution to this dilemma is to seek growth through integration and thus achieve further expansion by absorbing existing enterprises within or outside its own market. Integration takes three main forms:

(1) *Horizontal integration.*   This is a merger of two existing companies at present competing with each other in the same market, e.g. two frozen food packaging firms or two airlines. Where the two companies are both manufacturers but of vastly different products the integration is referred to as lateral, such as the merger of Cadbury and Schweppes.

(2) *Vertical integration.*   This consists of a merger between two companies in the same industry but at different stages of the productive or distributive process. It can be either forward vertical integration, e.g. a brewery buying up a free public house, or backwards, e.g. a manufacturer taking over the source of supply of its raw materials.

(3) *Conglomerate integration.*   This takes in any merger not included within the above headings and thus may well involve a merger between two firms with little or nothing in common at all. However, such mergers are rarely without some rationale, whether it be the opportunity to get into a new expanding industry or to apply financial or marketing skills to a compatible market.

While the primary justification for integration is that of growth the motives behind particular mergers may be quite varied in the objectives by which that growth will be achieved.

1. *Economies of scale.*   Many horizontal mergers are prompted by the recognition that advances in techniques within the industry have given rise to potential economies of scale which can only be realised through larger units of production. Merger may also achieve economies through rationalisation when both companies are producing similar products but the individual production of each firm is too small to achieve minimum costs. Rationalisation may also prompt mergers in declining industries to eliminate excess capacity as occurred in the textile industry in the 1930s, shipbuilding in the 1960s, etc. Vertical integration may also be inspired by economies of scale as, for example, when suppliers of components are too small to cope with the firm's demand and have not attained the same degree of technical progress.

2. *Market domination.*   If there is such a thing as the evolution of market forms it is from monopolistic competition towards oligo-poly, or even monopoly. The smaller the number of firms within the market the greater the potential for market domination either individually or collectively and so merger activity can be expected to reduce the danger from competitors, increase the firm's own market share and strengthen its position in competition with its remaining rivals. A merger may also permit two or more weak firms to strengthen their position against a powerful competitor who threatens their share of the market, notably when overseas firms threaten to acquire control of the domestic industry. This was the circumstance which led to the formation of Imperial Tobacco in 1902. Vertical integration, too, may be undertaken to achieve or resist market domination; in the former case it may deprive a com-petitor of supplies or market outlets while in the latter it may pre-vent a monopoly being formed by a firm's supplier of essential materials.

3. *Diversification.*   A main reason for diversification is to enter a new market when the firm's existing one is either static or declining and may thus permit accumulated reserves to be commercially ex-ploited. By taking over an existing firm in the market the firm will be able to take advantage of the former's market contacts, technical expertise, brand names and equipment and thus smooth the pro-cess of entry into this new area of activity. Diversification may also present an opportunity to take advantage of faster growth in other sectors of the industry or to enable the development of joint mar-keting strategies for complementary products or services as when the Grand Metropolitan Hotel Group took over Watney Mann.

Market concentration

Through a process of merger between some firms in the industry and the demise of others most of the major industries in Britain have, in the past century, evolved from a monopolistically competitive market to an oligopolistic one. While not all mergers have been successful in realising the economies of scale or market supremacy expected those firms which have indulged in merger activity have grown at a faster rate than non-merging firms and this factor has hastened the process by which most key industries have become dominated by a few large firms. By the late 1960s the degree of market concentration in British industry was such that roughly half the mergers considered on monopoly criteria to come within the domain of government legislation on mergers would have resulted in a market share of 50 per cent or more. Further market concentration since then has been hindered both by the constraints of government legislation and the tendency for a stalemate to develop between the remaining firms in the industry once their numbers have been reduced to three or four. This is because if the last three firms are all about the same size in terms of market share a merger between any two of them could severely threaten the position of the other. As a result oligopolists often indulge in defensive practices such as limitations on the number of shares that each may hold in the others. These major companies are unlikely, however, to refrain from merger activity once the limit has been reached within their original market and since the late 1960s an increasing number of larger mergers have represented diversification with the same firm having a substantial market share in several industries. It is thus possible for the same half-dozen firms to dominate several industries and as long as a firm can grow this way it need not risk government interest in its activities by trying to gain a larger share of its primary market. Thus the great conglomerates are able to increase their share of total industrial production without necessarily raising the level of concentration in any one industry. The process of increasing market concentration is as likely to occur during periods of economic depression as during periods of economic expansion since mergers may be attractive to reduce excess capacity in a dwindling market while the larger firms in the industry are better equipped in terms of resources and reserves to cope with losses or more difficult selling conditions than small firms which

Table 7.1   Mergers (1982)

	Expenditure (£ million)	No. of companies
Manufacturing	549	202
Construction	140	39
Transport & communication	9	13
Wholesale distribution	210	34
Retail distribution	581	17
Miscellaneous services	243	61
Agriculture & mining	270	20
Property	185	51
Mixed	20	26
Financial companies	162	24
Total	2,369	487

Source: *Annual Abstract of Statistics*

are more likely to go under. Increased market concentration among the domestic firms in the industry does not necessarily mean that the range of goods to the consumer is reduced. In many cases merged firms continue to operate on a semi-autonomous basis while strong foreign competitors may be able to break into the home market and reduce the market share of home producers even where they have a major slice of the market held by domestic firms. Indeed the great irony of increased market concentration among British firms is that in the last decade this development has been overtaken by the growth in market share held by foreign firms, most notably in such industries as motor vehicles, electrical goods and merchant shipping.

The importance of small firms

The fact that so many of the key industries in Britain are dominated by large firms tends to overshadow the fact that 70 per cent of all manufacturing establishments with more than ten employees have less than a hundred workers or that many small industries, as well as many of the service industries, are dominated by small firms. While the small firm has virtually been eliminated in those industries dependent on large financial resources or the development of economies of scale there are many areas in which its particular qualities enable it to play a significant or even dominant role. On the whole the continued success of many small firms is linked to the market or production conditions peculiar to the industry in which they operate.

1. *Economies of specialisation.* In many industries dominated by large firms small firms may concentrate on producing components or other specialised parts for the larger firms. Ford, for example, at one time produced their own car windows but found it more suitable to contract this work out as they could not benefit from the economies open to the specialist firm.

2. *Economies of small scale.* Particularly in the retail service industries such as dry cleaning or tailoring, economies of scale may be achieved at a relatively low level of output. This may apply too in manufacturing, although occasionally a major technological break-through will alter production techniques and make it either easier or more difficult for small firms to remain competitive.

3. *Provision of high quality goods or services.* In certain cases it is not

possible to develop economies of scale due to the nature of the product or service requiring intricate skills or individuality of items produced and in these cases while a larger firm may benefit from marketing economies it may also suffer the handicap of being less 'select' in the minds of potential clientele. In industries such as high quality fashion and jewellery, the small firm can not only thrive but also has advantages over larger organisations.

4. *Limited market size.* This is to some extent linked to the last point since high quality goods are certain to have a smaller market by virtue of their price. Yet while the firms themselves may be small, market concentration in such industries may be very high so that one firm has a monopoly of professionally hand-rolled cigarette manufacture yet employs only a handful of workers. Semi-monopoly situation also occur in the manufacture of test match quality cricket balls and so on.

5. *New industries.* While barriers to entry may prevent small firms breaking into long-established markets many new industries develop from small firms as the result of new product development or a technological breakthrough in the manufacture of existing products. Even where the industry is long established it may be possible for new blood to enter the industry if relatively little initial finance is needed such as some branches of retailing, the small workshop and the master craftsman. Unless they are exceptionally competent such firms will tend to stay small while others will fail. A few will grow to become major firms and the market leaders once the evolutionary path from monopolistic competition to oligopoly is traced.

In the above discussion the survival and importance of small firms is linked primarily to circumstances in which they have certain advantages over larger firms. Yet it is also the case that small firms do survive even in industries dominated by large firms. A major reason for this is the problem of diseconomies of scale encountered by larger firms. In contrast the small firm may be able to present an image of a friendly, flexible organisation able to take decisions more quickly, willing to adapt to a customer's suggestions and more likely to keep to deadlines. Furthermore in an industry dominated by mass production there may still be room for small firms producing high-quality articles for a limited market. In a sense these firms constitute an industry within an industry as competition with the larger firms is tenuous. Thus in the car industry Rolls-Royce, Morgan and Aston-Martin Lagonda can all be successful without posing a threat to the volume car producers. There is also a tendency for oligopolists to leave one or two small firms alone rather than taken them over and risk government interest in their already substantial share of the market.

The importance of the small firm in the maintenance and development of a healthy industrial structure has long been recognised. For statistical purposes small manufacturing firms are defined as those with 200 employees or less and on this basis 95 per cent of British manufacturing firms count as small firms, accounting between them for about a fifth of both net output and employment. The survival of small firms is essential if industry as a whole is to be successful for they provide the base on which industrial growth takes place. They provide not only an outlet for the talents of the true entrepreneur who might well be stifled and frustrated if working within a large organisation but also are the testing ground where the able young manager can learn his trade and show his potential before moving on to bigger firms. There is also strong evidence to suggest that, while large companies spend proportionately far more on research and development than do small firms and are responsible for the majority of minor innovative changes, it is small firms which introduce the bulk of major innovative changes and thus make a disproportionately large contribution to the process of innovative change, a prerequisite of economic development.

Despite the importance of small firms to the health of the economy their numbers and market share have declined steadily this century in an economic society more suited to the large business organisation. However, various governments have since the war attempted to stimulate the success of this type of enterprise by measures to ease their development and these will be considered in subsequent sections.

Case for discussion

Prior to 1960 the manufacture of aircraft in the United Kingdom was still dominated by a relatively large number of firms. Most of these had turned to aircraft manufacture to expand from their original activities or had developed it in parallel with other engineering activities. Being a relatively new industry the management of the various companies were frequently either the founders or had begun in the industry when still in its infancy. Whatever the size and stature of a particular company all shared the common dependence on the government who acted both as their principal customer and also their principal patron through the provision of funds for research and development. In 1960 the government of the day pressured the various companies to join to form large companies. None the less the uneasy relationship between government and industry remained until nationalisation in 1975 since the government saw the industry as profligate with public funds and failing to produce what was required of them while the companies thought of the government as short-sighted and liable to let the industry down by breaking contracts.

1. What special difficulties arise from having the government as an industry's main customer?
2. On what main economic grounds could the forced amalgamation of these companies be justified?
3. Consider the view that this industry shows that the phrases 'Small is beautiful' and 'Biggest is best' are not contradictory since they refer to different situations.

Chapter 8

THE DISTRIBUTION OF FACTOR EARNINGS

One of the most difficult areas of economic theory to apply to business practice is that of the distribution of factor earnings, i.e. the allocation of the revenue received by the business to the various factors of production, land, labour, capital and enterprise, which have contributed to earning that revenue. Before examining the theory itself it might be useful briefly to recapitulate the theory of the firm from which the theory of distribution can be developed. The theory of the firm postulates that the aim of the firm is to maximise profits and that the profit-maximising output will be the one at which marginal revenue is equal to marginal cost. The marginal revenue is the addition to total revenue accruing from the sale of one extra unit and the marginal cost is the addition to total cost arising from the production of that unit. It is possible, however, to break down both marginal cost and marginal revenue further into their various constituent parts. Suppose, for example, that a firm producing standard engineering components receives an urgent order for an extra 6,000 units at a price of 30 pence each, requiring the firm to work two hours' overtime in the course of the week. If it is assumed that the firm will maximise its profits on this operation so that marginal revenue is equal to marginal cost it is possible to produce a simple financial breakdown of the operation.

Marginal revenue = 30 pence
Marginal cost (the extra wages paid to workers, extra fuel and power costs, extra hidden costs (wear and tear on machinery, maintenance etc.) plus an allowance made for profit) = 30 pence

It should now be possible to calculate the marginal cost of labour by dividing the extra wages bill by the number of units produced so that if the extra wages bill amounts to £600 to produce the 6,000 units required the marginal cost of labour will be ten pence per unit. A similar calculation should be possible for the other factors of production used. But if the marginal cost of labour is ten pence it should surely follow that the marginal revenue contributed by labour is also ten pence otherwise labour is contributing less in earnings to the firm than it is costing and is therefore being used inefficiently. If the marginal revenue added by labour is ten pence then the following financial breakdown will apply.

Marginal cost of labour = 10 pence = $\frac{1}{3}$ of marginal cost

Marginal product of labour = 2,000 units ($\frac{1}{3}$ of production)

Marginal revenue product of labour = $\dfrac{2,000 \times 30}{6,000}$ = 10 pence

In the above calculation the **marginal revenue product** is found by multiplying together the marginal product added by labour and the revenue earned by that marginal product. So the marginal revenue product represents the portion of marginal revenue earned by the factor of production, in this case labour. As the marginal cost incurred by labour is one-third of the total cost (including an allowance for normal profit) of £1,800 it is assumed that labour has contributed a third of the total extra production and thus earned a third of the total extra revenue gained. Of course the right answer has been found by juggling with figures so that both the marginal product and the marginal revenue product have been calculated from the desired answer rather than the other way round. In practice how could the marginal revenue product of labour or any other factor of production be calculated? With extreme difficulty. In a modern industrial unit it is very difficult to separate out precisely the contribution made by any one factor. Furthermore the correct procedure should be to ascertain the marginal revenue product and then use the correct balance of factors of production to ensure that the marginal cost of each factor is equal to the marginal revenue product of that factor with each factor being used to its maximum efficiency, whereas in the example quoted marginal revenue product was worked out on the basis of known marginal cost. The fact that the marginal revenue product of a particular factor does not equal the marginal cost of that factor does not in itself negate the principle of marginal revenue and marginal cost being equal since if the marginal revenue product of labour were less than its marginal cost this could be balanced by the marginal revenue product of capital being greater than its marginal cost. The likelihood of the marginal revenue product of a factor being equal to its marginal cost is remote since in the example above such a factor as land may yield a zero marginal cost with no change in rent or rates yet still be making a contribution to the extra production. In addition such items as wage rates are agreed by management and workers under contractual arrangements and not costed for a particular job. None the less there must be some relationship between the contribution made by a factor and the cost of the factor and the theory of distribution goes some way towards quantifying that relationship.

The demand for a factor

Of the four factors of production one, enterprise or entrepreneurship, hires the other factors, land, labour and capital. In return for the use of their services the entrepreneur pays these factors rent, wages and salaries and interest. The entrepreneur's own reward is profit, which is effectively a surplus after all other factor payments have been met. If this surplus is not sufficient to cover his expected or normal profit the entrepreneur has made a loss while if it more than covers normal profit he makes super profits. The entrepreneur's demand for the factors of production is a derived demand since they are not wanted for their own sake but because, through their contribution to production, they offer the prospect of earning a profit for the entrepreneur. Since the marginal product of a factor is the extra product added by one extra unit of that factor while other factor inputs are held constant marginal product will tend to fall with every extra unit of the factor added because of the law of diminishing returns. The marginal revenue product will show a similar decline though in this latter case the decline will be much sharper if price is also reduced as output is increased.

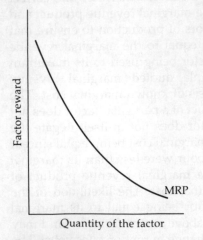

Fig. 8.1

As Fig. 8.1 shows, the marginal revenue product (MRP) line is similar to a demand curve and does in fact represent the demand curve for the factor. Not surprisingly the lower the value of input or reward to the factor the greater will be the quantity demanded as there will be an incentive for the producer to substitute that factor for more expensive ones.

The supply of a factor

Like the supply of any economic resource the supply of a factor of production will be responsive to price changes. Thus the higher the factor reward offered the higher will be the supply of the factor as units of the factor move from those uses which give lower returns to that offering the greater reward. In a competitive market, therefore, the price offered to a factor of production will be found by the intersection of the demand and supply curves of that factor. For the individual firm under perfect competition the supply of the factor will be perfectly elastic since the firm is unable to influence prices by its activities and thus can obtain as many units of that factor as it requires at the prevailing price. This situation is illustrated in Fig. 8.2.

Just as the firm maximises profits when MR = MC it achieves the same equilibrium point if it equates the MRP of each factor with its marginal cost so that the amount added to revenue by the use of one more unit of the factor will equal the cost of employing that unit. This theory of factor rewards is known as the marginal productivity theory under which the rate of reward offered to a factor

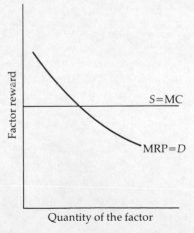

Fig. 8.2

will be equal to the value of the marginal product of that factor when the market is in equilibrium.

In Fig. 8.2 the firm is a perfect competitor and can therefore obtain each extra unit of the factor without raising the reward offered and thus the supply curve of the factor is the same as the marginal cost curve of that factor. However, where imperfect competition prevails the firm will not be able to attract extra units of the factor without raising the reward offered and thus the supply curve of the factor slopes upwards and to the right like a market supply curve. In its most extreme form the firm will be a monopsonist, i.e. the sole buyer of the factor who cannot attract units of the factor from other firms but must bring in new units of the factor into the market. In this case the monopsonist must offer a higher reward to attract new units of the factor but in doing so it will also have to offer the higher reward to existing units so that the marginal cost of employing the extra units will be above the supply curve. Thus supposing a monopsonist employs 100 workers at £100 each per week and then attracts a new worker for £101; the marginal cost of labour will be £101 plus (100 × £1) = £201, not £101.

By equating the marginal cost of labour, or any other factor, with its marginal revenue product the monopsonist will maximise profits by employing Q_1 units of labour at the wage rate W_1 instead of the competitive market situation in which Q_2 units of labour would be employed at wage rate W_2. Thus under a monopsony both the reward offered to a factor of production and the number of units of

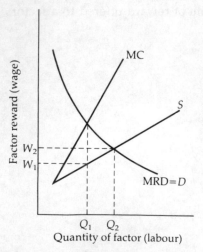

Fig. 8.3

the factor employed will be lower than under a perfectly competitive factor market (Fig. 8.3).

Clearly the existence of monopsonistic pressures in the factor market will provoke a response from the suppliers of the factor to protect their position and this is a subject to which we will return later in the chapter.

Economic rent and transfer earnings

In the above discussions the market rate offered to a factor of production means that all units of the factor receive the same reward despite the fact that some units would have been available at lower rates of reward. Thus it is possible to distinguish between two distinct payments made to each unit of the factor. Firstly there is the payment which must be made to keep the unit in its present use and secondly there is that payment over and above what is necessary to keep that unit in its present use. The first of these payments is known as transfer earnings and the second as economic rent. In Fig. 8.4 the market rate offered to all units of the factor is at the intersection of the supply and demand curves of the factor. That unit of the factor which enters the market at the equilibrium rate earns only transfer earnings since at any rate less than this it will transfer to another use. For all other units part of the reward received consists of economic rent payments since they would still be receiving their transfer earnings at lower rates of re-

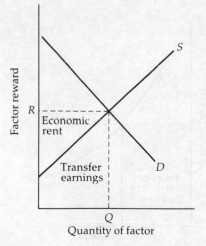

Fig. 8.4

ward. The firm employing these units is unable to avoid these economic rent payments since it cannot determine which units would be available at lower rates of reward. The term economic rent owes its origins to David Ricardo who first applied the term to land in the early nineteenth century. Contrary to popular belief at the time that high land rents were the cause of high farm prices he argued that land was fixed in supply with no alternative uses and its reward therefore depended on the demand for land. If food prices rose farming profits would also rise and this push up the rents paid to the most productive land giving the owners of such land economic rent payments. The term economic rent is now applied to any factor of production and in the case of profit applies to super profits just as normal profits are effectively the entrepreneur's transfer earnings.

It is clear that for most units of a factor part of their reward is transfer earnings and part economic rent; the ratio of one to the other depends on the responsiveness of the factor to changes in the factor reward offered, i.e. the elasticity of supply of the factor. In the two extreme cases shown in Fig. 8.5 that in Fig. 8.5(a) represents a situation in which the elasticity of supply is zero and thus all earnings are economic rent since the factor still available even if earnings fall to zero. In Fig. 8.5(b) all earnings are transfer earnings since the supply of the factor is perfectly elastic and at the prevailing price of the factor is infinite while below that price no supply is available. Since in the short run the supply of some factors is fixed such factors may temporarily receive economic rent

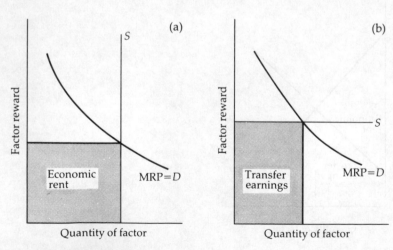

Fig. 8.5(a) & (b)

earnings which disappear in the long run. Such earnings are known as *quasi-rent*.

While the majority of factor units receive both transfer earnings and economic rent it is possible to find cases in which almost, if not quite, all earnings are economic rent, notably in the case of labour. Thus film stars can sometimes earn enormous sums for appearing in a particular film due to the fact that they are unique and the demand for their services is great. At the other end of the scale, people with religious vocations will take vows of poverty and work for virtually nothing at all. On the other hand there are also cases in which the worker receives only transfer earnings, as when there is a standard wage rate in an industry and nobody can be employed at a wage below that rate.

Limitations of marginal productivity theory

Thus far discussion concerning the demand for factors of production has been based on the assumption that firms can equate demand to the value of the marginal product of the factor, be it land, labour or capital. Each factor will then be employed until the point where the marginal revenue product of the factor equals the marginal cost of the factor. If, therefore, the MRP of capital exceeds the MC of capital while the MRP of labour is less than its MC the firm should reduce its demand for labour and increase its demand for capital until equilibrium is restored. When, however, this theory is applied to the real world it breaks down for several reasons. Firstly not all firms are profit-maximisers operating in a perfectly competitive market and thus relying on optimum efficiency to break even so that the typical firm will use some factors inefficiently and still survive. Secondly the theory assumes that all units of the factor are identical and thus equally efficient and this is obviously not true in the case labour or land. Thirdly it is assumed that changes can occur in one sector of the economy in isolation whereas if there is a general decline in employment levels demand for labour will drop even in those industries where wage rates have fallen. Finally the theory assumes that it is possible to measure the contribution of individual factors of production to output. In fact in most industries capital and labour are equally necessary to the tasks performed by the other and it is not possible to identify the exact contribution of each, let alone the contributions of individual workers or machines. Thus the theory of distribution based on marginal productivity theory cannot survive in the absence of a perfectly competitive environment. Rather than each factor receiving a reward commensurate with its contribution to output the factors of production are in competition with each other for the available returns – the final distribution depending upon the monopoly power of the factors involved. Nowhere is this situation more obvious than in the determination of wage rates.

Trade unions and the determination of wages

When examining the concepts of economic rent and transfer earnings it can be seen that because of the uniqueness of particular units of labour it is possible for some of these to receive enormous economic rent payments. While such uniqueness is rare, it is true that the various talents, skills, aptitudes and qualifications possessed by individual members of the workforce make mobility from one occupation to another often difficult or even impossible. The greater the difficulty in transferring labour from one occupation to another the more inelastic will be the supply of labour to that occupation and thus the greater the opportunity for economic rent earnings. By implication the converse will also apply – that where few skills or qualifications are required the supply of labour to a particular use will be highly elastic and only transfer earnings will be earned by many of the workers. It has already been seen, in Fig. 8.3, that a monopsonist will pay lower wages and employ fewer workers than a perfect competitor and where a monopsonist is employing unskilled individual workers with a highly elastic labour supply curve it follows that such workers will be unable to secure wages above the minimum to keep them in employment. For such workers trade unions offer the means by which they can acquire monopoly power comparable to that enjoyed by workers with highly specialised skills or qualifications. As with a monopoly in production the monopolistic union can control either output (the number of workers) or price (the wage rate) but it cannot control both simultaneously.

In Fig. 8.6 the entry of a union into the industry subject to perfect competition will mean claims for higher wages to push the wage rate above its competitive level and to establish a uniform minimum wage. Thus the wage rate rises from W_1 to W_2 with the supply curve for labour becoming a horizontal straight line until Q_3 where the original supply curve becomes applicable again for wage rates above W_2. The effect on employment, however, is that the demand

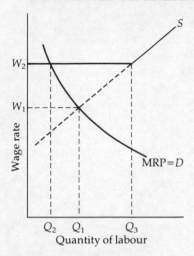

Fig. 8.6

for workers is reduced at the higher wage from Q_1 to Q_2 so that unemployment occurs in the industry. Unless the union can maintain the wage rate throughout the industry there will be a tendency for wage cutting as workers made unemployed seek to work for a lower rate. Frequently, a union is confronted by a monopsonistic employer whose actions will have some impact on wage rates. This situation of monopolist and monopsonist is described as a *bilateral monopoly*. This is shown in Fig. 8.7 where before the entry of the union the wage rate is W_1 and the quantity of labour employed is Q_1. The introduction of a union wage rate will raise the wage to W_2 and cause the supply curve to become perfectly elastic until Q_2. As the supply curve of the factor is the monopsonist's average cost curve for that factor the marginal cost curve will also be W_2 until Q_2 when it jumps to its original line above that point. The firm will employ Q_2 number of workers because at this level the marginal cost of labour is less than the MRP while beyond Q_2 MC is above the MRP. So the entry of a union into the industry has raised both wages and employment as the MC of labour is now lower than it was between Q_3 and Q_2. Only if the union attempts to raise wages beyond W_3 will there be any loss of jobs and thus there is scope for bargaining by both sides of the industry at wage rates between W_1 and W_3.

The bargaining process between management and unions reflects the relative power of the two groups in any given situation. The fact that a union's monopoly power does not of itself enable it to

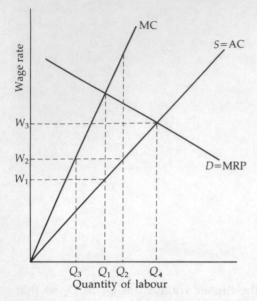

Fig. 8.7

protect its members' jobs and increase wage rates simultaneously has led to a number of other measures being developed by unions to strengthen their position.

1. *The closed shop.* This prevents non-union workers undercutting the union-negotiated wage and also controls the entry of workers into the industry.
2. *Pre-entry qualifications.* These include apprenticeships and examinations, again to limit entry into the industry.
3. *Manning and work rules.* The more complicated and detailed the rules the greater the demand for labour.
4. *Demarcation.* The existence of several unions in one industry emphasises the individuality of particular skills and thus maintains demand for such occupations.
5. *Establishment of union rights.* The attainment of time off for union meetings and for unpaid officials to do their union work ensures maximum communication and co-operation between members.
6. *Redundancy agreements.* These aim to minimise the number of jobs lost through increased capitalisation by the industry.

All these measures involve some restriction on the freedom of action of employers and must therefore be negotiated. The strength of a particular bargaining position depends on the extent to which each side can take sanctions against the other in defence or furtherance of its own position. While strikes immediately spring to mind they are usually the last, rather than the first, sanction adopted by a union. While strikes are obviously damaging to the firm in terms of lost production, orders and goodwill they are also extremely damaging to the union which sees its members suffer financial hardship, its funds depleted and, if the strike goes on long enough, a possible loss of jobs. In addition a protracted strike will almost certainly lead to a loss of income even if it is successful since the lost earnings will never be recovered. Thus unions prefer to use less dramatic methods of putting pressure on the firm, such as the go-slow, work-to-rule or overtime ban. It must also be remembered that not all industrial action centres on pay negotiation – very often the dispute arises over such matters as dismissal or other disciplinary measures, work allocation and demarcation or working conditions and supervision.

Trade unions and real earnings

In the theory of wage determination outlined above a union can only secure a rise in wage rates for its members and protect their jobs by an increase in productivity. This will raise the marginal productivity of labour and thereby lead to more workers being demanded at the same wage or the same number at a higher wage. In the absence of any increase in productivity the union is faced with the choice of either obtaining higher wages for a smaller number of workers or accepting the same wage as the price of maintaining the workforce at current levels. However, in practice unions have at their disposal various bargaining measures to ensure that wage rates can be raised without necessarily any fall in the numbers which are employed. In this case the firm must finance the higher wages bill either through a reduction in the rewards paid to the other factors of production (in practical terms this means profits) or through a rise in prices. This last course is more attractive to the firm but depends for its effectiveness in the degree of control the firm has over its own market and the elasticity of demand for its product or service. In the large oligopolistic industries of the private sector and the monopolistic public corporations there is considerable scope for passing on higher wage costs to the consumer but where the industry's markets suffer because of the higher prices there is likely to be a contraction of output with the resultant implication of lower profits and, ultimately, a threat either to wages or jobs in the industry.

When applying this analysis to real, rather than money, earnings the situation becomes even more complicated. Suppose that all workers achieve a 10 per cent rise in wages and all employers pass this rise on in the form of higher prices. The result is a 10 per cent rise in the level of prices so that there is no change in real earnings, provided that there has been no change either in productivity or market demand. If, however, some unions are more powerful than others and some industries better placed to charge higher prices it is possible, in fact likely, that with an average rise in wages and prices of 10 per cent some workers will achieve rises of more than 10 per cent and others less. There is thus a redistribution of income from the less powerful, less well-organised groups of workers to their more powerful colleagues in other industries. It is possible, then, for the latter to achieve a rise in real earnings without any increase in productivity. Thus while there is some correlation between rises in real earnings and improvements in productivity the bargaining power of the union is of equal importance. This power stems from two sources, the nature of the industry and the structure and organisation of the union. Oligopolistic and monopolistic industries may be better placed than others to pass on higher wage costs in the form of price rises because they do not fear a serious contraction in demand. Similarly such industries will probably be enjoying substantial super profits and will prefer to distribute part of these to the workforce rather than risk a costly strike. Alternatively the industry may consist of a large number of small firms confronted by a single well-organised union. In these circumstances the employers may well find it difficult to maintain a united front in pay negotiations, especially where some of them earn high profits and are more willing to grant the pay rise. With regard to the structure of the union the existence of a closed shop or voluntary high union membership in the industry will make industrial action more effective than where the union is weak or divided. In this context the possession of the funds necessary to sustain a long dispute will also be a strong bargaining weapon. Thus while wealthy unions like those in printing or mining may pursue a lengthy dispute weaker unions may soon be unable to continue to pay strike benefits and face disaffection among the membership. In addition to these factors the reaction of other forces in the economy is also important. Thus where other unions lend their support or where there is evident public sympathy for the union's case the chances of a successful outcome for the union will be greater than where there is public or governmental hostility to the union's case. The tightening and extension of legislation relating to union activities in the early 1980s placed a number of traditional union practices in conflict with the law and obviously hindered the ability of unions to pursue certain issues.

One other important complication with respect to the importance of trade unions in raising real wages relates to the value placed by society as a whole on the various occupations performed; a value often influenced by traditional or other historical factors. The nursing profession still suffers low earnings due to its origins in the mediaeval nursing orders of nuns and the daughters of well-to-do families in the last century with pay being an important consideration in neither case. Miners have traditionally, and rightly, received extra remuneration for the risks attached to working underground yet agricultural workers, who now suffer a higher fatality rate through industrial injury than do miners, remain among the lowest-paid workers in the country. Other groups who once received high earnings in return for specialist skills continue to receive the high rewards even though sometimes the skills have disappeared through technological change, as in some parts of the printing industry. Long-established differentials between various groups of workers may change slowly but tend to be maintained or even exaggerated by the practice of giving pay rises based on percentage figures. Furthermore while unions may campaign for those on low pay their members will be less successful in achieving rises in income than individuals who through high qualifications can enter the highest-paid professions or because of very inelastic supply can earn substantial economic rent payments. Thus white-collar workers were able to maintain their earnings differentials over manual workers at least until the 1960s even without strong trade union support because of traditional factors and sometimes, but not always, more formal qualifications. The need for earnings to be based on comparability with other similar groups has taken on an increased significance with the expansion of the tertiary sector, in particular the public sector. This is because a growing number of workers do not 'produce' anything and are therefore disadvantaged if rises in real earnings are to be measured only in terms of increases in productivity. The tendency for such workers to lose ground as their numbers have increased has led to a growth in trade union activism in the professions and other white-collar groups.

LONG-TERM TRENDS AND THE IMPACT OF TECHNOLOGY

The ability of workers to sustain high earnings is related to the maintenance of monopoly power which manifests itself in inelastic supply and high economic rent payments and is thus related to the importance of labour to the final product. In the absence of natural advantages the existence of a trade union can enable workers to enjoy the same bargaining position as a powerful individual. However, the higher the wage rate the lower the marginal revenue product of labour and the greater the attraction of replacing labour by capital, wherever possible. In the absence of union protection the turnround in wages can be catastrophic for the individual worker. In the late eighteenth century handloom weavers were able to command high earnings since the spinning process was already mechanised, creating a bottleneck at the weaving stage of production and a consequent demand for large numbers of skilled weavers. Once, however, the power loom was introduced the need for handloom weavers collapsed and their earnings fell rapidly as the decline in demand far exceeded the rate at which weavers were leaving the industry. Over the past hundred years the development of strong trade unions has enabled workers to resist their replacement by capital, sometimes resulting in overmanning where capital is introduced but the labour force is kept at previous levels. This situation only represents, however, a short-term respite for jobs since in the long term workers who retire will not be replaced and the industry will offer fewer new job opportunities. Furthermore the introduction of new technology poses greater threats to trade unions today than was the case when the handloom weavers disappeared. During the Industrial Revolution the introduction of machinery did lead to reductions in employment in the short term but by increasing production and leading to market expansion it enabled employment opportunities to rise in the long term. In the technological revolution of the late twentieth century long-established industries are unlikely to find that increased production will generate the demand for extra workers on the scale of the nineteenth century; rather increased automation will continue to reduce the numbers of workers employed. It is likely that white-collar occupations will suffer similar difficulties where basic clerical functions can be replaced by machine. Many essential skills will remain and new ones develop but the number of workers involved is likely to be relatively small. Trade unions may have to concentrate their energies more on seeking shorter working weeks as a way of raising real incomes rather than on seeking higher pay for those in work, otherwise the rift in living standards between those in work and those out of work will widen and the influence of the trade union movement itself weaken as its numbers decline.

Study questions

1. Explain how the MRP curve for a factor is the same as the demand curve for the factor.
2. What are the main constraints on substituting one factor of production for another?
3. Why does the monopsonist appear to be at a disadvantage compared to a perfect competitor when wishing to obtain more units of a factor? Is this true in reality?
4. Can it be argued that all economic rent payments are excessive?
5. Examine the view that hotel prices in London's West End are high because rents in the West End are high.
6. What are the main factors influencing wage rates apart from supply and demand conditions?
7. How would you expect the supply curves for architects, shorthand typists and dustmen to differ?
8. Consider the problems of comparing the occupations of bank clerk and salesman for pay award purposes.
9. Consider the advantages to a company of pay negotiations conducted under a closed shop agreement.
10. Consider to what extent in recent years there has been a growth in the numbers of wage-earners receiving rewards associated with the other factors of production.

Chapter 9

THE ROLE OF CAPITAL

The term 'Capital' is sometimes a source of confusion when used
in economics because of the way it is used in everyday life. In economics capital refers to man-made factors of production as opposed
to the natural factors of production, land and labour. Capital includes buildings, equipment, tools and so on which are produced
not for consumption but as aids to the production process, and, by
implication it also refers to those human skills acquired by education and training. Capital is thus the key factor of production in
the process of economic development and the attainment of economic growth since without it production methods cannot be improved and certain goods and services cannot be produced at all.
However, there is a cost attached to capital since if resources are
diverted towards the production of capital goods they must be
taken away from the production of consumer goods and services.
This cost is more than compensated for by the increased production
which capitalisation will bring and present consumption is thus forgone in order that greater consumption will occur in the future. The
allocation of resources to the production of capital goods is investment and again this word is frequently used to mean something
different. People often refer to their 'capital' being 'invested' in
shares or in a building society when they personally are neither
buying capital goods nor investing. However, the two meanings
of capital and investment can be reconciled. Investment is undertaken by firms to produce a stream of income in the future and the
decision to invest is made on the basis of whether or not the stream
of income earned will exceed the cost of the capital. Similarly the
private individual, by choosing to forgo current consumpton and
save, makes investment funds available to those who wish to use
them and in return receives a stream of income from these savings,
the investment funds themselves being used to buy capital goods.

In both cases the income earned is the interest received on the capital invested.

The investment decision

For the private individual the decision to allocate part of one's income to savings is relatively straightforward since the interest rate earned is known in advance, as is the sacrifice made in terms of the proportion of income diverted away from current consumption. It is also possible to convert these savings quickly into cash or to transfer them to other savings sectors. For the firm, however, the decision to invest is far more complex. The aim is to make profits and investment must be linked to a projected rise in revenue greater than the anticipated cost of the investment undertaken. In the short run this cost will consist of the revenue that could have been earned had the capital employed been allocated to working capital and thus assisted in current production, together with the interest which must be paid on borrowed capital or the interest forgone on the firm's own capital were it invested elsewhere. In the long run there will be the cost of lost flexibility since the value of investment goods in alternative uses is often negligible so that the failure of an investment project could have disastrous consequences for the viability of the enterprise. The benefits arising out of an investment project may be increased capacity and thus higher sales, improved quality of existing products, the development of new products or a reduction in costs. The decision can be based on favourable market conditions or arise out of a desire for greater competitiveness but underlying any motive is the potential for greater profit. Clearly capitalisation of production will offer greater opportunities for profits the greater the reduction in costs this brings. Whatever the capital cost involved the benefits to be gained will depend to a great extent on the savings on labour and other costs made – the higher the cost of labour the greater the incentive to invest in capital for production.

The fundamental difficulty of evaluating investment decisions is that uncertain future returns must be evaluated against present outlays. The future returns are uncertain because the longer the time period under consideration the less accurate will be predictions concerning market demand and cost and profit structures. Even when the firm perceives that it must invest to grow or to maintain its position in the market there may well be alternative investment projects available. In choosing between these various options the firms cannot be guided solely by the criterion of profit maximisation since the investment project may have serious implications for working methods or the size of the labour force and thus industrial relations. The choice made may well be a compromise between maximum profitability and the need to maintain stability in the firm – the behavioural theory of the firm thus seems more feasible than the profit-maximising one. Where, however, the various options would have a similar effect on the structure and workings of the firm and the choice is to be made on the relative profitability of the options there are a number of techniques available for investment appraisal. Most of these techniques solve the immediate problem of future changing money values by establishing the present value of sums to be received in the future. This is achieved by applying a discount factor to money which will be received in future years. This discount is related to the current rate of interest so that if an interest rate of 10 per cent is assumed £100 invested today will yield £110 in a year's time but the present value of £100 received in a year's time will be equivalent only to that sum which will, invested today at 10 per cent give a return of £100 in one year, i.e. £90.91. In general the present value (PV) of a sum due in the future (S) at a rate of interest (r) is

$$PV = \frac{S}{(1+r)^n}$$

where n is the number of time periods before the sum becomes due, in this case one time period being one year. Thus the present value of £100 received in one year when the interest rate is 10 per cent will be

$$PV = \frac{£100}{(1+0.1)} = £90.91$$

The same £100 in two years time has a present value at 10 per cent compounded discount of

$$PV = \frac{£100}{(1+0.1)^2} = £82.64$$

The present value of a series of cash inflows due over a number of years is thus shown as

$$PV = \frac{S1}{(1+r)^1} + \frac{S2}{(1+r)^2} + \frac{S3}{(1+r)^3} \quad \text{etc.}$$

Using this formula it is thus possible to measure the relative merits of several projects which will yield different returns over varying periods of time. To take one more example, if a firm undertakes an investment project which is expected to yield £100 one year from now and £300 for the three years following the present value of these future returns based on a capital cost of 10 per cent will be

$$\frac{£100}{(1+0.1)} + \frac{£300}{(1+0.1)^2} + \frac{£300}{(1+0.1)^3} + \frac{£300}{(1+0.1)^4}$$
$$= £90.91 + £247.93 + £225.39 + £204.90 = £769.13$$

Once the present value of the expected returns has been calculated it is possible to appraise the investment by deducting the outlays on the project (C) from the PV to give the net present value (NPV)

i.e. $NPV = \dfrac{S}{(1+r)^n} - C.$

If this formula yields an NPV greater than zero the project is justified because it will repay the original investment and compensate for the cost of tying up the capital. Thus in the example given above if the outlay is less than £769.13 the investment will be worthwhile but if it is £769.13 or more the investment is not worth undertaking.

The NPV method of discounting assumes a discount rate and then applies it to the revenue received. An alternative method of discounting is the internal rate of return (IRR) or marginal efficiency of capital method. This treats the rate of interest as unknown and calculates the rate which will produce a present value of return equal to the capital outlay. The rate thus calculated is the internal rate of return on the investment and if this rate is higher than the cost of capital, i.e. higher than the market rate of interest, the investment will be worth undertaking but if it does not the investment will be rejected. If, for example, an outlay of £600 yields a return of £120, £288 and £520 over the next three years a discount must be found which will reduce that total return of £928 to a present value of £600. Thus

$$£600 = \frac{£120}{(1+r)} + \frac{£288}{(1+r)^2} + \frac{£520}{(1+r)^3}$$

which when finally calculated gives a discount rate of 20 per cent.

In practice the two methods of discounting the cash flow produce the same decisions as to the acceptability of a particular investment. However, both methods are claimed by their supporters to have their own special attractions. The NPV method is said to be more accurate in ranking alternative projects in order of profitability and thus suits the objective of investment – profit. The IRR method is claimed to be more appropriate to the needs of businessmen in that the concept of a return on capital employed is more readily appreciated. Its also easier to compare the IRR result to the estimated cost of capital whereas the NPV calculation requires the estimation of present values for each possible cost. On balance the NPV method is considered more efficient by most economists but both are considered vastly superior to the various 'rule of thumb' methods used by many firms. Thus there is the 'pay-back' method which measures the time necessary to recoup sufficient profits to cover the initial outlay – the shorter the period necessary the higher a project is ranked. There is also the 'book rate of return' method which measures the rate of profit, after depreciation, to initial capital outlay. Thus if an investment earns £250 over ten years on an outlay of £100 the average rate of return is 25 per cent. The figure obtained is then compared to the cost of capital. Such methods, though popular, can never be regarded as more than a rough guide to deciding whether a project is worthy of more detailed analysis.

All the methods of investment appraisal outlined above depend to a greater or lesser extent on the rate of interest in deciding whether to proceed with a project, and in theory at least the level of interest rates should determine the willingness of firms to invest since the cost of capital affects the profitability of a project and therefore its viability. The higher the rate of interest on investment funds the less likely is any project to be worth undertaking. If the firms can borrow all the investment funds it needs at the going rate of interest it will go on borrowing until the rate of return of capital equals the rate of interest – this is the theory underlying the marginal efficiency of capital method of discounting future cash flow discussed above. The demand curve for funds is therefore the same as the marginal efficiency of capital curve (MEC).

In Fig. 9.1 the demand for loanable funds (D) is shown as a downward-sloping curve varying inversely to the rate of interest. As the rate of interest falls more projects become attractive since the rate of return on these projects will now at least cover the cost of borrowing or the foregone interest earned if the internal funds used are lent out on the market. The supply of loanable funds (S) for investment purposes is an upward-sloping curve varying directly with the rate of interest. The higher the interest rate, therefore, the greater the willingness of potential lenders to sacrifice liquidity or personal investment plans for an income from investment payments. The prevailing rate of interest in the market will be determined by the interaction of the demand for and supply of loanable funds, shown as I_1. For simplification it is assumed that there is only one market for investment funds. Changes in business

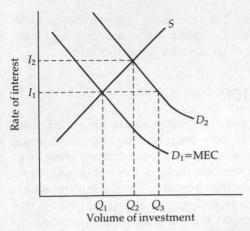

Fig. 9.1

expectations as to the yield from investment will cause a shift in
the demand for loanable funds irrespective of the prevailing interest rate so that a shift in demand from D_1 to D_1 indicates a greater
willingness to invest by firms and this will itself lead to an upward
pressure on interest rates, due to the increased demand at the prevailing rate of interest (Q_3). The outcome is that interest rates rise
and the final volume of investment demand is not Q_3 but Q_2, with
a new market interest rate of I_2.

It is the issue of expectations which does much to explain why
so many firms do not use sophisticated methods of investment appraisal and why even large firms give a relatively low ranking to
interest rates in determining their investment plans. Expectations,
whether positive or negative, about future performance tend to be
the dominant feature of investment decisions and this is likely to
be the case when one considers the nature of the entrepreneur who
prefers personal judgement and hunches to the more automative
decision-making imposed by investment appraisal techniques. So
individual entrepreneurs may be prepared to risk implementing an
expansion programme when generally business confidence is low.
It is also difficult for any theory to take into account the personal
dynamism and will to succeed of certain individuals. Throughout
the economy businessmen are influenced not only by their own
personal views but also by general business confidence in the economic and political system so that investment decisions may reflect
these trends as much as movements in interest rates. While one
cannot dismiss the current investment practices of firms who base
their decisions on 'rough guide' criteria because many firms are

successful using such practices it is a cause for concern that in some cases the management actually think they are making their decisions on scientific rather than abstract assumptions.

Sources of finance

A firm wishing to invest must use either funds generated from within the business itself or borrow from outside sources. Internal funds are more cost-efficient since there are no interest charges to be borne by the investment though there is the opportunity cost of using the funds to be taken into account, i.e. the income which could be earned if the funds were lent out elsewhere. When this latter point is taken into account the expected return on even internal funds needs to be considerably higher than the market rate of interest to make the investment worthwhile. To take the simple example of a company deciding whether to invest £1,000 in new equipment in the firm or to lend the funds out on the market and receive an interest rate of 10 per cent the return on capital used in the business must be considerably more than 10 per cent to compensate for the depreciation of the capital asset and the provision of funds for its eventual replacement. If the life-expectancy of the capital equipment is ten years the return on capital will need to be 20 per cent to equal the earnings of a risk-free investment in the market for ten years with no loss of capital value. If there is inflation in the economy the return on capital could rise in the latter years of an asset's life but this will be offset by a rise in the replacement cost of the asset. Given that the return on capital must be substantial to compensate for risk as well as the depreciation factor it is small wonder that during periods of low business confidence companies may prefer to lend out accumulated profits overseas rather than increase their own productive capacity.

Table 9.1 Sources of finance for industry and commerce £ billion, percentage of total in brackets

Year	Internal	Bank borrowing	Other loans & Mortgages	Capital issues	Overseas & import credit
1978	16.2 (75)	3.0 (14)	0.5 (2)	0.8 (4)	1.2 (5)
1979	17.5 (67)	4.8 (19)	0.7 (3)	0.9 (3)	2.1 (8)
1980	13.7 (56)	7.2 (30)	0.3 (1)	1.3 (5)	1.8 (8)
1981	15.5 (57)	7.1 (26)	1.1 (4)	1.7 (6)	1.9 (7)
1982	13.4 (55)	7.3 (30)	0.9 (4)	0.9 (4)	1.7 (7)

Source: *Bank of England Quarterly Bulletin*

External funds

The situation with regard to borrowed funds is more complex than that pertaining to internal funds since a firm which borrows to invest must earn enough from the investment to repay the interest owed as well as the capital borrowed and only the largest and most prestigious companies can expect to borrow at rates close to the banks' base rates. Furthermore as capital equipment is often highly specialist and of little resaleable value it is not always a good source of security against a loan. The commonest form of loan capital is the debenture, which is a secured loan against some of the firm's assets. The debenture holder is a creditor of the firm and receives a fixed-interest payment on his capital which must be paid annually – if not the debenture-holder has the right to put the firm into liquidation and recover his money from the sale of the security pledged against the debenture. The other main long-term external loans available to the company are the mortgage, usually associated with buildings, and the unsecured loan stock which is not redeemable against a particular asset but gives the stockholder similar rights to other creditors of the business.

In the short to medium term banks are an important source of finance for all companies, but especially for small firms in the form of overdrafts and bridging loans. Small firms, who have limited access to the markets for long-term funds also depend to a great extent on trade credit for HP facilities.

The other main source of external capital available to firms is the part-sale of the business itself, involving the formation or expansion of a partnership or the sale of shares in the company. The mechanisms associated with this expansion will be examined in the next chapter and this chapter concludes with a consideration of the importance of the various sources of capital finance. Internal finance is more attractive to firms for many reasons. Firstly it is cheaper so that the rate of return need not be as high as on external funds. Secondly the tax system discriminates in favour of retained rather than distributed profits and this encourages the accumulation of reserves. Thirdly it enables firms to retain maximum control over the company. Fourthly internal funds can be used for more risky projects than can external funds though there is the danger that projects financed from internal funds will not be costed as efficiently as those using external capital. None the less external sources of capital are vital to industry as a whole to enable structured and consistent growth to take place since few firms can rely entirely on their own resources for expansion.

Case for discussion

Your company is a small but successful manufacturer of kitchen utensils and associated products. A major chain-store has approached you with the offer of a contact to supply them exclusively for the next five years with a further review at that time. To take up this offer you will not only have to abandon your existing customers but will also have to expand the scale of your operations by the installation of extra capital equipment. The investment will cost £6 million and will yield £2 million per year for the first two years of the contract and £2.5 million for the remaining three years. The equipment itself will have a working life of about ten years.

1. Using the IRR method of investment appraisal calculate the worth of the project when compared to a market interest rate of 10 per cent.
2. What are the benefits to the company of this kind of offer?
3. What are the dangers inherent in such a scheme?

Chapter 10

THE ROLE OF FINANCIAL INSTITUTIONS

The importance of external sources of finance to both large and small business units necessitates the existence of sophisticated financial institutions to facilitate the flow of funds to where they can most effectively be used. In the absence of such institutions the market for funds would be less perfect than it is now and thus funds would be less likely to go to the most appropriate areas while the price of obtaining such funds would be higher and result in higher interest rates.

The capital market

In their desire to expand large public companies are forced to seek outside help when internal sources of funds are inadequate for their needs. The banking system plays a key role here, either as a provider of funds or as an intermediary between the company and the ultimate lender. While the clearing banks have traditionally been pleased to afford overdraft facilities and other short-term loans to both large and small companies the provision of large-scale capital finance usually requires support from more than one source and the merchant banks, in particular, specialise in the formation of consortia to assist with finance or the flotation of a share issue. Share and loan issues are made easier for public companies because of the existence of a market in existing stocks and shares – the Stock Exchange. While a company cannot float a share issue directly onto the Stock Exchange the fact that potential investors know that they will be able to dispose of the shares easily when they need to makes such an issue far more attractive than would be the case if there were no stock exchange. The issue of capital can be made in a number of ways.

1. *The offer for sale.* An issuing house (a merchant bank specialising in the flotation of new issues) takes the share issue from the company and then sells if off at a profit to the public.
2. *The public issue.* An issuing house acts on behalf of the company and advertises the shares for sale at a price decided by the bank. If the issue is under-subscribed the issuing bank buys up (underwrites) those not sold while if the issue is over-subscribed the bank determines the means of allocating the issue, e.g. by ballot or by proportional allotment.
3. *Placing.* The issuing bank sells large blocks of the issue to selected institutions such as unit trusts and pension funds.
4. *Rights issue.* The cheapest method of issuing new shares is for the firm to offer existing shareholders the right to buy new shares in proportion to their existing holding and usually at a lower price than that in the market.

Share issues involve in theory a transfer of control as well as sale of part-ownership of the company but though ordinary share-holders have voting rights the vast majority rarely exercise those rights so control tends to remain with the directors who can rely on substantial support from the main shareholders, if not necess-arily majority control. In any case it is possible to issue shares with no voting rights, notably preference shares which, unlike ordinary shares, are guaranteed a dividend at a fixed percentage and are thus attractive to pension funds and unit trusts because of their known income flow. Preference shares are effectively a hybrid of the ordinary share with its potential for high returns but no guaran-tee of a dividend and last place in the queue if the firm goes into liquidation and the loan stock with its guaranteed income but lack of control over the firm's activities. The ratio of an individual com-pany's loan capital and preference shares to ordinary shares is termed its 'gearing'. A company which has a large proportion of its issued capital in the form of loan stock and preference shares is highly geared while one which has most of its capital in the form of ordinary shares is low geared. As low gearing gives greater flexi-bility to companies in terms of dividend policy and loan stock com-mitments most large public-quoted companies tend towards low gearing while newly floated public companies are more likely to be highly geared.

While the Stock Exchange undoubtedly serves a useful function in the role of facilitating new capital issues the fact that it is a mar-ket in used securities leads to some activities which throw it open to criticism. Firstly much of the buying and selling activity that takes place in the market is speculative and as such probably contributes no more to the economy than the speculative purchase of works of art contributes to the development of painting. Furthermore the speculative buying of shares in some companies may divert investment funds away from new investment demands without in any way benefiting the firm whose share price has risen. A second criticism concerns the ownership of shares. Since 1963 the proportion of shares held by private investors has fallen from 54 per cent to less than 28 per cent in 1982. Over the same period the proportion held by insurance companies rose from 10 per cent to 20 per cent and by pension funds from $6\frac{1}{2}$ per cent to 27 per cent. Thus the market is dominated by large institutions who may use their substantial holdings to sway the market or to influence the policy-making of companies of which they are large shareholders. Finally there is the question of confidence. Throughout the world stock exchanges are regarded as indicators of the financial institutions' confidence in the economy and the direction in which it is moving. There is evidence to suggest that on occasion overreacting by the market to events can have severe repercussions for the standing of the economy among overseas observers and investors, the latter group being far more substantial in number than was the case in the past.

The money markets

The London money market and its various secondary markets operate not in one place, like the Stock Exchange, but throughout the City of London on a personal contact basis. At the centre of the money market is the discount market which grew up in the nineteenth century to discount bills of exchange for companies and thus ease the problem posed by delays in cash receipts. From this primary and still important function the discount houses and other institutions operating in the money markets have developed a whole range of operations in wholesale banking. Essentially the market borrows on a short-term basis of periods from overnight to a year and lends over the medium term. The fact that the market deals in such large sums means that it is highly competitive with regard to interest rates and represents an important source of medium-term credit for large organisations. At the same time the flexibility of the market had led to more and more firms lending money to the markets to be recalled in time to meet tax or other payments due at the appropriate time. Since the 1960s subsidiary markets have grown up in local authority bills and stocks and also in inter-bank lending. The inter-bank market is particularly important to large and small companies alike since the interest rate which operates in that market. LIBOR (The London Inter-Bank Offer Rate), is the rate which provides a key to the banks' base rates and thus the rates charged on overdrafts and other loans to customers. Of course LIBOR itself, like all the rates it influences, is subject to the pressures of the market for short-term liquid funds which reflects changes in the state of the market through alterations of the market interest rate. Money market rates are far nearer the pure interest rate than are the rates charged to the customers of the High Street banks. By pure interest rate is meant that rate which is based on a minimum of risk and inconvenience to the lender and is thus determined only by market forces.

The supply and demand for loanable funds

The demand for loanable funds has already been discussed. Since it approximates to the marginal efficiency of capital curve it is valid to assume that the demand for loanable funds will rise if there is a fall in market interest rates while a rise in demand itself because of increased business confidence will cause the interest rate to rise. Equally crucial to the interest rate, however, is the supply of funds. A rise in the market interest rate will presumably lead to more funds coming on to the market. The question is where these funds come from. They come from people with liquid funds who decide to lend them to the market instead of retaining them in liquid form or who choose to save rather than spend part of their income. An autonomous decision by savers to increase the supply of funds will tend to push down the market rate of interest as a temporary surplus of funds occurs. As economic growth increases the likelihood of a rise in the level of savings, and thus may push interest rates down, the classical economists believed that in the long term the pure rate of interest would be pushed towards zero so that eventually all profitable investment opportunities will have been taken up. This view did not take account of the fact that as the economy develops new investment opportunities are constantly appearing and thus tending to raise the marginal efficiency of capital and with it the demand for loanable funds. Thus the interest rate could be expected to rise as well as fall over the long term.

The classical view might also point to the tendency for savings to determine the level of investment as investors wait for the supply of funds to increase and make a potential investment worthwhile. In fact it is investment which determines savings rather than the reverse and this has important consequences for the economy as a whole as well as for individual firms. If firms were not willing to invest so that banks were unable to offer savers interest payments on their deposits the attraction of saving would be reduced and the desire to hold assets in liquid form would increase. At the same time an absence of investment activity in the economy would lead to the economy contracting, bringing down the level of employment and eventually the number of savers in the economy. How it is that investment generates saving is illustrated in the process by which bank deposits grow. In Table 10.1 example (a) shows a situation in which there is no demand for investment funds and the initial deposit of £1,000 leads to an increase in bank deposits of only that amount. In example (b), however, the willingness of a firm to borrow £800 for investment purposes leads to a further round of deposit creation.

Table 10.1

	Deposit (£)	Loan (£)	Reserve (£)
Example (a)	1,000	0	1,000
Example (b)	1,000	800	200
	800	640	160

In Table 10.1 the decision made in example (b) to borrow £800 leads to expenditure on capital goods of £800 and this will eventually lead to another firm making a deposit of £800 into the banking system. Provided that there is another customer willing to borrow part of that new deposit, say £640, the process will be repeated and eventually there will be a third deposit into the banking system of £640 and it, too, can be lent out. At each stage of this flow of funds to and from the banking system it is the loan which creates the new deposit rather than the reverse. Ultimately if 20 per cent of each new deposit is lent out the total growth in bank deposits resulting from the initial deposit will be £5,000. This figure is found by the formula:

$$\text{Total growth in deposits} = \text{Initial Deposit} \times \frac{1}{\text{Reserve Ratio}}$$

Thus $£1,000 \times \dfrac{1}{20\%} = £5,000$

In theory, therefore, if the banks kept no reserve ratio the total growth in deposits would be infinite. In practice the banks' deposits can only keep growing while they are able to lend out each new deposit received. Eventually the point will be reached when to attract new borrowers the banks would have to cut the interest rate charged while at the same time the interest rate offered to depositors would have to be kept high to ensure that the funds did not leak out of the system. Finally further lending would cease to be profitable and no new deposits would be created.

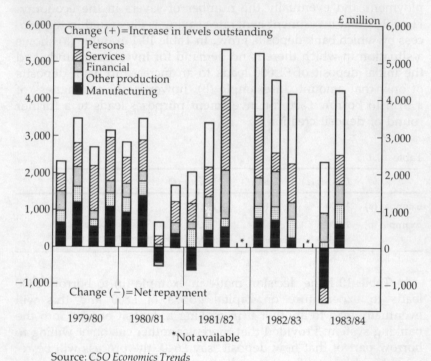

Source: *CSO Economics Trends*

Fig. 10.1   UK banks' advances and acceptances to UK residents

FLUCTUATIONS IN INTEREST RATES

The interest rate acts to equate the demand and supply of loanable funds. However, the interest rate at any given time may be a critical factor in deciding whether or not to proceed with a particular investment if the project under consideration is marginal in terms of its cost-effectiveness. Furthermore an apparently small rise in interest rates may well represent a substantial increase in the total borrowing costs. Thus when interest rates are volatile the ability to plan investment is strained because it becomes difficult to gauge the cost of borrowing in anticipation of the investment being put into operation – the decision as to when to invest may be postponed, for example, if interest rates are expected to fall. In Britain interest rates were very stable in the early post-war period but became more volatile in the 1960s due to various factors. Firstly inflation became more serious and itself more volatile. Secondly interest rate changes became more necessary to deal with recurrent sterling crises and balance of payments problems. Thirdly monetary policy resumed some of its former importance in dealing with economic problems. Associated with this volatility was a growing divergence between real and nominal interest rates. When account is taken of inflation the interest rate will be lower than its nominal rate and it may well become negative, as was the case for a time in the mid-1970s. None the less confidence and future expectations may be expected to counter the effects of interest rates so that even a negative interest rate may not stimulate new investment if confidence is low.

An important development of the 1960s was the growing need to recognise that allowances made for depreciation on a historical cost basis are meaningless during periods of high inflation. Thus in the 1970s an increasing number of firms introduced inflation-accounting methods to make more realistic assessments of the cost-effectiveness of investment programmes. Such attempts accord with the sophisticated methods of investment appraisal which also make attempts to make allowances for the changes that take place in the value of money.

Questions for analysis

1. What are the principal forms of financial assistance given by banks to commercial customers? Consider to what extent the advent of large-scale, centrally directed banking operations militate against the provision of a good service to commercial customers.

2. The Stock Exchange is often described as providing an essential service to the public company, the private investor and the international financial observer. Explain these functions and express any observations you may have as to the effectiveness or otherwise of performing these functions.

3. Discuss the arguments for and against the nationalisation or other means of taking into public ownership the deposit banks and the Stock Exchange.

Chapter 11

THE CONTROL OF MONOPOLY POWER

There have long been two areas of economic activity recognised as prone to monopolistic control and abuse – trade and industrial relations. In the first of these not only consumers but also small firms may be exposed to exploitation by manufacturers or distributors with powerful monopolistic domination of the market. In the case of industrial relations either a group of workers or an employer may enjoy considerably greater bargaining power than those on the other side of the negotiating table. The considerable legislation introduced by successive governments to deal with particular problems arising from monopolistic power is the subject matter of Commercial Law and Employment Law and the emphasis here will be not on the detailed legislative provisions relating to monopolistic practices but the impact of these on the economic structure.

The case for control over restrictive practices by firms

The two main accusations laid against the monopoly power of firms are that it results in economic inefficiency on the part of firms and that it leads to the exploitation of the consumer. Only in comparatively recent times has the question of exploitation concerned the economist since the classical economist, seeing the individual as capable of controlling his own environment and being an independent economic decision-maker, regarded the consumer as being a dominant force in the market. Thus early arguments against monopoly power were based on the harm it could do to the economy through its use of scarce resources inefficiently. Even this question posed a problem for the classical economists since they were forced to admit that market forces, which they applauded, could lead to one firm dominating the market to the detriment of economic efficiency. They eventually came to the uneasy compromise of suggesting that government interference with monopoly power was justified to remove the worst deviations from the perfect market and thus improve the level of economic efficiency. The tendency to regard monopoly as inherently prone to inefficiency while the perfect market was held to be efficient was based on the view, elaborated in the theory of profit maximisation, that under monopoly output will be less and price higher than under perfect competition. Furthermore in the long run there will be no tendency for the super profits of a monopolist to be eroded by competitive forces – as is the case with perfect competition. Thus monopolies and oligopolies have little incentive to innovate as their monopoly profits are protected by the various barriers to entry which prevent new firms entering the industry. This contrasts with the perfect competitor who can only keep ahead of his rivals through being innovative since in the long run he can expect only to break even and must therefore innovate to establish, if only for a short time, a cost advantage over his competitors. Whether these theoretical assumptions about the behaviour of monopolists contrasted with perfect competitors are justified is open to question. It is arguable whether the perfect competitor has any incentive to innovate when he knows that in a relatively short time his rivals will imitate him and cancel out his recently acquired advantage. The monopolistic firm, on the other hand, knows that barriers to entry will prevent new firms breaking into the industry while patent laws limit the ability of potential rivals to copy its products or production methods. Thus the profits arising out of innovation are not eroded in the long run so that the monopolist is more likely to build up the reserves to enable further research and development expenditure.

If the monopolistic firm is more likely to innovate it is also more likely to introduce new cost-cutting production techniques; thus the argument that perfect competition is more efficient than monopoly is a purely relative statement. The perfect competitor is producing at optimum efficiency and is more efficient than the monopolist using the same technical processes but it is likely that the monopolist will have introduced lower-cost methods of production. So the misallocation of resources by the monopolist in producing at less than the optimum output is outweighed by the greater absolute efficiency achieved through technical progress and the cutting of average costs – the perfect competitor using archaic production methods will be using more resources per unit of output than the monopolist using sophisticated production techniques even if the latter is not operating at optimum efficiency. None the less monopoly does remain capable of a greater wastage of resources if its monopoly power permits it to earn large profits without the need to eliminate wastage in its resource use. Thus government intervention against monopoly power is not to be justified on the positive attributes of competition but on the negative attributes arising from monopoly power.

In discussing firms with monopolistic power it is of course more likely to be an oligopolist than a true monopolist, though where oligopolists act in collusion they may achieve a joint monopoly. The behaviour of oligopolists acting in concert may well lead to the exploitation of the consumer through joint measures aimed at keeping prices high and controlling the level of output in the industry. Of course the fact that they are likely still to compete on the basis of non-price competition means that oligopolists will attempt to increase their market share by new product development and cheaper production costs which will help the consumer in the long run through better quality, lower-priced goods. Even when the oligopolists do compete on a price-cutting basis there is no guarantee that the consumer will benefit in the long-term since stiff price competition could reduce the number of firms in the industry and strengthen the position of those remaining. As the number of firms in the industry shrinks as it becomes an oligopoly further concentration may become difficult or even impossible. The tendency for oligopolists to diversify into other industries through conglomerate integration also raises problems for economic efficiency since such firms can exclude the possibility of new independent firms which might have grown up in the industry. They may also use the accumulated resources from their primary sphere of activity to finance short-run price cutting and advertising and so gain market leadership in more than one industry. Thus it is possible for a group of a dozen large conglomerates to compete with each other, in various permutations, across the whole range of industry.

Controls over monopoly and restrictive practices

Two main phases are recognisable in official attitudes towards monopoly and restrictive practices over the past hundred years. In the first phase, which predominated at least until the 1950s, the aim of control was to remove the worst excesses of monopoly and oligopoly in their mismanagement of resources while the consumer was expected to look after himself. Thus the industries which were nationalised in the 1940s were nationalised on grounds of economic efficiency rather than because they could exploit the consumer. This tendency to ignore the potential damage to the interests of the consumer arose partly out of the misguided belief in the independent judgement and self-determination of the individual and also in the belief that the worst excesses of restrictive practices were subject to legal remedy. In practice not only were individual consumers barely able to hold their own in dealing with their suppliers but the courts took a lenient attitude towards restrictive practices. Such legislation which did exist to protect the consumer's interest left the onus to prove the case on him rather than the supplier. Even in the area where economic concern was most expressed – that of monopoly power and the potential wastage of resources – opinion was split because of the gains which could be achieved by large firms in terms of economies of scale and international competitiveness – a major consideration in the support for monopolistic merger activity during the depression of the 1930s.

The first direct attack on monopoly power occurred under the Labour administration of 1945–51. Apart from the nationalisation of a number of natural monopolies the government introduced legislation to deal with potential monopoly abuses. Unfortunately the fact that attitudes to monopoly had been ambivalent in the past led the government to take a less firm line against monopolies *per se* as was the case in the United States. Instead the 1948 Monopolies and Restrictive Practices (Inquiry and Control) Act took a pragmatic view with each case being judged on its merits against the vague criterion of 'the public interest'. If the Board of Trade felt that a particular monopoly situation existed (a monopoly being defined as a situation in which one-third of the supply of goods in an industry or market is controlled by one firm or a group of firms acting together to restrict competition) it could refer the case to the Monopolies Commission for consideration and recommendation in the light of the public interest, applying guidelines laid down in the Act. The guidelines stressed the need to apply such criteria as efficiency and the development of both domestic and overseas markets but the guidelines were vague and open to wide interpretation. Even if the Commission felt able to report unfavourably in a particular case it was up to the Board of Trade to decide what, if any, action should be taken. Between 1949 and 1956 the Monopolies Commission completed twenty inquiries into specific industries but eighteen of these were concerned not with monopoly control but with restrictive practices leading to monopoly conditions. The restrictive practices brought to light during these inquiries reinforced the findings of the Commission in its general report on collective discrimination that such practices should be prohibited – a view taken also by the Lloyd Jacob Committee on collective resale price maintenance in 1949. This condemnation of collective restrictive practices arose from the Commission's antipathy towards cartels and the interference of these with the independent behaviour of firms. The mass of evidence produced by the Commission led ultimately to a revision of legislation in 1956, with the passing of a Restrictive Trade Practices Act.

The legislation passed in the 1950s and 1960s changed the emphasis of government control away from a concern with monopoly power and its inefficiency towards an assault on restrictive practices with, later, a growing awareness of the need for consumer protection being recognised. This legislation was brought together and expanded by the 1973 Fair Trading Act.

The Fair Trading Act

The name of the statute itself reflects the emphasis it places on the protection of the consumer and the recognition that the consumer is in an unequal position of weakness when dealing with any firm. The Act can be divided into two broad areas, one dealing with monopolies and mergers and the other with consumer protection.

As regards monopolies and mergers the Act replaced and consolidated the 1948 legislation and the 1965 Monopolies and Mergers Act. The Monopolies Commission is now the Monopolies and Mergers Commission with between ten and twenty-seven members; the market share for referral to the Commission is now a quarter instead of a third and both service industry monopolies and local and export monopolies are now also subject to investigation. Though the majority of eligible mergers are not referred for investigation the fact that a merger may be referred up to six months after it has taken place has led to firms approaching the Department of Trade and Industry for a ruling prior to commencement of the merger. In addition no merger of newspapers with a combined average daily circulation of 500,000 may take place without Department of Trade and Industry permission, a measure introduced in 1965 to halt the decline in daily newspapers. The major shift in approach to monopolies under current legislation is the fact that not only monopoly situations are subject to investigation but also mergers which could lead to a monopoly and therefore might pose a threat to the public interest. The fact that the Director General of Fair Trading (formerly the Registrar of Restrictive Trade Practices) has power himself to refer monopoly situations to the Commission and to recommend referral of mergers has further strengthened the supervisory controls on monopolies.

In line with previous policy on monopoly the Fair Trading Act does, however, reaffirm the principle that each merger shall be examined on its merits and if economic considerations point in favour of a merger there may well be a decision not to refer that merger for investigation. When a case is referred to the Commission the monopoly or merger is considered in the light of the public interest taking into account the desirability of promoting competition, the interests of consumers, reductions in costs, new product development and overseas markets. Only about 3 per cent of all proposed mergers are referred though of these some 70 per cent are subsequently abandoned or found to be against the public interest. Despite this it must be said that the existence and workings of the commission have done little to halt the drift towards conglomerate control of British industries since the working of the legislation does not demand that mergers positively benefit the economy, only that they are not demonstrably against the public interest.

The situation with regard to restrictive trade practices has also been rationalised in the 1973 Act. Collective resale price maintenance was effectively abolished under the Restrictive Trade Practices Act 1956. Any industry which wishes to maintain a collective agreement must register it with the Director-General of Fair Trading and then be prepared to justify the agreement before the Restrictive Practices Court on one of the grounds recognised as legitimate for a restrictive agreement. Of nearly 3,000 agreements registered only eleven have actually been successfully heard by the Court, mostly on the grounds that consumers benefited by the restriction. Since 1964 and the passing of the Resale Prices Act individual resale price maintenance has been under similar restrictions though even in the late 1950s it had been under attack from the growth in multiple retailers who wished to be free to engage in price competition. Once again few industries have found it possible to defend resale price maintenance, notable among them the manufacturers of books, maps, newspapers and proprietary medicines. Most industries were unable to put a strong case in the face of the overwhelming evidence suggesting that consumers on the whole benefit far more from the absence of RPM than from its existence. None the less it has proved difficult for the legislation to eradicate the natural tendency of firms to seek to protect themselves against costly price-wars through tacit understandings on pricing and supply policies. Thus in 1968 further legislation was necessary to close the loophole in the legislation opened by information agreements by which firms evaded the restrictions by informal agreements operated through an exchange of information. Further modifications were made in the Acts of 1976 and 1977. The attitude of firms in some industries is evidenced by the statement of one motor manufacturer in 1983 that stable prices were better for the consumer than the 'uncertainties' caused by periods of fierce price competition.

The Fair Trading Act also reorganised and modified many of the elements of consumer protection legislation, the aim being that the Act would provide an umbrella for the protection of the economic interest of consumers under which other specific legislation could be introduced as part of a protective environment rather than as isolated attempts to deal with certain abuses. The Director-General of Fair Trading has personal powers to collect information on practices detrimental to the consumer and to refer such information to the Consumer Protection Advisory Committee and also to take action against producers or traders persisting in such practices. Finally he is able to publish information for consumers and to encourage the adoption of voluntary codes of conduct by trade associations.

The growth in consumer protection generally since the 1960s is the result of a recognition by successive governments that the bargaining power between consumer and producer is by no means as balanced as economic theory would suggest. Far from being the sovereign consumer taking independent decisions based on demand patterns formulated by himself, the consumer is often an insignificant member of the mass market who is influenced by producers in his demand patterns and often feels intimidated in his dealings with producers or traders. The primary aim of consumer protection is thus that it should enable the consumer to inform himself of the properties possessed by a product before he commits himself to buying it, to protect him from being deceived into thinking a product is something which it is not and to eliminate misleading information from producer to consumer. Prior to the 1960s there was consumer protection legislation but it tended to concentrate on such areas as weights and measures, dangers to health and so on. The presumption in most legislation, such as the Sale of

Goods Act 1893, was that the consumer was a fit person to assess the quality of goods offered for sale and could not take as implicit that such goods were of a suitable nature. Unfortunately there was an ever-growing number of goods available where the layman was in no position to make an individual informed assessment and was thus forced to depend on the worthiness of the trader with whom he dealt. Legislation since the 1960s has shifted the burden of proof concerning quality from the producer to the trader and increased the protection afforded to the consumer in such areas as trade descriptions, consumer credit and unsolicited goods. Nevertheless the only remedy available to the consumer in the vast majority of cases where he has a complaint is through the courts and this probably deters many consumers from standing up for their rights, especially where the value of a defective article is low. In one main area in which the consumer is most likely to be manipulated – advertising – such controls as exist are voluntary except for legislation governing food, drugs and medicines and all advertising which is transmitted under the control of the Independent Broadcasting Authority, which is expected to enforce strict advertising standards on commercial radio and television. As far as advertising in general is concerned, the Advertising Standards Authority is quick to act on complaints of misleading advertising but frequently the damage has been done before the advertiser agrees to withdraw the advertisement.

The impact of legislation on firms

In the sections dealing with monopoly and mergers it was noted how few mergers are stopped by the legislation and it is probably no exaggeration to say that legislation has barely halted the natural evolution of British industry towards oligopolistic domination. However, its existence has deterred the development of monopoly situations which would have been undoubtedly against the public interest. Furthermore while restrictive trade practice legislation cannot stop entirely the development of informal or tacit price and output agreements, it has made them unenforceable by law and thus more likely to collapse. The abolition of resale price maintenance in all its forms has opened the way for quite fierce price competition among retailers, at least in some products, which itself has generated two developments. Firstly the growing power of the large retailing groups in terms of the total retail sector has been made possible by their ability to maintain finer profit margins. Secondly the balance of power has swung away from the manufacturers to the retailer who has been able to insist that manufacturers, too, accept lower profit margins so that price competition has been strengthened among manufacturers.

Consumer protection legislation has been concerned directly with the consumer in his dealings with a manufacturer, trader or retailer and recognises that it is not necessarily, or even predominantly, the oligopolist which is most intimidating in its dealings with the public. Most large retailers have been aware for many years of the importance of a good public image and while consumers may be passive in their response to a retailer's prices they will 'vote with their feet' if the retailer appears to be less than fair with regard to service, quality and the willingness to exchange faulty products. The legislation has made it more difficult for the scrupulous retailer or supplier to make this aspect a marketing tool since the public will regard that behaviour of all firms as merely complying with legislative pressure. There is no doubt, however, that the consumer can now approach the business of exchanging goods and obtaining a refund with less trepidation than twenty years ago. The fact, too, that the consumer can obtain satisfaction either from retailer or manufacturer in the case of sub-standard products and no longer has to go through a complicated procedure to ensure that a guarantee is valid has removed most of the shabbier practices by which either manufacturer or retailer or both dodged their responsibilities. Naturally there will always be those sellers who 'try it on' with customers and there will be cases where consumers are deterred from obtaining their rights by a frustrating or unhelpful response, especially in such areas as mail order where the ability to get the matter resolved face-to-face is limited. None the less the legislation has redressed the balance between seller and buyer and this itself has done much to improve the attitudes and behaviour of less scrupulous firms. One major area of concern remains that of marketing methods. Though some sharp practices, notably those connected with 'sales' and price reductions, have been repressed it tends to be the letter rather than the spirit of the law which is observed particularly in the case of advertising and product description. On the other hand the public consciousness of dubious marketing methods has been raised considerably over the years and it is doubtful if the advertiser's ability to manipulate the market has increased to any great extent.

Questions for analysis

1. Consider the view that British legislation has been more successful in dealing with restrictive practices than monopoly in the post-war period.
2. 'The existence of consumer protection legislation and voluntary codes of conduct by advertisers and traders is conclusive evidence that the concept of consumer sovereignty is a myth.' Examine this statement and go on to attempt to define the relationship between consumer and trader.

Chapter 12

THE CONTROL OF MONOPOLY: THE LABOUR MARKET

Concern about monopoly power in the factor markets tends to centre around the labour market since it is difficult to talk in terms of a market for entrepreneurs while the market for capital is as perfect as any. Even the market in land is exceptional in that the government already has considerable powers to purchase or control the use of land while most major private transactions take place between approximately equal parties. In the labour market, however, there has always been concern at monopolistic advantages enjoyed either by the suppliers or purchasers of labour, though no generally accepted solution to the problems raised has resulted.

The economic problems raised by restrictive trade practices could be dealt with by legislation since it was universally recognised that such practices could threaten efficiency by removing competition while they could also be seen as damaging to the consumer. Similarly consumer protection legislation, while not necessarily being justified on economic grounds, raised little controversy or opposition since the consumer was generally seen as being in need of protection from unscrupulous manufacturers and traders. The situation with regard to restrictive practices in the labour market is much more complicated since it is not always clear who needs protection from whom and how best would the cause of economic efficiency be served. However, two types of legislation can be distinguished; that to protect individual workers who might otherwise be exploited by powerful employers and that to deal with restrictive practices by organised labour to control the market for labour and thus exert pressures on the industry in which they operate and on the economy in general. As in the last chapter on consumer protection legislation it is not proposed here to analyse the detailed provisions of employment law but to examine the problems raised and the economic implications for such legislation.

Restrictive practices in the labour market

The operation of restrictive practices by trade unions as monopolistic suppliers of labour has often been compared to restrictive practices operated by producers and therefore a worthy object of government attention. It is true that such practices as the closed shop, national wage rates and standard conditions of work do reduce the degree of competition between individual suppliers of labour, i.e. workers, so that the buyer of labour, the employer, is forced to buy at a higher price than might otherwise be the case. However, there are a number of differerences between the situation pertaining in the labour market compared to that in the product market. Firstly the absence of restrictive practices in the product market does not mean that the seller is reduced to a weak position in his dealings with consumers; indeed the oligopolistic supplier may still benefit from a considerable degree of monopoly power in the market. But if workers lose their capacity to co-operate together each one has virtually no bargaining power at all and is reduced to an inferior position in dealing with the buyer, his employer. Secondly there has in the past been a greater legislative bias against labour restrictive practices so that there is less need for legal enforcement to make them prone to constraint by society. Thus though the courts were loath to take action against firms under the conspiracy laws this was not the case with regard to workers' unions which were suppressed and even banned during the early nineteenth century under the Combination Acts. Thirdly, restrictive practices are not confined to the labour side of industry and the removal of restrictive practices from the labour side would still leave many industries in a monopolistic position, and it would be difficult to prevent firms combining together for bargaining purposes. In short, in the absence of their ability to manipulate the labour market, unions would be severely weakened and it is doubtful whether the power of employers could be similarly reduced.

This being said is there still some limit that should be placed on the ability of the trade unions to use their monopolistic powers in the pursuit of their aims? Thus, given that peaceful picketing is an acceptable practice to publicise and present their case, should there be limits on secondary picketing and so less effective means for carrying their case in a dispute? Should unions be held liable for contracts they enter into as are other bodies and should they be liable for the individual actions of their members? In these and similar questions the problem has always been to what extent restrictive practices could be controlled without emaciating the union. In effect even if it is not possible to eliminate or severely reduce restrictive practices is it at least possible to afford some element of 'consumer protection' so that an employer is at least able to rely on certain contractual procedures being met and some commitment on such matters as productivity and time for completion? Attempts to deal with these questions have not been particularly successful since in the absence of legislation traditional patterns of behaviour have often prevented the adoption of acceptable solutions, while legislation has merely seemed to polarise the attitudes of union members to make co-operation with the law unlikely. Thus ninteenth-century attempts to deal with picketing by legislation and the action of the 1979 Conservative government with regard to secondary picketing suffered from the problem that no lawful picketing could go beyond the limits of reasonable behaviour yet legislation seriously weakened the unions' right to promote its case. Similarly the attempt to make unions responsible for the actions of individual members (the Taff Vale judgement in 1901) was too prone to be abused by employers to discredit unions, and in the matter of contractual agreements between an employer and his workforce it does appear unfair to hold the trade union as a whole liable for breaches of agreement by individuals or groups of union members. None the less the relative failure of Britain's economic performance in the 1960s compared to that of other advanced countries was partially ascribed to the poor state of Britain's industrial relations. This was the result of various historical influences which pervaded the relationship between management and unions. Firstly, there was the strong class-based social structure largely unruffled by the social upheaval affecting the rest of Europe in modern times. Secondly, and partly the consequence of this, there was an obsession with 'them and us' in the conduct of working relationships militating against effective communication between the two sides of industry. Thirdly, the historical structure of trade unions remained intact so that there was a multiplicity of unions complicating the process of collective bargaining and causing friction in the conduct of industrial negotiations. Fourthly, there was an excessive number of unofficial strikes, in part arising from the practice of collective bargaining agreements being made at the local level, and often being disruptive out of proportion to the number of workers involved due to the increased specialisation and interdependence within the economy. The Labour government elected in 1964 had made a commitment to modernising British industry and as part of this aim established the Donovan Commission on Trade Unions and Trade Associations in 1965. Many of the findings of this Commission, which reported in 1968, were incorporated in the white paper 'In Place of Strife' which introduced the Industrial Relations Bill of 1969. This bill aimed at establishing a code of conduct under the direction of a Commission on Industrial Relations, with penalties for employers or workers who broke the code. It also proposed a 'cooling off' period for strikes, and strike ballots, while also proposing reform of the trade union movement to rationalise their numbers by making grants available for mergers, etc. Despite its mild proposals the bill was opposed by the TUC and trade union movement, by substantial sections of the Labour party and the Conservative opposition, and was eventually dropped.

If the Labour party had hoped to reform the trade union movement and the system of collective bargaining through their special relationship with the unions it was the Conservative Party which became committed to reform in the 1970s. The 1971 Industrial Relations Act attempted to deal with labour restrictive practices in the way in which the restrictive trade practices acts had operated in the trade area, via the establishment of a legal framework within which disputes would be settled. Thus there would be a Chief Registrar of Trade Unions and Trade Associations with whom all unions would have to register and obtain approval for their rules. A national industrial relations court was set up to deal with disputes arising from the act and the court could, on a request by the Secretary of State, issue a restraining order delaying industrial action for up to sixty days, or order a ballot where a strike could endanger the economy. The legislation also provided for ballots when there were doubts as to the wishes of the majority of workers being met and aimed at the ending of closed shop agreements. The antipathy of the unions was such that the TUC expelled unions which did register under the act and all unions worked for the repeal which came with the return of Labour to office. Indeed the return of Labour and the passing of the Trade Unions and Labour Relations Act 1974 virtually restored the pre-1971 status quo to the conduct of industrial relations so that the trade union movement was guaranteed the right to use restrictive practices without there being any legal code of conduct on these practices.

The Conservative attempts to control labour restrictive practices in the 1970s were hampered by the concentrated opposition of the trade union movement and the likelihood that these controls would be removed with the re-election of a Labour government. During the late 1970s, however, the continuing decline of Britain's manufacturing base and the consequent contraction of trade union membership and power coupled with a rising tide of support among voters for industrial relations reform led to the possibility that a future government would be in a stronger position to tackle reform. Certainly the Conservative government elected in 1979 was strongly committed to reform, a commitment reinforced by the decline in Labour support even among trade union members – a decline which was extended in the 1983 election. Thus a more strongly armed government felt able to introduce the Employment Acts of 1980 and 1982. The 1980 Employment Act restricts lawful picketing to the pickets' place of work, made secondary picketing unlawful where not directed at the business of the employer in dispute, gave protection against unfair dismissal for non-union workers employed in a closed shop environment, encouraged greater use of secret ballots and made a number of changes in unfair dismissal legislation to help relieve the burden of that legislation on small businesses. The 1982 Employment Act went further and brought trade union practices under legal control even more than had been attempted by the 1971 Industrial Relations Act. Thus trade unions lost their immunity from legal proceedings if they organised unlawful industrial action and it now became possible to seek injunctions against (and sue for damages) trade unions in such matters as negligence and nuisance. In short, trade unions were put on the same legal footing as individuals, while the term 'lawful trade dispute' was to be more strictly interpreted. The act also gave further protection from unfair dismissal for non-union employees in a closed shop and increased the compensation available to such workers. It also promoted regular reviews of existing closed-shop agreements by secret ballot, made illegal pressure by unions on employees to discriminate against non-union firms and reformed employment protection legislation in certain areas, a subject returned to later in the chapter.

The effect of legislation introduced by the Conservative government, and other proposals for further legislation in the field of industrial relations, is to place collective bargaining into an institutional framework similar to the situation with regard to trade between consumer and supplier. The toll taken by the depression and the continued shrinking of the traditional industries has put the trade union movement on the defensive and this situation has made the implementation of such legislation possible so that employers like the *Stockport Messenger* (in 1983) have successfully used the law in a struggle with the unions whereas ten years previously the law would have been unworkable against concerted union pressure. While current legislation certainly attacks the abuses of traditional labour restrictive practices it makes little attempt to get to the roots of the difficulties which led up to the legislation. Thus the attack on the closed shop has not been accompanied by an effort to understand and compensate for the importance of the closed shop in collective bargaining. Like all legislation it will make little impact in those firms with excellent industrial relations and effective communication between management and unions; its importance lies in the long-term impact in areas of industry beset by poor industrial relations. Here there are three likely possibilities. Firstly, the trade union movement will expect the repeal of the legislation by a future Labour government and will accept the situation until then, albeit from a hostile position. Secondly, the trade unions may accept the limitations imposed by the law and, like firms which previously enjoyed legally-sanctioned restrictive practices, adapt their behaviour to improve their bargaining position in other ways. Thirdly, the legislation represents a substantial and permanent shift in the balance of power to employers from labour so that restrictive practices matter less than productivity deals, etc. as a way of maintaining and improving living standards – already in such industries as coal-mining the negotiation of productivity agreements has become much more common. Each of these possibilities, or combination of them, depend for their likelihood on the future patterns of the economy since if union power continues to decline due to its being in a defensive position then the ability or even will to reverse current legislation will also fade. One point worth making is that union power has visibly contracted under current legislation whereas the legislation on the restrictive practices of firms can hardly be said to have seriously damaged their profitability or power, especially where they have international links.

Employment protection

The 1970s saw the passage of a great deal of legislation aimed at assisting the position of individual workers' employment rights and thus equalising the bargaining position between employer and individual worker. Such legislation was not new since the Liberal government of 1906–1916 had introduced Wages Councils to deal with the task of settling wage rates where trade unionism was too weak, or even non-existent, and thus workers would be prey to the power of their employers. However, the new legislation, much of which was brought together in the Employment Protection (Consolidation) Act, 1978, dealt with other areas of concern such as un-fair dismissal and redundancy payments. Furthermore other legislation aimed to protect traditionally weaker sections of the em-ployed community through the banning of race and sex discrimi-nation in employment and the institution of equal pay and maternity leave provisions to help improve the pay and career pros-pects of women; tentative steps were also taken to encourage posi-tive discrimination though such proposals failed to win sufficient approval generally to become common practice. While such legis-lation as that on employment protection was desirable on social and ethical grounds, such considerations only apply to the economic viewpoint if resources are used more effectively. There is no guarantee that this will always be the case since some of the legis-lation has led to counter-productive action by firms, such as keep-ing workers on to delay heavy redundancy payments or preferring less-qualified workers who would, nevertheless, be unlikely to seek maternity leave in preference to appointing young married women. In addition the law itself has been evaded by firms with regard to sex or racial discrimination just as it has with regard to minimum wages for many years, so that workers are employed for short periods to avoid their becoming eligible for redundancy payments and part-time workers are used to avoid their being eligible for all benefits under the legislation.

The high-water mark for such legislation was 1978. Since then the Employment Acts of 1980 and 1982 reduced the number of cases in which workers can claim unfair dismissal, abolished the man-datory minimum basic award and modified the law on maternity leave to assist small firms. As employment opportunities have de-creased those groups most prone to losing out have done so – in the 1980s there has been little or no progress on the equalisation of pay for men and women. While the legislation has undoubtedly sincerely tried to help the position of individual workers and dis-advantaged groups it is probably true that where the legislation has posed substantial cost or lack of flexibility problems, firms have either evaded the law or adopted alternative plans so that the groups who should have benefited may in some cases have suf-fered because of the existence of the legislation. The position of the unions with regard to the legislation has been clearly in favour but the legislation may pose a threat, indirectly, to the power of the unions. Since the more institutionalised becomes the relationship between employer and employee the more indirect becomes the union in the settlement of an individual dispute, so trade union membership may be less important than the ablity to go to law.

Case for discussion

Your company is a small private company employing 100 workers, many of whom are female and work part-time. The majority of the many other firms in the industry are also small, indeed smaller than your own, though there are several large companies and groups. All have similar types of workforce to your own.

Traditionally trade union representation has been weak throughout the industry. This has been due partly to a lack of interest among employees but also, especially in recent years, to resistance by employers to union recognition. Accordingly wage settlements have been settled for many years through a Wages Council.

1. What advantages and disadvantages would firms like your own encounter if the Wages Council was abolished and individual firms arrived at agreements with appropriate trade unions regarding union recognition and wage settlements?
2. Compare the differences you would expect to see in the role of a trade union in your company compared to that in a large firm in a high-technology industry.

Chapter 13

GOVERNMENT ASSISTANCE TO INDUSTRY

In the mixed economy governments are expected not only to control the abuses which can arise from monopoly power and restrictive practices but also to play an active part in the growth and development of the economy. Central to this latter role is the promotion of a healthy industrial and commercial structure without which growth will be held back, or even stifled. The government may assist industry and trade in one of two ways. Either it can do so indirectly by promoting growth and development throughout the economy and thus stimulate demand for goods and services or it can act directly on the industrial structure to enable efficiency to be improved, new products developed, and capacity and markets to be expanded. Policies designed to affect the economy in general are examined later while in this chapter direct assistance to industry is considered. To improve efficiency and capability action must be taken to raise the quality and effectiveness of the three factors of production involved in industrial production, capital, labour and enterprise. Successive governments have therefore stepped up the services available to industry in the raising of capital through financial assistance, for raising the efficiency of labour through manpower policy and for stimulating enterprise through the assistance given to small businesses. Such assistance has inevitably increased with the continuing decline of British manufacturing industry and while all trades and industries can and do benefit from this assistance it is the manufacturing industries which have needed most help and attracted the greatest attention.

Financial assistance

Government financial assistance to industry covers aid at all stages of a company's development from its establishment and has taken over the years various forms, notably generous tax and depreciation allowances, grants and loans for expansion, relocation and merger, and direct investment in the company. As indicated above the rationale for such assistance has been the need to promote modernisation and efficiency in British trade and industry so that the assistance given is frequently linked to overall government objectives – as with regional policy. Of these various forms of assistance one generally considered to be most open to abuse is that of tax allowances on capital expenditure since the allowances were so generous that firms could consider a project worthwhile on these grounds alone, irrespective of the commercial feasibility. Thus capital expenditure on machinery and plant carried a 100 per cent first year allowance and buildings a 79 per cent first year allowance until the 1984 Budget phased out tax relief on capital projects in favour of lower rates of Corporation Tax. This decision was taken because it was felt that the prospects of industrial efficiency and industrial innovation are more likely to be achieved through a policy of tolerance towards profits rather than through blanket tax concessions to efficient and inefficient alike.

Government policy has also sought to aid industry by stimulating the availability of funds for expansion and modernisation, particularly for the small- to medium-sized company denied the range of opportunities provided by the capital market. Thus in 1945 both the Industrial and Commercial Finance Corporation (ICFC) and the Finance Corporation for Industry (FCI) were set up with capital subscribed by the deposit banks and the Bank of England. The ICFC's role is to assist the growth of small firms through the provision of loan capital. Loans of up to £1 million can now be obtained as the ICFC acts as agent for the EEC in the provision of funds. The role of the FCI is to assist larger companies which experience difficulty in raising capital through the normal channels and thus has tended to help industries in difficulty such as steel and shipbuilding. The ICFC and FCI were brought together under one co-ordinating body, Finance For Industry (FFI) in 1974, now Investors For Industry. Other organisations operate to provide funds with government backing in such areas as technical innovation and the introduction of micro-processors and other high technology aids to improved productivity.

More direct government involvement in industry has consisted of the part-ownership of companies to assist their development. Thus the Industrial Reorganisation Corporation of 1966 – 70 was established to promote mergers considered desirable as part of the government's industrial strategy, either by the provision of advice on undertaking a merger or by the purchase of equity in the companies concerned to facilitate the merger. In 1975 the National Enterprise Board (NEB) was set up by the Industry Act and given finance facilities of £1,000 million together with the right to buy into any manufacturing industry. The NEB soon became a source of financial assistance for many small companies and it was hoped that it might be instrumental in revitalising ailing firms like British Leyland or Rolls-Royce and stimulating the growth of new high technology industries by giving financial assistance. The return of the Conservative government in 1979 led to the activities of the NEB being severely curtailed under the 1980 Industry Act as part of the new government's commitment to reduce direct government participation in industry.

Regional incentives

In addition to the financial assistance given to industry and commerce generally, successive governments have also given considerable additional help to firms operating in, or willing to move to, the less prosperous parts of the United Kingdom. The need for such assistance was first discerned in the 1930s when certain regions – the industrial belt of Scotland, much of Wales, Northern Ireland and the North of England – were clearly suffering more in the depression than were other parts of the country. The fact that regional assistance has continued to be necessary, whatever the state of the economy as a whole, throughout the post-war period is evidence of the deep-rooted industrial decline of these areas. This decline stems from the dependence of those areas on the closely related and interdependent industries which brought them prosperity at the peak of the Industrial Revolution but which were unable to sustain this success as the twentieth century wore on – coal, iron and steel, shipbuilding, heavy engineering and textiles. Historical factors had necessitated such industries being located closely together near their sources of raw materials and power, rather than near their markets. The slump in world trade and output inevitably hit these industries in the 1930s, already under pressure from cheaper foreign competition. The result was structural unemployment on a massive scale which had come nowhere near to being solved when the outbreak of war led to a revival of demand in these industries. Meanwhile the new growth industries of chemicals, radio and electrical goods and light engineering were drawn to the Midlands and South-East where both capital and labour were more flexible and where the more prosperous markets were located.

After the post-war boom had subsided and the regional problem began to reassert itself successive governments looked to the fact that industry was becoming more footloose for their solution. An industry which is footloose can be sited in a variety of locations without any detrimental effect on performance, and the growth of footloose industries arises from several factors. Firstly new industries are not tied to traditional sources of fuel. Secondly the decline in the relative importance of transport costs coupled with the greater flexibility of road transport has led to proximity to either markets or supplies becoming less important in the determination of industrial location. Thirdly an increasing number of industrial processes entail the assembly of components from several areas and no one site is therefore transport-minimising. Thus with industry less disadvantaged by one site rather than another governments could seek to encourage firms to move to the depressed areas.

The case for regional aid is based both on economic and social grounds. Economically there is the problem of structural unemployment and the consequent wastage of labour resources. Capital is also wasted with the under-utilisation of buildings and equipment leading to low productivity and low profits so that funds are not generated for modernisation and capital replacement projects. In addition there is the problem of unbalanced growth with regional variations in the level of economic activity resulting in differing rates of economic growth and widening differences in living standards. Attempts to alleviate problems in depressed areas through national economic policies are likely to encounter the difficulty that such policies will result in inflationary pressures in the more prosperous sectors of the economy. Thus regional inequalities can inhibit national planning for economic growth. The social problems arising from regional deprivation are of equal concern. The economically more mobile sections of the community are likely to seek employment elsewhere and the residual population becomes increasingly unbalanced, often with a high proportion of elderly people. This migration creates congestion and excessive demands on services in the prosperous areas while leaving the depressed areas with declining resources to meet static or even growing demands for social services. The depopulation of depressed areas results in under-utilisation and decay of social capital with schools empty and hospitals closed. At the same time lack of adequate local financial resources prevents the replacement and modernisation of antiquated and obsolete buildings and equipment. Even transport becomes a problem with rail and bus services being cut through declining demand, leading to a further weakening of outlying communities. The strain placed on the social services inevitably leads to a decline in health and educational standards in some areas while the atmosphere of economic and social depression is likely to provoke a severe response. The high unemployment rates in the big cities of Scotland and the North of England in the 1980s must be held partly to blame for the outbreak of such severe social problems as inner-city violence and a massive increase in heroin addiction. The complex problems of Northern Ireland, too, owe much to the economic stagnation and social deprivation of that province in the 1960s when the rest of the country was enjoying full employment and growing prosperity.

The measures adopted by successive governments since the 1930s to deal with the regional problem have tended to encourage industry to move to the workers rather than the other way round. This has been partly because industry was seen as more geographically mobile than labour but also because the southward drift of the population had already led to an increasingly unbalanced population without the government encouraging it further. The main measures have included taxation and capital allowances for expansion in the development areas, restriction on expansion in prosperous parts of the country through the strict allocation of Industrial Development Certificates (IDCs) which are required by firms wishing to increase the scale of their operations, financial inducements to take on more workers, retraining schemes and the provision of government factories and workshops for sale or lease. By the time that the 1972 Industry Act was passed the development areas – classified into different grades according to the severity of their problems – had spread to include Northern Ireland, Scotland, Wales, Cornwall and Devon and England North of Nottingham. Despite the temporary success of many of the measures tried, the scale of decline of British manufacturing has outweighed the assistance given and further decline in the 1970s was to bring even the Midlands within the category of development area as defined by the EEC. Under the 1980 Industry Act the Conservative government reduced the areas qualifying for special assistance as shown in Fig. 13.1.

In addition to the regional development grants and selective financial assistance available under the Industry Act, 1980, Enterprise Zones have been established in a number of areas most sev-

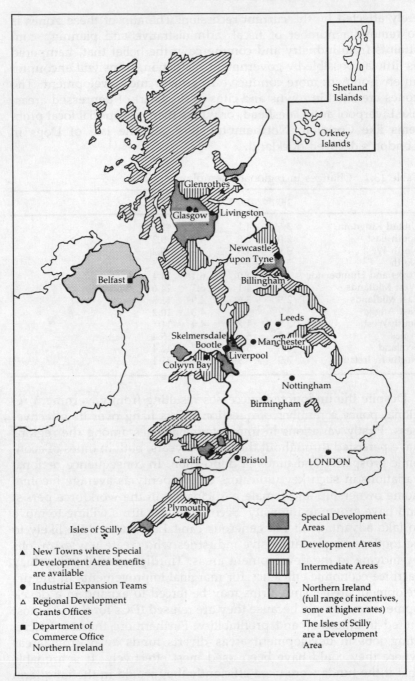

Fig. 13.1   The assisted areas

erely affected by the current recession. The aim of these zones is to remove a number of fiscal, administrative and planning constraints from industry and commerce in the belief that, hampered as little as possible by government restriction, firms will encounter an environment more conducive to growth and development. The zones are sited in towns and cites in the heart of depressed areas, like Liverpool and Gateshead, or where there are special local problems like Corby in Northamptonshire and the Isle of Dogs in London's decayed dockland.

Table 13.1   Changes in regional unemployment (%)

	1971	1975	1979	1984
United Kingdom	3.5	4.1	5.4	12.6
South-East	2.0	2.8	4.4	9.3
North-West	3.9	5.3	7.6	15.3
North	5.7	5.9	9.2	16.5
Yorks and Humberside	3.8	4.0	6.1	13.4
West Midlands	2.9	4.1	6.1	14.6
East Midlands	2.9	3.6	4.9	11.5
East Anglia	3.2	3.5	4.3	10.2
South-West	3.3	4.7	4.4	11.1
Wales	4.4	5.6	9.9	15.4
Scotland	5.8	5.2	8.7	14.4
Northern Ireland	7.9	7.9	11.1	21.1

Despite the undoubted successes resulting from government regional policy a number of question marks hang over its effectiveness. Firstly variations in unemployment rates among the regions have persisted throughout the last fifty years, both in times of economic prosperity and times of depression. In consequence regional variations in such key indicators of prosperity as average income, home ownership and female participation in the workforce persist and have grown in intensity. Secondly those firms willing to move to take advantage of the generous capital allowances are likely to be footloose capital-intensive industries who create few extra jobs by moving to the development areas. Thirdly regional policy may sacrifice economic efficiency for marginal improvements in the development areas. Thus firms may be forced to expand in a development area simply because they are refused IDCs for the site most suited to efficiency and profitability. Furthermore the cost of creating jobs in development areas diverts funds away from areas where they could have been used most effectively. It is arguable that if the funds were used efficiently they would in the long term create the prosperity for the country as a whole required to regenerate the most depressed areas.

Manpower policy

In its broadest sense manpower policy aims to ensure that industry and commerce are provided with the skilled labour they require in sufficient numbers to ensure the maximisation of labour resource allocation in the economy. The need for such a policy has grown as the pace of economic and technological change has quickened since old skills become redundant faster and new skills are required more immediately. The implementation of such a policy is therefore linked to policies on employment, future industrial development, education and training and long-term economic goals. Ideally this would involve the assessment of future industrial and commercial manpower needs and policies to ensure that these needs are met, using the educational system, training and retraining facilities and other measures to optimise the geographical and occupational mobility of labour. In practice there are many difficulties encountered in the implementation of manpower policy. With regard to long-term planning, circumstances frequently change to nullify intelligent estimates as governments have found when changes in the birth-rate have more than once led to miscalculations as to the numbers of doctors and teachers required in the post-war period. The other main problem arises out of the nature of the mixed economy. In a totally *laissez-faire* society economic necessity would force workers out of occupations where they were no longer needed into new areas of opportunity while in a state-directed economy workers can be ordered to move from one occupation to another. In the mixed economy people exercise choice and the imperfections of the market system support their ability to do so. Thus workers may be slow to leave one employment to which they are accustomed but where they are no longer needed even when their services are urgently required elsewhere. This situation will occur even in an expanding economy but where the economy is stagnant and unemployment high, workers will be much less likely to risk changing occupations, especially if this entails a period out of work. The most effective period in British history from the point of view of successful direction of manpower was 1939–45 when the authorities assumed dictatorial powers in allocating workers to the various sectors of the economy.

Since the war government manpower policy divides into two phases. Firstly there was the period up until the 1960s when there was full employment and the government sought ways of increasing the size of the workforce and moving workers from declining industries to expanding ones. In the early part of this period employment in manufacturing was still rising and even as late as 1965 the Labour government was still trying to induce workers out of the service industries into the manufacturing sector. However it was in the service industries that employment opportunities grew fastest, especially after the post-war manufacturing bubble burst in the early 1950s. The answer to the problem of labour shortages was to encourage more women to enter the workforce, especially in the service sector where part-time employment enabled a rapid rise in the number of married women at work. The proportion of married women at work rose from one in five in 1951 to one in two at the end of the 1970s. At the same time the government increased the provision of training centres to enable those displaced by structural unemployment in the depressed areas to gain new skills. Unfortunately the fact that it was often a shipbuilder in the North-East who lost his job while there was a vacancy for a secretary in the South-East prevented harmonisation of job vacancies and those available for work.

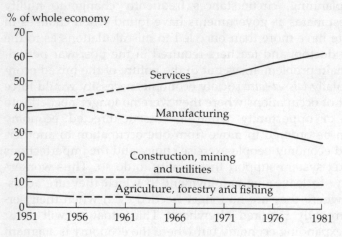

Source: Treasury, *Economic Progress Report*

Fig. 13.2   Shares of total civilian employment GB, 1951–1981

The second phase of manpower policy develops with the decline in employment opportunities in the 1970s and the growing momentum of technological change which poses a threat to more jobs in some sectors in the future. The emphasis has increasingly shifted to employment growth in the service sector as the manufacturing sector has declined at an accelerating rate. This view is based on past trends and on the rise in disposable income which enables a growing share of income to be spent in the service sector. This presupposes that technological unemployment will not in the future hit the service sector just as hard as it did the manufacturing sector. The other key area of current policy, and one linked to the hopes pinned on the service industries, is a greater provision of training and retraining arranged under the auspices of the Manpower Services Commission (MSC). While there has been a rapid decline in traditional apprenticeships all school leavers without a job are encouraged to enter the Youth Training Scheme (YTS) which, it is hoped, will give them a better chance of securing employment – though if everybody becomes better qualified and work opportunities are limited some will still find it impossible to gain employment. Similarly many of the retraining schemes mounted by the MSC may inevitably only be shifting a person from one unemployed occupation to another. Where the government has made little progress has been in recognising the need for work to be more evenly distributed in the society of the future. It could do this by reducing its own workers' hours and encouraging other sectors to do the same. This would require changes in the tax and national insurance schemes too, since at present it remains cheaper for firms to use overtime working rather than take on more staff.

Table 13.2   Changes in employment: Great Britain

| | Employees (000) | | | Change 1973–83 | |
	1973	1979	1983	No. 000s	% per annum
All industries and Services	22,180	22,590	20,460	−1,720	−0.8
Agriculture, Forestry & Fishing	420	360	340	−80	−2.1
Mining and Quarrying	360	350	310	−50	−1.5
Manufacturing	7,660	7,050	5,370	−2,290	−3.5
Construction	1,340	1,250	970	−370	−3.2
Gas, Electricity and Water	340	340	320	−20	−0.4
Service industries	12,060	13,240	13,150	+1,090	+0.9

Source: Department of Employment

Small businesses

The small firm has always received sympathy and support from post-war governments because of the high esteem in which this form of business organisation is held, both economically and politically. The small business is typically seen as enterprise in its purest form with the entrepreneur working hard and struggling against the odds for a small return, unlike the large company which has settled down to enjoy its monopoly profits and has ceased to be an innovative force for growth in the economy. Although such descriptions are caricatures of the relative worth of large and small firms they emphasise the important point that however good a small firm is it will find it harder to raise the funds it needs for expansion or development because it is a greater risk than the large firm. Yet despite the fact that the need for practical help was recognised long before the Second World War it was only in 1945 that ICFC was established. The establishment of ICFC was a step forward in solving the twin problems of the small firm – a lack of internal reserves for expansion and a lack of access to the capital market. It was followed in the following decades by the establishment of specialist bodies to help develop technical innovations and to support small firms in danger of being crippled by death duties. Since Britain joined the EEC small firms in Britain have also become potential beneficiaries of the various European schemes to help small firms. The funds in the main come from the European Investment Bank and the European Coal and Steel Community and are channelled through the banks and other institutions to qualifying applicants. The European Investment Bank is able to offer loans of £15,000 to £250,000 at or near capital market rates in non-development areas but in assisted areas funds of up to £2 million can be obtained via ICFC. These loans are for the purpose of buying fixed assets or other capital spending projects such as modernisation. In addition other forms of finance are available for training or energy conversion (from gas or oil to coal). Where firms take on redundant steel or coal workers as trainees the European Coal and Steel Community will help pay their wages during training, an invaluable subsidy for the small firm that wishes to take on more labour but cannot afford to train extra workers on full pay.

Despite progress in the capital funding of small firms the movement of the mixed economy towards larger and larger units acts against the small firm since investors have so many much safer outlets for their funds; part-ownership of a small company is less attractive than a safe unit trust with a guaranteed return. But small firms must in part be held responsible for their difficulties. Few small firms are willing to part with some control of the business in return for assistance while they often fail to meet the needs of potential investors in the supply of financial data and other information necessary for a decision. Finally it must be remembered that management expertise is not always at its best in the small firm since people can enter business without any formal training. To remedy this defect an increasing number of management teaching establishments offer courses in the setting up and running of small firms.

Question for analysis

'Where a firm's location decisions come into conflict with government regional policy the government should back down since the firm is the best judge of its own interests and efficiency.' Discuss this statement as underlining the contradiction inherent in regional policy – micro economic measures to deal with a macro economic challenge.

Case for discussion

Highqual Plc is a company in the heavy engineering industry which manufactures a wide range of high-quality equipment entailing a considerable emphasis on skilled workers. Unfortunately demand for the equipment is prone to fluctuate considerably over a three to five year period. As a result manning requirements also vary a great deal over time and this leads to the company being faced with two unsatisfactory alternatives.

1. Over-manning during downturns in demand and thus rising costs.
2. A shortage of skilled workers during periods of high demand.

In the past the company has tried to solve the problem by expensive training schemes for new workers in times of high demand and redundancies during periods of low demand. This has proved unsatisfactory in terms of labour relations and has been made more difficult due to increased legislative protection affecting both employment and redundancy.

Consider how new solutions might be sought to the problem on the basis of recent government initiatives on training and recent changes in society with regard to patterns of employment.

Chapter 14

THE PUBLIC SECTOR OF INDUSTRY

The public sector is used as a general term to refer to all those economic activities performed by the government directly or through one of its agencies. In practice it is important to distinguish between those activities performed by the various government departments in providing such public services as health, education and social security and those which are provided on a commercial basis by the nationalised industries. The public ownership of industry has always been an emotive subject because of the tendency to identify nationalisation with political rather than economic policies. It is true that the Labour Party has advocated nationalisation as a principle for many years under clause four of its constitution which aims 'to secure for the producers by hand or by brain the full fruits of their industry, and the most equitable distribution thereof that may be possible, upon the basis of common ownership of the means of production and the best obtainable system of popular administration and control of each industry or service'. Yet while this clause literally provides for the nationalisation of most industries, Labour governments have in practice applied the principle of nationalisation mainly to industries where there have been economic rather than political reasons for intervention. Long before the first Labour government came into office public ownership had been applied to the telegraph in 1870, the telephone system in 1911 and the Port of London in 1909. Indeed so appropriate was public ownership seen to be for some industries that in the two decades before the First World War many local authorities established municipal gas, water, public transport and electricity services operated on a commercial basis. Thus many of the modern nationalised industries have their origins as much in the public sector of the economy as the private.

During the course of the twentieth century greater state intervention in industry became inevitable, both because of the need for the co-ordination of industry during two world wars and because of the damage done to a number of key industries by the depression of the 1930s. When the 1945 Labour government announced its intention of nationalising many key industries in the economy it was effectively bringing under state ownership industries which had all been subject either to state control or to state financial assistance prior to 1945. Thus were nationalised the railways, which had been heavily subsidised since before the First World War, the coal-mines which were badly in need of funds for modernisation, the gas and electricity industries which were already partly state-owned and required rationalisation and the Bank of England which had acted as if it were owned by the government for the past fifty years anyway. Only in the case of iron and steel, cable and wireless and road haulage was there much room for manoeuvre in deciding whether the industries would best be left in private hands or taken over by the government. Although the Conservative Party attacked this major extension of public ownership the only important industries it felt able to denationalise when returned to office in 1951 were road haulage and iron and steel, while in the latter case the Iron and Steel Board continued to supervise price and development policies. While the debate over nationalisation is a political as much as an economic one, it is more apt to examine nationalisation in the context of economic considerations since these have underlain the decisions taken to nationalise most of those industries now in the public sector.

Arguments for nationalisation

The grounds for nationalisation are many but they can be classified under the three broad areas discussed below. In fact most of the nationalised industries have qualified on more than one criterion and in one or two cases it is difficult to find an argument for their not being nationalised.

1. *The natural monopoly.* It is in the nature of some industries that competition and efficiency are incompatible, competition resulting in wastage of resources through the duplication of services and excess capacity. In the nineteenth century a period of disastrous competition among the railway companies was followed by mergers and regionalised monopolies; similarly it was inevitable that the gas, electricity and telephone companies would develop as regional monopolies. As natural monopolies such industries

must be subject to some form of public control and nationalisation is the most direct means by which the government can exert control, but it is only one among several available to the government in a mixed economy. Thus it can choose to legislate to control monopoly power or it can interfere in the pricing and output policies of individual firms and both these measures are available under the current legislation on monopolies and restrictive practices. The decision to nationalise in the case of the railways, gas and electricity lies partly in the other economic reasons for nationalisation.

2. *National economic efficiency.* The phrase 'On the commanding heights of the economy' was frequently used to describe those industries vital to the effective running of the economy and those in which society as a whole should have a key interest. Included within this group are those industries providing essential raw materials such as iron and steel, those providing fuel and power like gas and electricity and those concerned with essential communications such as the railways, some road transport and cables and wireless. The degree to which these industries operate efficiently has repercussions for the rest of industry and for the economy as a whole and if they are in private hands there is the possibility that conflict will occur between the interest of shareholders and the public interest. Such a conflict may be due to the desire of shareholders to increase profits excessively but equally may arise where the national economy demands new investment and modernisation to take place while private owners are unable or unwilling to provide the necessary capital resources. Indeed while the first of these possibilities could be dealt with by government regulation of prices the second requires more direct government action. In both world wars the government had to take over the direction of key industries to ensure that production and distribution of essential materials could be effectively co-ordinated. After the Second World War it was apparent that industries such as coal and the railways would be unable to maintain their contribution to the economy and still remain viable as profitable private enterprises. It is also important to the workings of the economy that essential services such as transport, communications and power are provided to rural and other relatively inaccessible areas and private companies may be unwilling to provide such services except at prohibitive prices.

3. *Development and reorganisation.* Even where private owners are willing to provide funds for modernisation and expansion their companies may be too small to accumulate the necessary reserves

or to benefit from economies of scale. Most of the industries nationalised in the late 1940s were badly in need of structural re-organisation to achieve their full potential and even profitable industries like gas operated in relatively small units with backward technology. Similarly the electricity industry, already under government co-ordination through the National Grid, was in need of massive government aid to enable it to build the new generation of power stations. In the 1950s and 1960s the growing importance of research and development costs were to make it increasingly difficult for all technology-based industries to progress without government assistance and thus made the nationalisation of the British aircraft industry inevitable.

4. *Social and political considerations.* While governments may be able to control the prices charged by companies in the private sector they cannot force them to provide a service where this is un-economic. In the mixed economy governments have felt it part of their responsibility to ensure that those key services essential to the maintenance of a reasonable quality of life are available to all the population at a reasonable price so that some form of subsidy is necessary. While it is true that such subsidies could be paid to firms in the private sector it is arguable that a less contentious solution can be found in the service being provided by the state at a price standard for all. As well as protecting consumers, nationalisation might be argued also to prevent the economic power emanating from ownership of these industries being in the hands of a few families, as was the case with steel. In fact nationalisation did not involve much redistribution of income since generous compensation payments were made to shareholders in the nationalised industries, and they could then reinvest their funds in more attractive sectors of the economy. Another important political consideration is that of national security. Since some industries have been regarded as vital to national security in the contribution they make to defence and related matters it seemed appropriate to place such industries in public hands, as was the case with Cables and Wireless and the development of nuclear energy. Similarly the government felt it had to take over Rolls-Royce, when it failed in 1971, due to the importance of the aero-engine division to national defence.

The problems of nationalised industries

The nationalised industries have never been popular with the public despite the intention that they were to be run for the benefit of the nation as a whole. This unpopularity stems mainly from a confusion in the public mind between efficiency and profitability. While many people recognise that enormous profits earned by some private sector firms are the result of monopoly power rather than efficiency, they are reluctant to accept that losses in the public sector could be due in part to demands made upon them rather than through inefficiency. While the public corporations established to run the nationalised industries were expected to combine the best of private enterprise and government control they are frequently perceived as combining the worst of both. To some extent the public is justified in its view of the public sector of industry because of the way in which successive governments have failed to resolve the contradictions inherent in the structure and aims of the nationalised industries.

THE CONFLICT BETWEEN ACCOUNTABILITY AND INDEPENDENCE

The nationalised industries were established as public corporations rather than as government departments since the latter are accountable in detail for their actions to Parliament and such a structure would impose severe limitations on the industry's freedom of action in determining its policy and long-term strategy. The public corporation on the other hand is established as a company with its own legal identity and control over its own assets. It is run by a board who deal with the day-to-day matters of administration as well as being responsible for recruitment of staff and the determination of policy. It is thus similar to a company in the private sector except that it is ultimately responsible, through the appropriate minister, to Parliament rather than a group of shareholders. The minister is empowered to give general directives to the board on matters affecting the public interest while the Act of Parliament establishing the public corporation lays down instructions as to the responsibility of the board with regard to the interests of consumers and employees.

On the face of it there is a compromise between commercial independence and public accountability. Unfortunately the results have been less fruitful than expected. Firstly the minister within whose sphere of government the industry is located is expected to defend the actions of the industry to parliament and yet because of the sensitivity of governments to criticisms of the nationalised industries ministers frequently find it difficult to support the actions of the board and conflict between minister and board is common. Thus a minister may refuse to support his board's decision to modify services if there is strong criticism of the decision inside and outside parliament. Even more serious problems occur because of the decision by governments to use the nationalised industries as part of their overall economic strategy. Successive governments have manipulated the prices of gas and electricity as part of their policies on inflation and energy irrespective of the wishes of the industries themselves. Furthermore as governments are in power for periods of only a few years they frequently take a short-term view of an industry's structure. While the public corporations frequently need many years of planning to achieve their aims, many of them have been subjected to repeated changes in targets imposed by regular changes of government.

THE CONFLICT BETWEEN THE SOCIAL SERVICE PRINCIPLE AND COMMERCIAL OBJECTIVES

All of the nationalised industries have been expected both to provide a service to the public beyond that normally expected of a firm in the private sector while at the same time also prove a profitable enterprise – or at least break even. Throughout the 1950s the nationalised industries found their applications for price rises refused or moderated and most of them found it difficult to balance their revenue account when expected to maintain loss-making services to fulfil their social commitments. In the 1960s the government white papers of 1961 and 1967 tried to specify commercial objectives by requiring that deficits be balanced by surpluses over a five-year period while trying to link pricing policy more closely to the cost of the goods and services provided through the use of marginal cost pricing. While attractive in principle marginal cost pricing is impractical when applied to the nationalised industries since neither short-run nor long-run marginal cost pricing ensures that average cost is covered by average revenue and therefore that the industry is breaking even. This is because most of the industries in question are capital-intensive with high fixed costs in the short run and increasing returns to scale in the long run so that over the normal range of outputs marginal cost falls continuously and is below average cost. This means that when marginal cost is equal to average revenue (i.e. price) average cost is higher than average revenue and the industry makes a loss. Though it proved difficult to implement a policy of marginal cost pricing, government policy did at least accept the principle of flexible pricing and price discrimination, while some steps were taken to distinguish between services which could be provided profitably and those requiring government subsidy, notably with regard to the railways.

INDUSTRIAL RELATIONS

Prior to nationalisation pay and working conditions in many of the industries were very poor, reflecting the state of decline of the industries themselves. The new public corporations were expected, therefore, to pay due attention to the needs of the workforce in their policy and planning decisions and thus seek to promote good industrial relations. This has resulted in the problem of excess labour in many of the industries being dealt with by natural wastage rather than redundancies and thus periods of severe overmanning in the declining sectors. Industrial relations themselves have not improved significantly because in most of the industries bi-lateral monopolies pertain with a sole buyer of labour, the public corporation, dealing with a sole seller in the form of an industrial union – conditions rarely conducive to a placid negotiating environment. Generally speaking, however, both sides of most of these industries are loyal to the industry and considering the 'muscle power' of the unions, disruption is less prevalent than might be expected.

INVESTMENT AND RETURN ON CAPITAL

One of the avowed aims of nationalisation was the modernisation and increased efficiency of the industries concerned. Yet from the outset the public corporations were saddled with the requirement to meet from their revenue interest on all capital *including* the original compensation stock. This, coupled with price restraint imposed by successive governments, made it very difficult to build up the reserves necessary for capital investment programmes required to modernise and maintain their high rate of capital intensity. Inevitably the 1950s saw the government having to step in to assist in the financing of new capital investment. The 1967 White Paper attempted to tighten financial responsibility towards investment by laying down that discounted cash flow techniques were to be used in investment appraisal while social cost-benefit analysis was to be the basis for the evaluation of investment projects. More specific attention was given to investment appraisal in the 1978 White Paper. Financial targets were henceforth to be decided industry by industry and to be set for three to five years. Each target takes into account the 'required rate of return' of 5 per cent in real terms which was set to reflect the opportunity cost of capital in the economy but allowance is made for the various social objectives set for an industry, and on the earning power of existing assets. The financial target set for each industry to a large extent determines the price level in each industry and between 1978 and 1980 there were rapid price rises in the fuel and transport industries in line with financial targets. Higher profitability allowed self-financing to rise also from 27 per cent in 1975–76 to 60 per cent in 1977–78, thereby reducing their borrowing requirement. A further change was introduced with regard to long-term financing in 1980. The nationalised industries do not borrow from the domestic market other than for short-term borrowing. Instead the public corporations borrow from the National Loans Fund and the government in turn borrows from the market. In 1980 the government set new guidelines by which it would adminster the industries' external financing limits (EFLs) which control the amount of finance which an industry can raise in any financial year from external sources. The main changes involved firstly a greater flexibility in the raising of finance, with borrowing linked to future cash flows rather than to the life of a particular asset. Secondly stricter controls were announced on EFLs in that the nationalised industries could not

Table 14.1   External financing limits for the nationalised industries (1984–85)

	(£ million)[1]
National Coal Board	1,103
Electricity (England and Wales)	−740
North of Scotland Hydro-Electric Board	−2
South of Scotland Electricity Board	261
British Gas Corporation	−100
British Steel Corporation	275
British Telecom	−250
Post Office	−52
National Girobank	−1
British Airways Board	−160
British Airports Authority	10
British Railways Board	936
British Waterways Board	43
National Bus Company	66
Scottish Transport Group	16
British National Oil Corporation[2]	−4
British Shipbuilders[3]	175
Civil Aviation Authority	20
Water (England and Wales)	286
Total	**1,882**

[1] Figures are shown rounded to the nearest £1 million.
[2] The figure for BNOC is not a limit. BNOC's trading results are likely to fluctuate from year to year given the uncertainties of oil trading.
[3] The British Shipbuilders EFL is provisional pending decisions on the industry's corporate plan.

Source: Treasury

rely on deficits being met by a further injection of external finance. In future EFLs would be adjustable during a financial year but only when no further action is possible to keep the industry within its limits and the government could deduct any such adjustment from the following year's EFL.

Despite the many changes introduced into the pricing and investment structures of the nationalised industries to give them greater freedom of action the problems discussed above have not been adequately resolved. Such environmental constraints as lack of certainty concerning the precise role of the nationalised industries and the conflict between commercial and social objectives persist. Thus assessments of efficiency and performance are blighted by the inconclusiveness resulting from the different criteria for evaluating one industry compared to another or any one of them against a private sector industry. The present government has not been convinced of the ability of the public sector to use resources as efficiently as the private sector and has sought to reverse the nationalisation of the past forty years through the process of privatisation.

Privatisation

From its election in 1979 the Conservative government stated its purpose as transferring ownership from the state to the private sector to extend market forces and competition in order to improve resource utilisation and efficiency. Privatisation has taken a number of forms including the disposal of public sector shareholdings in companies and the contracting out of local government services but its most dramatic impact has been in the sale of shareholdings in the nationalised industries. The government's arguments in favour of privatisation centre on the belief that in the private sector managers are free of government interference and are stimulated to enterprise and risk-taking by the spur of profit, absent from the public sector. Furthermore the consumer will benefit because competition will increase and this will widen choice. The government also believes that privatisation presents an opportunity to widen share ownership and have sold many of the shareholdings to employees. Finally the sale of assets is seen as helping to reduce the burden on the exchequer by providng funds through the sale of assets and removing from the PSBR any future borrowing made by the industries in question.

The progress made on privatisation in the first four years to 1983

Table 14.2   Major privatisation undertakings (1980–83)

Sale	Proceeds (£ million)
British Aerospace (51%)	43
Auction of oil licences	210
Motorway service areas	28
Local authority land and housing	3,918
Cable and Wireless (50%)	182
Oil stockpiles	63
Amersham International	64
Britoil (51%)	548
Associated British Ports (49%)	22
British Rail hotels	35

raised slightly over £2 billion through the sale of strategic share-holdings in British Petroleum, Cable and Wireless, Britoil and British Aerospace. Plans for 1984 and beyond envisaged the sale of £2 billion of public assets each year for four years through the privatisation of British Airways, the British Airports Authority, the Royal Ordnance Factories and parts of British Gas, British Steel, British Shipbuilders and British Rail. Furthermore the privatisation legislation has removed the telecommunications monopoly enjoyed by British Telecom, relaxed the licencing system for bus and coach services and given the Secretary of State power to suspend, should he so wish, the Post Office's monopoly on the postal system.

Problems posed by privatisation

There are a number of interrelated problems arising from the policy of privatisation some of which arise from such a drastic alteration of the structure of British industry while others echo the reasons why nationalisation was adopted in the first place. Firstly asset sales of £8 billion between 1984 and 1987, including £4 billion alone in the sale of British Telecom, will impose a strain on the capital market in its attempt to manage such large sums. Indeed there is the danger that assets will not realise their valuation, resulting in a loss to the Treasury of expected revenue. Secondly one avowed aim of privatisation is the ending of a public monopoly and the introduction of greater competition yet since some of the nationalised industries are natural monopolies it is difficult to avoid the view that a public monopoly will become a private monopoly and therefore a potentially greater threat to the public interest. Thirdly, and related to the last point, privatisation removes ultimate control of the industry from ministers and civil servants and places it with those interests having a controlling stake in the industry so that the public loses any say it previously had in the administration of industries, many of which provide essential services. It is thus difficult to see how public services can be maintained at current levels when private enterprise, which after all is concerned with the profit motive, finds that such services threaten the maintenance of profits. Fourthly privatisation is assumed to give greater efficiency by relieving management from governmental control and by worker share-participation schemes to increase the commitment of workers to the industry. In practice some of the industries are so important that, like the railways in the nineteenth century, they will inevitably have to be subject to some form of official supervision especially where monopoly power is present. As to worker-shareholders if the pattern of shareholding follows that in other public companies the majority of shares will be in the hands of the great financial institutions – pension funds, insurance companies and unit trusts rather than with workers. Finally the privatisation programme is likely to be so far-reaching that even if it proved to be unsuccessful in its aims no future Labour government will be able to contemplate renationalisation of all the privatised industries without prohibitively high tax rates and interest rates.

Case for discussion

'Privatisation represents by far the most effective means of extending market forces and in turn of improving efficiency and the allocation of resources.' Lord Cockfield, Minister of State, Treasury, 19 November 1981.

1. In this context what is meant by 'market forces' and 'efficiency and the allocation of resources'? How valid is the view that the private sector is more likely to achieve these ends than the public sector?
2. Given that in the long term British Rail is a possible candidate for partial privatisation:
   (a) What problems would face British Rail if it were partially privatised?
   (b) Consider possible measures which might be adopted to try to deal with these problems.

Chapter 15

NATIONAL INCOME FLOWS

The term national income refers to the total flow of goods and services in society over a period of time. As the name suggests it is an attempt to quantify the total income earned in society and by implication to quantify total output and total expenditure since all members of an economic society perform more than one economic function; as consumers they buy the goods and services which have been produced while as owners of the factors of production they receive the incomes derived from the use of those factors, which in turn are used in the production of society's total output of goods and services. If the members of society are treated as income-receivers, or as producers or as consumers it is possible to calculate three measurements of economic performance over a given period each of which should be identical since each is viewing the same process of economic activity from a different viewpoint. That this is the case can be seen in a simple example of where a person undertakes his own car maintenance so that the work done (output) benefit received (income) and time spent (expenditure) result in no monetary transaction since the value of each is equated. In a sophisticated economy income, output and expenditure must also be equal though this is not nearly so obvious, since it is impossible in most cases to equate the income of any one individual with the output of that person or the expenditure undertaken on his behalf. None the less if the example of a car is taken which sells for £5,000 of which £4,200 are taken up by the total costs of using land, labour and capital the remaining £800 must consist of profit retained by the firm or distributed to shareholders. Similarly total output must equal total expenditure as if the car is not sold it will be put into stock and thus count as investment expenditure with the firm effectively buying its own production. The relationship between

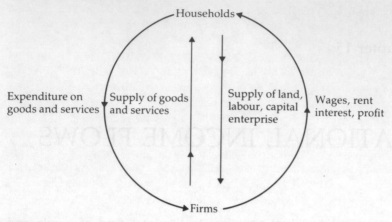

Fig. 15.1

the three methods of measuring national income is illustrated in Fig. 15.1.

In Fig. 15.1 the expenditure method of measuring national income is on the left-hand arc of the circle, the output method is represented by the supply of goods and services and the income method is represented by the right-hand arc. In this basic diagram the national income is seen exclusively in terms of the flow of income, output and expenditure between households and firms though in practice there are further flows to and from the circular flow due to the activities of governments and trade with other countries. The importance of these flows will emerge as the various methods of measuring national income are examined in detail.

THE INCOME METHOD

National income is found by totalling all factor incomes. This would include not only rent, wages, interest and profits but also any surpluses earned by public corporations and other public bodies. Not included, however, are transfer payments, i.e. those incomes or parts of incomes received without any contribution to output being made, and these would include pensions, unemployment and social security benefits and other income which is transferred to the recipients from the factors of production via the tax system. The total figure calculated is the national income at factor cost before the distortional effects of redistributional transfers are taken into account. However, allowance must also be made for the fact that those firms with stocks will have seen the value of these rise without any production taking place and so a figure for stock appreciation must be deducted to yield a figure for gross domestic product at factor cost. So far allowance has been made for redistributional effects and for changes in stock values but other adjustments are necessary to arrive at an accurate reflection of national income. Firstly, account must be taken of income earned from abroad by British residents and income paid abroad by British residents and companies. When this is done *Gross domestic product at factor cost + Net property income from abroad = Gross national product at factor cost*. Finally the total so far obtained makes no allowance for the fact that some capital assets have worn out during the year and represent a reduction in national income. When the figure for capital consumption is deducted from gross national product at factor cost a figure for net national product is obtained.

THE EXPENDITURE METHOD

This method arrives at a figure for national income by measuring total expenditure by consumers, by the public sector and by firms through investment (including additions to stocks). This total domestic expenditure figure must be adjusted, however, to take account of the impact of overseas trade and the activities of the government in influencing prices. Thus export expenditure must be added to the figure since the purchase of goods and services by overseas buyers adds to domestic national income while the corresponding figure for imports must be deducted for opposite reasons. Furthermore the figure so far obtained for total domestic expenditure is based on market prices which do not correspond to the factor costs incurred in production since they are distorted by the effect of taxes and subsidies – the price of a bottle of whisky, for example, bears little resemblance to the cost of producing the product. Thus taxes on expenditure must be deducted from and subsidies added to total domestic expenditure to arrive at the gross domestic product at factor cost. Then the same process as under the income method can be followed to arrive at the net national product.

THE OUTPUT METHOD

This measurement is based on the value of the production of the various firms and public enterprises in the economy. In arriving at this figure it is important that only the value added by each firm in the production process is counted, otherwise the problem of double counting will occur with both the suppliers and the users of raw materials counting them as part of their output. The value added is the total revenue of the firm less what has been paid to other firms for goods and services supplied. While it is possible to

Table 15.1   National income statistics (1982)

Expenditure method	(£ million)	Income method	(£ million)
Consumers' expenditure	167,128	Income from employment	155,133
General govt. consumption	60,082	Income from self-employment	20,068
Gross domestic fixed capital formation	42,172	Gross domestic trading profits of companies	33,344
Value of physical increase in stocks	− 1,162	Gross trading surplus of public corporations	9,068
Total domestic expenditure	268,220	Gross trading surplus of general govt. enterprise	124
Exports of goods & services	73,128	Rent	16,166
Total final expenditure	341,348	Consumption of non-trading capital	2,507
Less imports	−67,165	Total domestic income	236,410
Gross domestic product at market prices	274,183	Less stock appreciation	−3,907
Less taxes on expenditure	−47,082	Gross domestic product	232,503
Subsidies	5,452	Residual error	50
Gross domestic product at factor cost	232,553	Gross domestic product at factor cost	232,553
Net property income from abroad	1,577	Net property income from abroad	1,577
Gross national product at factor cost	234,130	Gross national product at factor cost	234,130
Less capital consumption	−33,057	Less capital consumption	−33,057
Net national product = national income	201,073	Net national product = national income	201,073

assess the value of services supplied by private enterprise it is not quite so simple to assess the value of those provided by the government where no charge is made and thus these are valued at the cost incurred by the government to provide these services in the form of the salaries and wages paid to the public servants giving the service. The figure obtained is the gross domestic product at factor cost, as with the other two measurements of national income.

Whatever method of calculating national income is used errors are bound to occur, not only through double-counting in the output method but also through such factors as non-declaration of incomes, illegal imports, output which is not registered and so on. These errors are dealt with by the inclusion of the residual error which has been approximately 0.7 per cent of total GNP for the last decade. Also included in the output section is an estimated value of owner-occupied houses which provide a service but would not otherwise be included. Left out, however, are services provided by oneself for oneself such as housework or decorating and, of course, the 'black economy' of output, income and expenditure which takes place but is not declared to any government department and is excluded from the various measurements of national income.

Because of errors, omissions and other inaccuracies the measurement of national income is important not for the figures it gives in a particular year but for the indications it gives concerning trends in the economy. These trends will be accurate as long as the methods of measurement remain constant but the use of figures in forward planning or other forecasting requires that certain factors are taken into account in interpreting the figures. Firstly allowance must be made for changes in the value of money which exaggerate movements in national income; thus in the 1930s a rise in the value of money gave the impression that national income fell throughout the period whereas this was not the case. Similarly in the post-war period inflation has made the national income appear to grow rapidly while in fact growth has tended to be less than 3 per cent per annum – indeed the national income changes very little from one year to another with the bulk of capital investment replacing worn out capital rather than representing new investment. Secondly living standards may change without any movement in national income as when output and income are maintained at existing levels but workers receive longer holidays or a shorter working week. Thirdly depending on the form the extra national income takes will be the effect on living standards. Thus if all national income growth goes into capital formation, as happened in the Soviet Union during the 1930s and for much of the period following the last war, there will be national income growth with virtually no change in living standards. It is also possible for living standards to rise while national income falls, at least in the short term, if resources are devoted to consumer goods and services while capital formation is negative so that current capital formation is less than current depreciation. Finally it is extremely difficult to compare the national incomes of different countries due to such differences as population size, rate of inflation, relative cost of living and the value of the domestic currency both in terms of its exchange rate and its local purchasing power. Thus while *per capita* income is undoubtedly very low in most African countries a weekly income of £2 per head buys more there than it would in the UK. Many British workers who have been comfortably off while resident in India, for example, find that their income is totally inadequate when applied to the British cost of living.

The national income flow

At the beginning of the chapter a simple national income cycle was depicted with national income flowing exclusively between house-

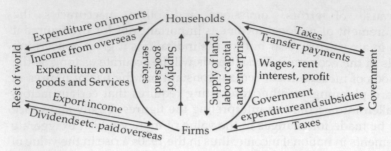

Fig. 15.2

holds and firms. Yet as the calculation of national income showed the role of the government and external trade must be taken into account in any model of the circular flow and these are brought in in Fig. 15.2.

In the above figure flows to and from the government and to and from the rest of the world are depicted as outside the main circular flow of income because such flows are the result of transactions taking place apart from the normal transactions between firms and households. Thus exports represent income earned by firms from external sources while imports are taken from the circular flow to be spent on foreign goods. Similarly payments to the government either by households or by firms are taken out of the circular flow of income while government expenditure either directly to firms or indirectly via transfer payments represents an external flow into the national income. Not shown in the diagram is another loop connecting households to firms, that of saving and investment. This line is omitted because there is no guarantee that savings will be pumped back into the firms as investment; furthermore it is investment which, we have seen, generates savings rather than the other way round. It is also the case that some investment funds flow into firms from abroad and from the government. Those payments into the circular flow from outside are known as injections while payments and leakages from the circular flow are withdrawals. Injections consist of investment + government expenditure + exports; withdrawals of savings + taxation + imports. The circular flow of income and expenditure leads to income both being generated by expenditure and itself generating further expenditure. The level of domestic output is thus determined by the level of aggregate demand which consists of consumption of domestically produced goods and services by households plus injections. Provided that expenditure, output and income levels are maintained at the same level through successive time periods the national income will show no tendency to rise or fall since it will be in equilibrium. Any reduction in aggregate demand will automatically lead to an equivalent fall in income and output so reducing the level of national income. Thus if consumers switch expenditure from home-produced to imported goods or the government cuts its expenditure in the economy without a corresponding cut in taxation firms will experience a fall in their income which will in turn lead them to lower output and thus employ less factors of production so that incomes received by the households also fall. On the other hand if there are autonomous increases in export sales or investment in firms then national income will rise in response to the higher aggregate demand. But what of the relationship between injections and withdrawals? If withdrawals are increased all that can be predicted is that there will be a tendency for national income to fall unless the increase in withdrawals is matched by a simultaneous increase in injections. This is hardly likely. Why, for example, should the Japanese buy more British goods just because nine out of ten new video-recorders bought in Britain in 1984 were made in Japan, or a firm in Manchester embark on a new investment programme because the population of East Anglia or Cornwall decide to save more of their income? On the other hand an increase in injections will have an influence on the level of withdrawals. This is because a rise in injections will lead to a corresponding rise in national income so that both output and income will rise; households will thus have more income to spend not only on home-produced goods but also on imported goods. Furthermore higher incomes will mean that the levels of tax paid and savings made will also be higher. Thus while an increase in withdrawals cannot be assumed to affect the level of injections a change in injections themselves will alter the level of withdrawals. The precise effect of a given change in injections on the level of withdrawals will become apparent when they are examined in relation to a given level of national income.

In Fig. 15.3 the level of injections is assumed to be constant whatever the level of national income since there is no direct correlation between the size of national income and injections. Thus the key issue affecting investment is the expected return, the level of government expenditure depends on the political aims of the government while exports relate to their attractiveness to overseas buyers. Thus even though it is likely that investment at least will rise as national income rises it is impossible to predict accurately the path followed by injections collectively. Withdrawals, on the other hand, are assumed to rise with national income since the higher

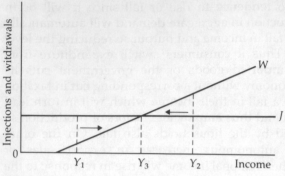

Fig. 15.3

the income the greater the likelihood that some income will be saved, spent on imports or paid in taxes. The equilibrium level of national income is at Y_3 since at any point to the left of Y_3, say Y_1, injections exceed withdrawals and aggregate demand outstrips output so that stocks fall, profits rise and prices increase. Firms respond to the situation by increasing output through using such spare capacity as is available. Expansion of national income will continue until withdrawals have risen to meet injections since at this point, with injections and withdrawals equal, the flow of income between households and firms will be in equilibrium. Since national income equilibrium is reached at the point where injections and withdrawals are equal it can be predicted that a given increase in injections must generate an equivalent increase in withdrawals. Alternatively if in Fig. 15.3 the income were at Y_2 demand would fall short of current output so that stocks build up while sales and profits fall. Only in the unlikely event of firms opting to continue to produce at current levels and thus increase their investment in the form of higher stocks will it be possible to maintain income at this level. If they choose to reduce output, employment and income levels will also fall until the level of withdrawals has fallen to that of injections and income is again in equilibrium. In the above analysis there is no automatic relationship between the equilibrium level of income and a healthy national income, thus in Fig. 15.3 the income level Y_2 could be that at which full employment exists but is not sustainable since the economy is out of equilibrium. This is the problem of national income equilibrium – it is quite possible for income to be in equilibrium at a high level of unemployment. By the same token it is also true that national income cannot by definition increase beyond its full employment position.

Short and long run national income changes

It would appear from the foregoing analysis that it is possible to make two definitive statements with regard to savings and full employment. Firstly savings are a bad thing since they are a withdrawal from the circular flow of national income and thus cause a reduction in national income. Thus the advice given to all children to save is apparently bad advice! Secondly national income can only grow to a certain point before it comes up against the barrier imposed by full employment. In fact both these statements are only partially true in the short run and hardly true at all in the long run. Firstly with regard to savings they are only a bad thing in the sense that autonomous attempts to increase savings without reference to investment demands in the economy will tend to reduce national income. However, where higher investment generates a growth in national income and permits savings growth in response to the demand for investment funds, there is an expansionary, not a downward, pressure on national income. Furthermore long-term future investment plans will depend for their implementation on the availability of investment funds and, therefore, of a pool of savings. With regard to the limits imposed on growth by full employment it is true that with full employment it is difficult to expand output in the short run beyond more intensive use of existing resources. However, in the long run the economy as a whole can extend the limits of total output by a more efficient use of existing resources and the development of new methods of production. It is of course perfectly possible for both productive capacity and utilisation of existing capacity to rise or fall at the same time and it is difficult to isolate the two components. However, changes in the utilisation of existing capacity can be regarded as short-term fluctuations associated with the trade cycle while productive capacity changes much more slowly and is associated with the growth in national income which occurs over a period of twenty or thirty years. Thus while aggregate demand, which reflects short-run national income, may exhibit wildly varying rates of growth or decline over a period of a few years most countries have experienced a consistent economic growth in the post-war period.

The consistent economic growth of the 1950s and 1960s outstripped the long-term rate of growth at any period apart from the peak years of the Industrial Revolution, and was a cornerstone of government policy of both parties during this period for social reasons. Firstly economic growth enables living standards to rise – an annual average growth rate of 3 per cent will double living standards in a quarter of a century. Secondly economic growth permits all sections of society to enjoy higher real incomes so that policies to redistribute income may be adopted without anyone suffering a cut in living standards. Finally sustained growth creates a climate of confidence and stability among businessmen and this will encourage new efforts to raise productive capacity. It also leads to society as a whole being willing to accept temporary austerity in return for longer term benefits when resources have to be directed from consumption goods to long-term investment. Yet despite a general commitment to growth governments have found themselves confined by short-term policies designed to deal with immediate problems, leaving the long-term target to hope rather than action.

CAUSES OF GROWTH

Without the various factors discussed below economic growth would rely almost entirely on the growth of population to provide

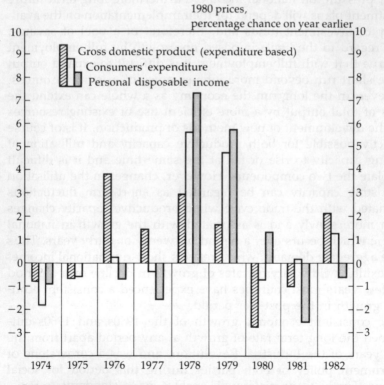

Source: *CSO Economic Trends*

Fig. 15.4 Income, product and spending *per capita*

more labour resources and thus increase production and even then labour on its own is limited in its stability to feed itself let alone offer prospects of growing output per person.

1. *Invention and innovation.*   While invention is the discovery of new products and new techniques, essential if society is to develop, innovation is the process by which these discoveries are put to economic use. Thus economic progress depends both on the scientist and the technologist but equally on the entrepreneur. The strong streak of conservatism and safety first in human nature places a premium on the willingness to take risks and try new ideas and ensures that in the free market economy, and to a lesser extent in a mixed economy, entrepreneurial rewards can be high. Even in the absence of the profit motive entrepreneurial expertise is necessary if industries in the public sector are not to stagnate. Without innovation society would quickly exhaust all the potential investment projects available and would reach a plateau of economic stagnation. Innovation provides constant sources of new growth through opening up areas of potential profitable investment opportunities for funds generated by the economy. Even technical and scientific research apparently undertaken with no direct economic benefit in mind can have important economic spin-offs as space research has shown.

2. *The accumulation of capital.*   Together with entrepreneurial activity capital is the key factor of production in economic growth since the supply of land is fixed and increased labour adds only marginally to the productive capacity of the economy. The growth of the stock of capital depends on the maintenance of a strong flow of investment funds and thus of a pool of available funds in the economy. Greater use of capital enables the costs of production to be reduced as skilled expensive labour is replaced by machine thus allowing prices to be reduced and demand to increase so setting in chain another round of growth. Furthermore the replacement of labour by capital both permits output to be accelerated while also releasing labour for other sectors of the economy.

3. *Human capital.*   Economic growth consists not only of greater output but also of better quality output. But to prove successful technological progress must be matched by a rise in the quality of labour. Improvements in the quality of labour depend not on marginal increases in physical quality but in developing its technical expertise, i.e. the capital part of labour. Thus training and edu-

cational facilities must be developed to suit the needs of a technology-based society. The view that many workers need no intellectual skills but merely physical ability and a minimum of training may have been true, if cynical, in the past but such occupations are eventually to be replaced by machine and the whole population at work in the future can expect to become more human capital than labour.

4. *Demand conditions.*   Economic growth requires a willingness to innovate and invest on the part of businessmen and such willingness springs from an expectation that demand will respond sufficiently to justify their enterprise and the risk this involves. In a modern consumer-based society this necessitates a broad-based demand in most cases so that buoyant demand is associated with rising living standards *and* a reasonably equitable distribution of income so that new products can be offered to the public as a whole rather than to a small group of very wealthy consumers. This points to one of the problems facing all industries during a depression; higher unemployment inevitably narrows the potential market for new products and services and this can be a critical factor in deciding on the launch of a new product. On the other hand conditions of high demand help to make growth self-perpetuating by stimulating increases of productive capacity and thus employment opportunities while these in turn will further assist demand growth.

5. *Foreign trade.*   Overseas trade helps countries to counter domestic resource shortages and to develop greater economies of scale thus lowering average costs and raising living standards. A strong export market also encourages confidence and thus helps create an environment conducive to economic growth. Finally exports represent an injection into the national income and thus are automatically a source of national income growth.

Of equal concern in the long-term maintenance of economic growth, possibly even of the status quo, is the position of the Third World countries. In order that the developed countries can continue to expand their markets for consumer goods they must develop their trade with the potentially vast markets of Asia and Africa. Unfortunately for both parties concerned but especially the developing countries economic growth there continues to be slow or non-existent. The reasons for this are that in the areas making for growth discussed above they are lacking. Instead a cycle of poverty prevents the accumulation of a pool of funds which can be used for investment and thus the modernisation of agriculture and industry. Unlike the countries of Western Europe in the nineteenth century or Japan and Eastern Europe in the twentieth they have not reached that point in their economic development where growth is both spontaneous and self-supporting – indeed it becomes less likely all the time that such a situation can occur as they must compete with all the current industrialised and developed nations who can outbid them for resources and already dominate world markets. They depend for their development on the investment in these countries of funds from overseas which can be used to develop their resources. While such action will inevitably lead to fears for the industries of the developed countries in terms of competition from new cheaper producers there will be compensatory growth from newly-expanded overseas markets in industries where the developed countries retain an advantage. However, these markets can only develop if investment is used partly at least to establish indigenously controlled industries rather than being used entirely to finance cheap production using the local workforce while profits are repatriated to the company's main country of operation.

Questions for analysis

1. What are the main difficulties encountered in attempting to measure national income? What further difficulties arise when comparing the national income of the UK with that of a developing country?
2. Examine how the different factors which contribute to economic growth interact with each other and show how it is possible to achieve either a cycle of growth or of decline.

Chapter 16

NATIONAL INCOME DISEQUILIBRIUM

When national income analysis was introduced in the last chapter the problem arose that it is quite possible for national income to be in equilibrium at high levels of unemployment so that at the full employment level national income is in disequilibrium with withdrawals exceeding injections. Expressed another way this means that at the full employment level of national income aggregate expenditure in the economy is inadequate and national income must therefore contract. This is illustrated in Fig. 16.1 where the 45° line represents possible equilibrium levels of national income where income is equal to aggregate expenditure (consisting of consumption together with injections). Any points above or to the left of the 45° line represent levels of aggregate expenditure which exceed current income while points below and to the right are those where aggre-

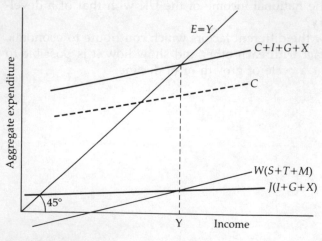

Fig. 16.1

gate expenditure is less than current income. As injections are being held constant for the purposes of this analysis the aggregate expenditure line will have the same slope as the consumption line and at the equilibrium level of national income (Y) withdrawals will equal injections and aggregate expenditure will be equal to income.

It is thus possible to predict on the basis of this analysis that a rise in injections will lead to an expansion of national income as higher aggregate demand generates higher national output while conversely a rise in the level of withdrawals will cause income to fall as the contraction in aggregate demand leads to a fall in output.

The multiplier effect

While it is now apparent that changes in the level of either injections or withdrawals lead to changes in the level of national income the question remains as to how much national income will vary as the result of a given change in either injections or withdrawals. An increase in investment of £100 million must cause national income to rise by the same figure but it could rise by more than this initial injection. Thus if the £100 million investment programme is the construction of a ship this will result in extra income being paid to the owners of the factors of production involved in supplying materials and resources for the building of the ship. So far national income has risen by only that £100 million but if the recipients of this extra income then choose to spend some of it on goods and services provided by the rest of the community there will be a second wave of extra income creation more widely dispersed through the economy. This process will continue until no further new income is created by another round of consumption. Quantifying this multiplier effect is a complex task since different injections of the same amount will have differing effects depending on the nature of the injection and in which sector of the economy it has its greatest impact. However, the multiplier effect must relate ultimately to the proportion of income which is transmitted back into the circular flow of income in each round of income generation. Thus if the £100 million investment programme did not result in extra production and income in this country but was subcontracted for completion overseas there would be no multiplier effect at all while the greater the proportion of extra income generated that is fed back into the circular flow of income the larger will be the multiplier effect.

The size of the multiplier effect relates, therefore, to the proportion of new income allocated by those who receive it to consumption, i.e. *the consumption function*. Consumption is a function of income in that consumption increases as income increases, though not necessarily at the same rate. The remainder of any extra income not consumed must be withdrawn from the circular flow of income as savings, taxes or payment for imports. Thus *Income = Consumption + Savings + Taxes + Imports*. The proportion of each extra unit of income devoted to consumption is the **marginal propensity to consume (MPC)**. Similarly the proportion of each extra unit of income allocated to savings is the **marginal propensity to save (MPS)** and there are also **marginal propensities to pay taxes (MPT)** and to **buy imports (MPM)**. Together the marginal propensities to save, to pay taxes and to buy imports make up the **marginal propensity to make withdrawals** from the circular flow **(MPW)**. Each member of society has his or her own marginal propensity to consume etc. based on the person's lifestyle and patterns of expenditure while the marginal propensity to consume will change for an individual as that person's income changes. Thus if a person receives a large increase in income it is likely that he or she will pay more taxes and perhaps save more of the extra income. In order to be able to discuss the multiplier as a principle it will be assumed that the various marginal propensities are constant.

Table 16.1

Income (Y)	Consumption (C)	Savings (S)	Taxes (T)	Imports (M)	MPC	MPS	MPT	MPM	MPW
100	40	10	30	20	—	—	—	—	—
120	48	12	36	24	0.4	0.1	0.3	0.2	0.6
140	56	14	42	28	0.4	0.1	0.3	0.2	0.6
180	64	16	48	32	0.4	0.1	0.3	0.2	0.6

In the above table, of each new £ received 40 pence is spent on consumption, 10 pence on savings, 30 pence on taxes and 20 pence on imported goods. Thus the MPC is 0.4 and MPW totals 0.6. Obviously MPC + MPW must equal One. On this basis it can be predicted that if there were an extra injection into the economy of £100 million, £40 million of that would return into the circular flow and thus create further income of £40 million to add to the original £100 million. The growth in national income will continue on this basis as shown in the following table.

This process could be continued until the nth generation when one pound will be added to income of which 40 pence is spent on consumption and 60 pence withdrawn from the circular flow. However, as in the case of the credit creation multiplier discussed in

Table 16.2

	Increase in Income (£ million)	Consumption (£ million)	Withdrawals (£ million)
Initial injection	100.0	40.0	60.0
1st Regeneration	40.0	16.0	24.0
2nd Regeneration	16.0	6.4	9.6
3rd Regeneration	6.4	2.6	3.8
4th Regeneration	2.6	1.0	1.6
5th Regeneration	1.0	0.4	0.6

Chapter 10 a simple formula can be used to calculate the change in income arising from a given injection, i.e.

$$\text{The Injection} \times \frac{1}{\text{MPW}} = \text{Total growth in national income}$$

In Table 16.2 £100 million $\times \dfrac{1}{0.6} = $ £166.7 million.

The multiplier effect is thus a 1.67 magnification of the original injection so that the multiplier is the reciprocal of the marginal propensity to make withdrawals – in this case the reciprocal of 6/10 which is 1.67. The multiplier effect continues until there has been sufficient generation of extra income that withdrawals have risen by the level of the original injection so that injections and withdrawals are once again in equilibrium. Clearly the smaller the MPW the greater the circular flow of income must expand by stages until withdrawals once again match injections and thus the greater the multiplier effect of some injections on national income than others.

So far multiplier effects have been considered only in respect of changes in the level of injections but they apply equally to changes in the level of withdrawals. Thus an increase in the level of taxation will have a downward multiplier effect on national income, as would a fall in the level of government expenditure. If taxes are increased, with injections held constant, national income must contract until withdrawals as a whole are back to the level at which injections and withdrawals are equal. The effect of the multiplier is always to exaggerate the rise or fall in national income resulting from a given change in injections or withdrawals. Provided that some resources in the economy are unused a rise in injections or a fall in withdrawals will lead to a multiplied growth in the equilibrium level of national income while a fall in injections or rise in withdrawals will tend to dampen economic activity and lead to a multiplied decline in the level of economic activity.

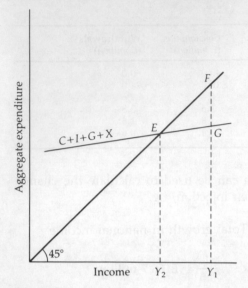

Fig. 16.2

In Fig. 16.2 aggregate expenditure is less than income at the full employment level of income (Y_1) so that withdrawals from the circular flow of income exceed injections into it. The shortfall of full employment expenditure to income is known as a deflationary gap and is depicted by the distance between F and G. The national income is now in disequilibrium with output in excess of demand and firms finding their stocks building up. Full employment is no longer tenable as producers seek to cut back output and lay off workers and leave plant and equipment idle. National income thus contracts until equilibrium is reached at Y_2. The total fall in national income will be greater than the original deflationary gap due to the action of the multiplier. The inherent danger in this situation is that investment (which until now has been regarded as constant) may fall as profits wane and business confidence sags so that another deflationary gap opens up and the equilibrium level of income falls below Y_2. Fortunately there is a point at which decline bottoms out since investment cannot fall to zero and such economic activity as food and energy production will not cease no matter how low business confidence sinks.

When a deflationary gap exists an increase in injections or fall in withdrawals will result in a multiplied growth in national income. If, however, the economy enjoys full employment equilibrium any increase in aggregate demand will be unable to generate further

growth as there are no unused resources available. Instead there
will be excess demand in the economy with upward pressure on
prices. Higher prices lead to firms making, at least temporarily,
higher profits and attempting to increase output by the employment of extra factors of production. With full employment this can
only be done in the short run by bidding up factor rewards to
attract land, labour and capital from other firms but as higher factor
incomes result in increased demand for goods and services the upward spiral of prices and factor rewards is given another boost.
This situation of excess demand in the economy is an inflationary
gap and is illustrated in Fig. 16.3. With an inflationary gap equilibrium can only be restored beyond the full employment level of income and since no level beyond the full employment level is
possible the inflationary spiral will continue until there is a reduction in the level of aggregate demand or until the money supply
is no longer sufficient to fuel further increases in demand.

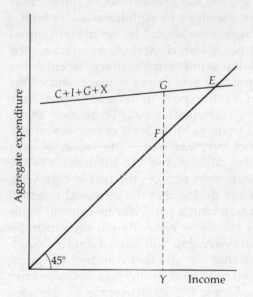

Fig. 16.3

The trade cycle

Thus far both the deflationary gap and the inflationary gap have
been described but questions about the level of national income
remain. Which, for example, is the natural state of national income
– at full employment or with a deflationary gap or with an in-

flationary gap – or is there no natural state? Furthermore once one of these situations is established why should national income deviate from this in the absence of some external pressure on the economy? In answer to the first question there is no evidence to support the view that a full employment equilibrium is the one toward which national income will gravitate. In fact national income analysis shows that a deflationary gap is just as 'natural' as a situation of full employment while an inflationary gap is self-perpetuating without ever reaching a true equilibrium. Yet while the economy may be in a state of full employment or suffer from either a deflationary or an inflationary gap for a certain period of time such a situation will not endure indefinitely. If, for example, the economy is suffering from a deflationary gap with high unemployment and a relatively low level of demand a time must eventually be reached when output expands in response to increased demand and the economy moves out of recession. This development must presumably be the result of some autonomous change in the level of either injections or withdrawals – or both – but why should such a change come about? In the modern mixed economy it is government action which springs to mind as the likely cause of this change but it is only comparatively recently that governments have taken an active role in the management of the national economy and yet in the past deflationary gaps have opened and closed without government action. There must therefore have been spontaneous changes in the level of investment and savings and in the pattern of overseas trade. The causes of such changes are a mixture of the rational and the irrational. On the rational side a deepening depression reduces the cost of borrowing and some firms may eventually decide that the increased potential profits justify the risk of undertaking a particular investment while other firms realise that they can delay replacing old equipment no longer. Furthermore a deflationary gap will have a depressing effect on prices and, provided that not all other countries are going through a similar depression, will tend to increase overseas sales of domestic goods while reducing the attractiveness of imported goods; as a result injections increase and withdrawals fall. Sooner or later there may also be a rise in the level of investment if those firms still experiencing relatively healthy demand decide to expand output.

In addition to these rational indicators of a revival in business activity there is the all-important question of business confidence. If businessmen think that the economy is about to pick up and increase the demand for their products, they will respond accordingly and renew capital equipment and so on and in so doing they will raise both the level of injections and output and the economy will expand – just as they expected it would. Thus if they know from past experience that after a depression has lasted for three years economic activity revives, businessmen will respond accordingly and the trade cycle will behave with predictable regularity. A similar phenomenon is observed at the opposite phase of the trade cycle when the economy is enjoying boom conditions and there is an inflationary gap. Higher prices will eventually price exports out of overseas markets and encourage imports while at the same time new investment will slow down, especially when firms expect the boom to end, based on past experience. On the evidence of the trade cycle, then, the national income is always in a state of expansion or contraction with full employment one of the phases through which it passes on its way from inflationary gap to deflationary gap and back again. In the diagram of the trade cycle (Fig. 16.4) the long-term trend is shown as upwards, in line with long-term economic growth, despite short-term contractions in national income.

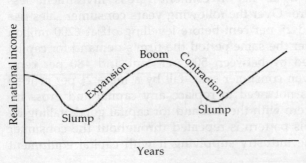

Fig. 16.4

While business confidence is obviously a factor helping to explain the trade cycle, once a cyclical trend is established it is likely to continue, even in the absence of changes in business attitudes, especially since there is evidence to suggest that in addition to the standard business cycle of three to five years there are longer cycles of around ten and twenty-five years duration and perhaps even longer cycles of seventy-five years. One explanation for this rhythmic pattern of national income change is the accelerator theory.

The accelerator

This theory relates changes in investment not only to changes in the level of national income but also to the rate of change of national income. Thus if income is increasing steadily investment will rise in anticipation of higher sales in the future and to provide the extra capacity required. But if national income levels off, net investment will drop and a recession set in. This recession will not be the result of a decline in consumer demand but will occur simply because sales of consumer goods have stopped growing. Three predictions follow from the theory of the accelerator. Firstly that capital goods industries are subject to greater fluctuations in demand than are consumer goods industries. Secondly that cyclical demand fluctuations for capital goods are inevitable and will lead to alternating periods of growth and decline. Thirdly that a stable buoyant economy is still liable to experience a downturn in activity unless consumption is capable of continuous expansion. The working of the accelerator is shown in Table 16.3 where a firm manufacturing consumer goods has initial sales of £100 million. Its capital stock is £200 million consisting of 20 machines of varying ages, one of which is replaced each year as it wears out; gross investment is thus £10 million while net investment (gross investment less depreciation) is zero. Over the following years consumer sales rise by between 11 and 25 per cent before levelling off at £200 million in year six. Yet over the same period the firm's demand for capital goods has changed by between 500 per cent and −80 per cent. Finally in year seven consumer sales fall by a mere 2½ per cent so that the firm does not need to replace any capital and gross investment falls to zero with the demand for capital goods falling by 100 per cent. If this pattern is repeated throughout the consumer goods industry the industry supplying it with capital equipment

Table 16.3

			Investment		% Change in	% Change gross
(£ million)						
Year	Consumer sales	Capital stock	gross	net	consumer sales	investment
1	100	200	10	0	—	—
2	120	240	50	40	20	500
3	150	300	70	60	25	40
4	180	360	70	60	20	0
5	200	400	50	40	11	−28
6	200	400	10	0	0	−80
7	195	390	0	−10	−2½	−100

would suffer a major recession. If now the pattern of consumer sales remains static for decades there will nevertheless be periods when several machines need to be replaced at once and others when none do, resulting in recurrent booms and slumps in the capital goods industry.

The fact that the trade cycle is associated with fluctuations in the demand for capital goods explains why there are several trade cycles of different lengths which overlap each other. Since different replacement periods will apply to different industries the booms and slumps associated with capital replacement in each will occur at different times. Thus the trade cycle associated with the construction industry or shipping will be longer than that identified with furniture or clothing. If there is indeed a long term cycle of seventy-five years or so it is less likely to relate to a specific industry than to a major technological change like the introduction of steam power in the nineteenth century or atomic energy or computerisation in the twentieth. As the various cycles overlap there will be times when they are in conflict so that when the economy is going through a deep, prolonged depression there will be minor upswings during this period as shorter cycles reach their peak. Obviously the greatest dangers lie where all cycles, whatever their length, are moving in the same direction simultaneously. The impact of the accelerator does not end with the surge in demand it produces in the capital goods industries since the extra income so created will then operate through the multiplier to affect the economy as a whole. The brief revival enjoyed by some shipyards during the construction of rigs for the North Sea oilfields in the 1970s led to a multiplied growth in income for the economies of local communities. The multiplier therefore acts to exaggerate the cyclical effects on national income induced by the accelerator.

While a neat and valuable theory, the accelerator is not able to provide a comprehensive theory of investment since it ignores a number of key factors. The most important of these is the time-lag in investment decisions as most manufacturers choose to wait to see if an increase in demand for their product is sustained before committing themselves to new investment. In the meantime they will use existing capacity more intensively with shift and overtime work. Thus investment increases only after income has already been rising for some time. The accelerator also ignores the entrepreneurial motivations behind investment decisions such as developing new production techniques to lower costs or attempting to anticipate increased demand. Finally it ignores the importance of profitability and the marginal efficiency of investment which leads to firms taking into account the cost of borrowing when considering new investment. In any case the confidence of firms about the future remains in practice the key issue in investment and this alone can be enough to generate cyclical investment even in the absence of the accelerator.

Revision test

1. Define and explain the terms 'injection' and 'withdrawal' as applied to the flow of national income.
2. Of what does aggregate expenditure consist?
3. In the UK flow of national income, the foreign tourism multiplier is valued at 3. What does this mean?
4. Why is the multiplier effect of the £10 Christmas bonus given to pensioners greater than that of a similar total sum being given out in the form of tax cuts?
5. A British company receives an export order valued at £2 million. Given that the completion of the order will entail the purchase of raw materials from abroad worth £0.8 million and that the MPS = 0.2, the MPT = 0.3 and the MPM = 0.2 what will be the total growth in national income resulting from the order?
6. In what sense is an inflationary gap unstable?
7. If there is a deflationary gap of £5 million and the taxation multiplier is 3 what fiscal measure should the government adopt to close the gap?
8. Give two reasons why the trade cycle can be considered self-perpetuating.
9. What is the accelerator and what are the main criticisms of it?
10. Under what circumstances could withdrawals from the circular flow of income be negative? Could injections be negative?

Chapter 17

INFLATION AND UNEMPLOYMENT

According to the fluctuations of the trade cycle the level of national income alternates between boom and slump. However, the underlying trends in national income dictate the precise nature of each phase of the cycle. Thus if the economy is in the slump phase of a long-run cycle the boom of the smaller business cycle will reduce unemployment and generate some growth but not necessarily lead to a situation in which full employment is attained, let alone an inflationary gap appear. Where, on the other hand, there are long-term inflationary pressures at work even the slump of the business cycle may not be sufficient to eradicate the inflationary gap completely. None the less if all inflation and unemployment were the direct result of the fluctuations of the trade cycle, it would be possible to see the role of government as attempting to maintain a national income equilibrium level between the two extremes of inflation and deflation where there is full employment and yet prices remain relatively stable. Unfortunately neither all employment nor all inflationary pressures are attributable to the trade cycle so that both the problems themselves and the policies to deal with them are inevitably quite complex.

The causes of unemployment

The unemployment examined so far is the direct result of the trade cycle and is thus caused by a deflationary gap. While this **cyclical unemployment** is extremely serious and, during a major slump, can lead to millions of workers losing their jobs it is not the only form of unemployment which can lead to massive job losses. Before looking at these serious forms of unemployment mention must be made of **frictional unemployment**. This covers those workers who, voluntarily or involuntarily, leave employment for a short period but then, perhaps after a period of retraining, are quickly reabsorbed into the workforce. This process is inevitable in periods of economic and industrial change when some industries are contracting while others are growing. The greater the mobility of labour and the more buoyant the economy the faster will people made unemployed in this way rejoin the ranks of the employed. Other workers laid off temporarily due to strikes or other disruptions in the industry also count as frictionally unemployed and when all these various groups are taken together they account for about 1 per cent of the workforce being unemployed at any one time.

Structural unemployment

This results from a fundamental change in demand causing an industry to contract permanently and possibly quite rapidly so that jobs in the industry decline at a faster rate than workers are leaving the available workforce. Thus unemployed workers still seek employment in the industry despite the disappearance of employment opportunities. In the UK the post-war period has witnessed the decline of several key industries concentrated together in certain areas and structural unemployment is thus closely identified with regional unemployment. Since the 1970s the structural problem has taken on a deeper seriousness with the rapid decline of many of Britain's manufacturing industries and 100,000 jobs a year being lost from the manufacturing sector during the late 1970s and early 1980s. This rapid and seemingly irreversible de-industrialisation of the British economy poses a grave threat to the restoration of full employment even if demand overall were to expand strongly through the 1980s. The lack of competitiveness of many British manufacturing industries has meant that problems which began as cyclical through a downturn in world trade have become structural as demand for British goods has not responded in the following upturn.

Technological unemployment

It is not always the case that the contraction of employment opportunities in an industry is the result of decline in the industry itself. Technological unemployment is the result of labour being replaced by capital in the production process so that output levels are maintained or expanded despite the reduction in required manpower. Firms are prompted to replace labour by capital both to reduce costs and to enable output to be increased – though clearly the two motives are interrelated. Because there are costs incurred both in the development and introduction of new technological processes the incentive to replace labour by capital will be the greater the higher the proportion of total costs represented by labour; either because wage rates in the industry are high or because production is labour-intensive. Technological unemployment is associated with long-term economic growth as it results, indirectly, from innovation and because it releases resources which can be utilised to expand output in other sectors of the economy. Provided that workers who lose their jobs through technological unemployment quickly rejoin the workforce their position is similar to that of the frictionally unemployed. However, if technological change occurs so rapidly that too many workers are displaced for them to be reabsorbed into the workforce within a reasonable time, their position more closely resembles that of the structurally unemployed. Furthermore attempts by firms to become more competitive can lead technological unemployment to occur during times of economic depression and then there is little prospect of new work opportunities arising, at least in the short term. In the last quarter of the twentieth century technological unemployment has taken on a more profound significance both because of the scale it has attained and due to the economic climate within which it has occurred. In the past technological change led to some occupations disappearing but new skills were created and new industries developed with their own demand for workers. At the same time sustained economic growth and the progress in working conditions enabled any tendencies towards an excess supply of labour to be offset by reductions in the available pool of labour through, for example, free education for the young and pensions for the old. In the 1970s, however, the pattern of technological change, involving micro-technology and robotics, has altered the scale to which labour can be replaced by machine and has begun to reduce employment opportunities in the service sector – which had been expected to accommodate the workers displaced by technological change in the primary and manufacturing sectors. At the same time the prolonged recession in the economy has acted against any serious attempts by society to adopt measures to reallocate the work available.

Seasonal unemployment

Government unemployment figures are always adjusted to take

account of seasonal fluctuations in employment and although the factors contributing to such fluctuations have declined in recent years their influence it still felt. Thus the construction and other industries affected by weather conditions traditionally provide greater employment opportunities in the spring and summer months while some sectors of agriculture are still in greatest need of workers in late summer and early autumn. However, in most of these industries technological change has reduced the demand for labour and thus the impact of seasonal factors while new all-weather materials have been introduced into some parts of the construction industry. Nevertheless seasonal demand presents a serious problem for workers in the various entertainment industries while school-leavers are affected by the fact that most are searching for work when firms are not recruiting so much, i.e. in the summer months.

Inflation

If the causes of unemployment are varied they are at least universally accepted as such. Inflation, on the other hand, has for many years been the source of much acrimonious debate as to precisely what are the root causes of a general and persistent rise in prices. The key causes of inflation must arise either from the demand side or the supply side of the market.

Demand-pull inflation

This is associated with an inflationary gap since it is generated by excess demand so that high demand leads to higher prices and sets off a cycle of rising factor rewards and prices with only marginal increases in output, if any at all. Demand-pull inflation thus has tended to be regarded as quite healthy in the past (provided it did not go beyond a modest rate of increase) since it was associated with a situation of full or near-full employment. The phenomenon of demand-pull inflation is generally accepted among economists but disputes have arisen over the cause of this excess demand and thus the appropriate measures to be adopted in dealing with it. Principally these disputes stem from the precise role played by the money supply in the inflationary spiral.

The Keynesian theory of money regards money as an asset which people may wish to hold instead of other assets and which can be analysed in terms of supply and demand. Thus the supply

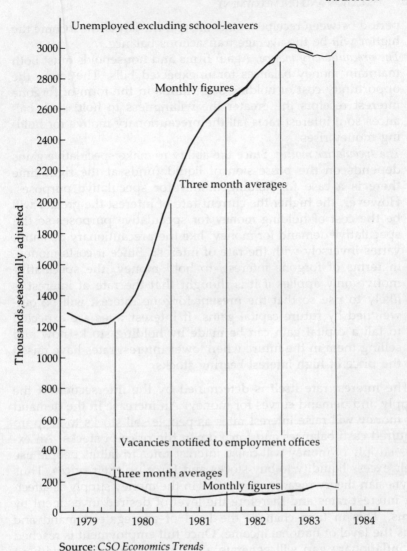

Source: *CSO Economics Trends*

Fig. 17.1 Unemployment and vacancies

of money is determined by the banking system and the demand for money represents the desire to hold money instead of other assets, i.e. liquidity preference. The demand for money is classfied under three headings:

(a) *The transactions motive*. Money balances are held by both firms and households to meet bills as they arise. The longer the period between receipts of income and the larger the income the higher will be the average transactions balance.

(b) *The precautionary motive.* Again firms and households must both maintain money balances for unexpected bills. The lower the opportunity cost of holding such funds in the form of forgone interest receipts the greater the willingness to hold such balances so if interest rates fall the precautionary motive for holding money rises.

(c) *The speculative motive.* Since the ability to make speculative gains depends on the possession of liquid funds at the right time there is a case for holding money for speculative purposes. However, the higher the current rate of interest the greater will be the cost of holding money for speculative purposes so the speculative demand for money, like the precautionary demand, varies inversely with the rate of interest. Since it costs money, in terms of forgone interest, to hold money, the speculative motive only applies if it is thought that the rate of interest is likely to rise so that the present forgone interest will be outweighed by future capital gains. If interest rates are expected to fall a capital gain can be made by holding stocks now and selling them in the future when lower interest rates have raised the price of high-interest-bearing stocks.

The interest rate itself is determined by the intersection of the supply and demand curves for money. An increase in the demand for money will raise interest rates as people sell stocks to keep up required cash balances and force down the price of stocks. An excess supply of money will cause interest rates to fall as people use their excess liquidity to buy stocks and force up their prices. Thus Keynesian theory regards an increase in the money supply as affecting interest rates and therefore the level of desired investment by firms. This in turn changes the level of aggregate demand and thus the level of national income. Once full employment is reached an inflationary gap will generate a spiral of rising prices without the need for any further change in the money supply. The money supply is thus not the cause of inflation but is seen as essentially neutral in the inflationary process.

The quantity theory of money explains changes in the general level of prices by reference to changes in the stock of money. The theory originated at least as long ago as the eighteenth century and was based then on observation of the effects of large increases in the money supply as occurred in the sixteenth century throughout Europe and the rapid rise in prices which followed. The theory resulted in the 'Quantity Equation of Exchange'

$$MV = PT$$

where M is the quantity of money, V the velocity of circulation of money (how frequently each unit of money exchanges hands in a time period), P the level of average prices and T the number of transactions in the economy in the period in question. The two sides of the equation are by definition equal because they are two aspects of the same process. The left-hand side of the equation comprises total spending by consumers, i.e. the quantity of money multiplied by the number of times each unit is used in a given period. The right-hand side represents spending on output, which consists of the number of transactions taking place times the price at which they take place over the same period. The quantity theory of money's proponents argued that the velocity of circulation is constant since it is derived from the custom and institutions of society. The level of transactions in the economy is also seen as fairly constant due to the natural state of the economy being one in which there is full employment. The two variables are thus the money supply and the price level, changes in the former resulting in an equivalent response in the latter. If the money supply is increased it will lead to a rise in the price level once any excess capacity has been taken up in the short term.

This crude quantity theory of money enunciated by the classical economists was discredited in the twentieth century, especially after the depressions of the inter-war years illustrated that the equilibrium level of national income could be well below the full employment level so that changes in the money supply were likely to have their effect on national income as much as on the price level. Instead the Keynesian view that the money supply responded to, rather than determined, the level of demand held sway until the revival of interest in the quantity theory in the 1950s. In 1956 Milton Friedman of the Chicago School restated the quantity theory in claiming that there was a close relationship between changes in the United States money supply and changes in the money national income over a long period of time. Subsequent research led Friedman to claim that changes in the nominal money supply were actually the cause of changes in money national income. Since the 1960s three strands of modern monetarism have developed based on the arguments of the modern quantity theory. All three groups agree that prices are flexible and that the market acts to allocate resources in accordance with relative prices. In the long run the price level is determined by the quantity of money while output and unemployment both settle at their 'natural' level. Where they differ is in their views on the degree of flexibility of prices, the process by which changes in money lead to changes in output and prices and the part played by expectations. Firstly there is the New Classical school which believes in totally flexible prices and the efficiency of market forces. Thus changes in the quantity of money lead to rapid adjustments by output and prices while expectations are formed rationally and also react quickly to the economic situation. Secondly the Gradualist school sees prices as being much less flexible so that there is a time lag between the change in the money supply and the consequent change in the price level which may lead in the interim to disruption of national income and output. They also regard expectations as being formed not by rational analysis on the part of groups or individuals but in response to experience. Thus expectations that prices will fall can only arise after prices have already started to fall. Finally there is the Pragmatist school which believes that, as wages are very resistant to downward pressure, control of the money supply is likely to have disruptive effects on the economy itself so that the price of bringing down inflation is likely to be a recession which will ultimately alter expectations and bring down the rate of wage inflation.

Despite the resurgence of monetarist theories in recent years such theories have not achieved universal acceptance and both the neo-Keynesians and the anti-monetarists reject the emphasis on money supply growth as the prime cause of inflation and thus the need to control the money supply as the main anti-inflationary weapon.

Cost-push inflation

For all the various schools of monetarist thought demand-pull inflation is the only cause of inflation. The neo-Keynesians, on the other hand, tend to point to inflation being not only the result of excess demand but also the consequence of rises in costs which occur outside the national flow of income itself. The initial rise in costs leads to the price of many goods and services rising and there follows a fall in living standards which prompts workers to campaign for higher incomes which themselves constitute rises in costs for the industries in which they work, so that another round of price and wage rises is generated. Two examples of events which could be blamed for starting off cost-push inflationary spirals are the devaluation of sterling in 1967 which led to the prices of all imported raw materials rising and the oil price rise of 1973 which led to rises in costs for all industries, either directly or indirectly.

The natures of demand-pull and cost-push inflation are com-

(a)

(b)

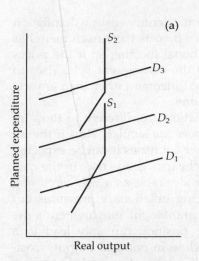

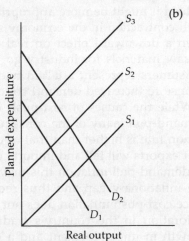

Fig. 17.2(a) & (b)

pared in Fig. 17.2. In Fig. 17.2(a) excess demand is shown by the increase in aggregate demand from D_1 to D_2. With full employment the aggregate supply of goods and services is unable to respond to the increased demand but the resultant higher prices lead to the rewards paid to factors of production being increased so that supply shifts from S_1 to S_2. However, the increased factor earnings give another upward push to aggregate demand from D_2 to D_3 and so the process continues with rises in *money* aggregate demand and supply but no change in real national income. In Fig. 17.2(b) the initial change is that of aggregate supply from S_1 to S_2 due to rises in the costs of production. In theory total demand in the economy should fall due to the higher prices and consequent fall in living standards but in practice workers and other groups receiving factor rewards push these up to compensate for the fall in living standards so that demand rises from D_1 to D_2. These increased factor rewards represent a rise in costs to producers so that supply shifts upwards again to S_3 so once again there are rises in money aggregate demand and supply but no change in real national income.

It can be seen that whether initiated by demand-pull or cost-push pressures an inflationary spiral, once in operation, follows a similar path with factor earnings rising in response to rising prices. The important distinction between demand-pull and cost-push inflation is that while the former is synonymous with an inflationary gap and is thus associated with full employment and a buoyant economy, the latter can occur whatever the state of the economy since it is a response to a rise in costs rather than to a rise in demand.

Indeed it might be more appropriate to identify cost-push inflation with contraction in the economy since if costs have risen there has been a downward effect on real national income; so if the prices of raw materials for industry go up the consequent price rises to consumers represent a fall in national income rather than any response to increased demand conditions.

While the causes of cost-push inflation are different to those of demand-pull many of the consequences are similar. Thus if the inflation rate is higher than that of other countries it can be expected that exports will fall and imports of cheaper goods rise. In the case of demand-pull inflation this may be desirable as a way of closing the inflationary gap and thus reducing inflationary pressures but since cost-push inflation does not guarantee full employment a deterioration in the country's trading position can only lead to a growth in unemployment and a decline in national output. Cost-push inflation is also likely to be self-perpetuating and the experience of Britain in the 1960s and 1970s points to cost-push inflation eventually becoming built in to the psychology of society so that both pay and price rises tend to incorporate some expectations of further inflation which itself generates an upward movement in the rate of price increases.

The need to control inflation

In recent years inflation has achieved as much notoriety as unemployment, after the period between the 1940s and 1960s when a mild inflation rate was considered healthy due to the likelihood that it would be accompanied by full employment and a healthy economy. This view was based on the belief that inflation is preferable to unemployment and is still supported in countries like Israel and Iceland which have coped for many years with very high inflation rates. None the less it is recognised that there are distortional effects in the economy as a result of high inflation rates and these may become so very serious that the economy as a whole suffers.

1. *Distribution of income.* It is impossible that all sections of the economy will be equally affected by inflation. Those who are on fixed incomes, for example, will suffer a fall in living standards at the same rate as the annual inflation rate. Those who are debtors tend to find that the debt diminishes in real terms unless they are charged interest rates well in excess of the rate of inflation. Creditors, on the other hand, see their savings or deferred payments

due to them lose value. There is also a redistribution of income from those in weak bargaining positions with regard to rises in income to those groups who negotiate from strength. Finally cost-push inflation in particular is certain to affect different groups unevenly, for example a rise in oil prices will affect most those who spend a considerable proportion of their income on energy, such as the elderly.

2. *The effect on business activity.* An inflationary gap is associated with boom conditions in the economy so that firms enjoy high profits and are encouraged to expand both output and investment. However if the inflation rate gets much above 5 per cent future plans become increasingly more difficult to determine and less attractive to implement due to the uncertainty associated with future costing, pricing and profitability. Where the economy is suffering from cost-push inflation there may well be no boom conditions at all so that inflation merely adds to uncertainty and costs and thus inhibits confidence.

3. *The external position.* If the domestic rate of inflation is higher than that of overseas competitors exports will tend to fall and imports rise thus endangering the balance of payments position and leading, via a balance of payments deficit, to a contraction in national income. The effect is that while demand-pull pressures are reduced cost-push ones are increased and if the exchange rate falls in response to exports being over-priced this will add further to cost-push inflation.

4. *Built-in inflation.* Once inflation has become established expectation of further inflation leads to price and wage increases outstripping current rates of inflation so that future rates rise even faster. Furthermore the faster that prices rise the less price-conscious are consumers and buyers in general so enabling 'price push' inflation whereby firms increase profits by adding to the price rises caused by inflation a further margin for their own benefit. Clearly,too, there is the danger that under extreme circumstances inflation rates could get out of control as happened in Germany after the First World War and Hungary and China after the Second.

Revision test

1. In Britain structural unemployment is usually associated with regional unemployment. Why is this and why is this relationship tending to weaken?
2. Consider the view that technological unemployment is always treated as a disaster when it should be viewed as an opportunity for economic and social development.
3. Explain the three motives for holding money according to Keynes.
4. What is the basic difference between Keynesians and Monetarists as to the causes of demand-pull inflation?
5. Not all monetarists are politically right-wing yet monetarism tends to be associated with right-wing policies and was even before the election of a Conservative government supporting monetarist views. Why is this so?
6. How is it that demand-pull inflation helps cure unemployment while cost-push can actually cause it?
7. Which groups benefit most from demand-pull inflation? Do exactly the same groups benefit from cost-push?
8. Explain the statement 'Demand-pull inflation arises from totally inelastic supply while cost-push is due to totally inelastic demand.' To what extent is it true?

Chapter 18

GOVERNMENT AND THE NATIONAL ECONOMY

Governments have always been associated to some extent with the success or otherwise of the economy. Thus even in mediaeval times successful governments were those who could provide 'peace and prosperity' since taxes were raised principally to wage wars and the absence of war meant both lower taxes and less disruption of the economy. Later on, and especially after the Industrial Revolution, the role of the government in the economy was extended to providing an environment in which trade and industry would flourish – though without intervening itself to regulate the economy. In the twentieth century the role has been broadened again to include direct intervention to promote the well-being of the economy, a role made easier by the increased direct involvement of the government and its agencies in industry, trade and the provision of social services.

The aims of government economic policy

In modern times the economic aims of all governments have had similar patterns. Yet while there has been close accord on the objectives the means by which these might be achieved and the importance to be ascribed to each have been the subject of endless debate, on economic as well as on political grounds. The main objectives generally agreed upon are as follows:

1. *Full employment.* As there is the ever-present occurrence of frictional unemployment it is impossible to achieve literally full employment. In 1944 the government set a target of 3 per cent unemployment as constituting an approximation to full employment and in fact this proved a realistic target for the period up to the early 1970s. Indeed for most of the 1940s and 1950s the unemploy-

ment rate was 2 per cent or less. Full employment was viewed as taking high priority for several reasons. Firstly on economic grounds unemployment represents not only unused human resources but, except in the case of technological unemployment, unused capital and other resources too so that the economy is operating at a level well within its full potential. Secondly unemployment widens income and wealth differentials and requires redistribution of income from the employed to the unemployed via taxation and social security transfers. None the less since unemployment is not evenly distributed there will be serious economic decline in the areas it affects most. Thirdly unemployment is socially divisive and can lead to political unrest which has serious repercussions for the successful conduct of the economy.

2. *Stable prices.* The discussion of inflation in the last chapter indicates that inflation must be controlled to some extent in order to avoid those severe distortional effects in the economy which may well inhibit the attainment of other economic objectives. Where falling prices can be achieved through greater efficiency they are clearly desirable and such a situation occurred in the nineteenth century. This century falling prices have been associated with a severe recession so a low rate of inflation is a reasonable price to pay for the achievement of full employment and growth in the economy.

3. *Economic growth.* This objective is important not only because it represents an increase in the long-term potential of the economy but also because if offers the prospect of rising living standards to the whole population without the necessity of transferring income from one group to another. Indeed during periods of sustained economic growth the government is more likely to enjoy full national support, and thus greater hope of success, in its attempts to achieve all its objectives.

4. *Balance of payments equilibrium.* A balance of payments deficit represents an excess of imports and other foreign payments over exports and other foreign earnings and thus an excess of withdrawals over injections so that national income contracts. A surplus conversely could be expected to lead to expansion of national income through injections exceeding withdrawals. While a surplus is thus more desirable than a deficit a permanent surplus can result in a shortage of goods for the home market and initiate demand-

pull pressures in the economy. Ideally the economy should alternate between small surpluses and deficits.

5. *An Equitable distribution of income.*   Governments must attempt to achieve a distribution of income which will foster the success of its other objectives. This does not mean that income is distributed equally throughout the economy but that it is distributed so as to promote initiative and enterprise and yet also eradicate the worst excesses of the free enterprise system through the taxation of high economic rent payments and the provision of subsidies to the poorest sections of the community. An equitable distribution of income is not only more likely to command general support for the taxation system; it is also more likely to stimulate economic growth than a distribution of income leaving wealth concentrated in the hands of the few since this latter case is less likely to promote the development of new industries and stimulate the growth of mass markets on which industrial development depends.

BALANCING THE OBJECTIVES

The attainment of these objectives involves inevitably some choice between them in terms of the priority to be accorded to each. In theory there need be no conflict since the government could moderate the trade cycle to produce a situation of full employment but without an inflationary gap. From this basis the government could then go on to promote economic growth and rising living standards, both of which flow from a strong buoyant economy and also would be able to redistribute income without the need to reduce the living standards of any one section of the population. Finally a healthy growing economy is more likely to provide an environment conducive to the expansion of trade and the resolution of balance of payments difficulties. In practice this ideal is obstructed by the various frictional pressures on the workings of the economy. Thus the existence of frictional unemployment makes it impossible for all unemployment to be eradicated before inflation sets in while the fact that inflationary pressures are not evenly spread throughout the economy means that unemployment will rise in some sectors while inflationary pressures still persist in others. This trade-off between inflation and unemployment was noted by A. W. Phillips and a typical Phillips Curve applicable in the 1950s is shown in Fig. 18.1.

In the 1950s the trade-off between inflation and unemployment was small with an unemployment rate of 2 per cent being sufficient

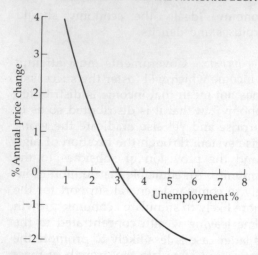

Fig. 18.1

to eliminate inflation. However the government's problem in seeking to balance its objectives is not simply one of riding a see-saw of demand-pull inflation and cyclical unemployment. As the last chapter showed there are forms of unemployment and inflation which do not owe their origin to the trade cycle while the relationship between cost-push inflation and unemployment is unpredictable. Furthermore the need to protect the balance of payments position may prevent the adoption of policies to cure unemployment for fear of causing a rise in demand for imports. Again the promotion of long-term economic growth may necessitate the acceptance of a short-term fall in living standards, and perhaps a temporary rise in unemployment. Yet despite these complications the management of demand in the economy is central to the attainment of the government's objectives since the level of aggregate demand has important repercussions for each of these objectives.

Demand management

This term applies to the manipulation of aggregate demand, and thus aggregate expenditure, in the economy to further the achievement of the government's objectives. Most clearly this management would relate to the closing of inflationary and deflationary gaps in the economy though it would indirectly affect too the long-term growth rate, the level of living standards and the state of the balance of payments. Aggregate expenditure, it will be remembered from Chapter 16, consists of consumption plus injections (investment, government expenditure and exports) and in the absence of natural economic forces acting to solve the problem of either excess or insufficient aggregate demand the government may intervene to reduce excess demand and close an inflationary gap or increase demand and close a deflationary gap.

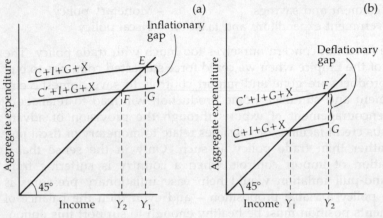

Fig. 18.2(a) & (b)

In Fig. 18.2(a) the economy suffers from an inflationary gap ($E - G$) with the equilibrium level of national income at the unattainable level of Y_1 but a decrease in aggregate expenditure from $C+I+G+X$ to $C'+I+G+X$ leads to national income being brought into equilibrium at the full-employment level of Y_2. In Fig. 18.2 (b) there is a deflationary gap ($F - G$) with the equilibrium level of national income at Y_1 well below that necessary to sustain full employment. If now there is a sufficient rise in the level of aggregate expenditure there will be a multiplied rise in national income until the full employment level of national income is attained (Y_2).

Government action to deal with either inflationary or deflationary gaps is necessary because of the fact that there is no guarantee that natural economic forces will eventually act to correct the problem. Even if eventually the economy will tend to move out of a depression or from a period of high inflation government intervention would be justified to speed up the process of correction or to attempt to prevent its occurrence. Government action may take several forms, depending on which aspects of aggregate demand it seeks to influence. Thus the government may act on one of the three injections, investment, government expenditure or exports or it may seek to change the level of consumption. Since the level of consumption is that level of income which is not withdrawn from the circular flow, changes in consumption are the result of changes in the three withdrawals, savings, taxation and imports. It is now possible to classify government policy according to which injections and withdrawals it is seeking to manipulate, i.e.

Exports and imports   – Trade policy
Investment and savings   – Monetary policy
Government expenditure and taxation – Fiscal policy

We need not concern ourselves too much with trade policy. The days of the Empire when we could force subjected countries to buy our products are gone and import controls to save domestic employment and stimulate home production will lead to retaliation. The encouragement of exports through the provision of advantageous credit facilities or subsidies relate to monetary or fiscal policy rather than trade policy as such. Only in the sense that a relaxation of import controls when a country is suffering from demand-pull inflation would help ease inflationary pressures is trade policy a viable proposition – and even then the balance of payments position must be healthy enough to support this option.

Monetary policy

Like trade policy the emphasis in monetary policy lies not so much in direct changes in the level of government intervention in the economy as in alterations in the environment within which expenditure decisions are made. Monetary policy aims to regulate the level of aggregate expenditure through manipulation of the money supply and thus of the availability of credit to finance that expenditure. Before considering the money supply and its control it is important to remember that the money supply expands through increases in borrowing rather than lending and that it is investment which determines the level of savings rather than the other way round. Thus the techniques of monetary policy are concerned with regulating the process of credit creation and are effected mainly through the working of the banking system.

There is considerable confusion surrounding the term 'Money Supply' due to difficulties of definition. This problem of definition arises once an attempt is made to go beyond the narrowest possible definition of the money supply being notes and coins in circulation, in the tills of banks or held as working balances at the Bank of England (M0). The various wider definitions of money attempt to take into account those balances held by the banks or other financial intermediaries.

M1 = M0 + bank sight deposits (current accounts)

M2 = M1 + bank seven-day deposit accounts

Sterling M3 = M2 + all other sterling interest-bearing deposits held by the banking system excluding public sector deposits

M3 = Sterling M3 + the foreign currency deposits of UK residents

The main definitions currently used by the government in its monitoring of the growth of money supply are M1, Sterling M3 and PSL2 (Private Sector Liquidity 2) which is the broadest definition of all and takes into account Building Society deposits and National Savings Bank deposits. This proliferation of measurements of the money supply arises from the artificial distinctions drawn between current accounts and deposit accounts – the latter for many people being used as interest-bearing transactions accounts – a situation further confused by the clearing banks establishing interest-bearing cheque accounts.

In exercising its control over the money supply the government operates through the Bank of England which occupies a pivotal position in the banking system being banker both to the government and the deposit banks.

OPEN MARKET OPERATIONS

This is the long-established and principal method whereby the Bank of England can intervene in the market for funds to expand or contract the supply. If the Bank sells some of its holding of government securities on the open market to members of the public these purchases will be settled by withdrawals from the buyers' bank accounts and result in a cash drain from the deposit banks. Since the deposit banks endeavour to keep a certain level of liquidity relative to their liabilities this reduction in their cash holdings will lead to a multiplied contraction of bank loans and deposits. This process is shown in Table 18.1.

An open market sale of £1 million reduces deposit bank reserves by £1 million and induces a £10 million drop in total demand deposits on the basis of the banks maintaining a 10 per cent liquidity ratio, as the deposit banks cut lending by £9 million to restore their required level of liquidity. Conversely to expand credit the Bank can buy securities on the open market and thereby cause a multiple expansion of bank credit. Open market operations can thus be used to cut the supply of credit and make borrowing less attractive so

Table 18.1

	Bank of England		
Assets		Liabilities	
Government Securities	−£1 million	Deposit banks' deposits	−£1 million

	Deposit Banks		
Assets		Liabilities	
Reserves	−£1 million		
Loans and Investments	−£9 million	Demand deposits	−£10 million
	−£10 million		−£10 million

forcing down aggregate expenditure or to make credit easier to obtain and thus encourage an upward shift in aggregate expenditure. Open market operations also affect interest rates in two ways. If the government sells securities to engineer a contraction of credit, banks will have less to lend and will push up rates charged to borrowers to reduce the excess demand for loans. At the same time the increase in the supply of securities resulting from the government's sale will lead to their price falling and effectively raise the true interest rate paid, the yield. If, for example, a £100 stock with an interest annually of 10 per cent falls in price to £90 the yield is now 11 per cent (a return of £10 on £90) as the price of the stock does not change the value of the interest coupon due. The reverse will occur if the price of stocks rises.

INTEREST RATES

The monetary authorities exercise monopoly control over the money supply. However, like any other monopolist, they must choose either to control output (the supply of credit) or price (the interest rate) since they cannot simultaneously determine both. In the section above it was noted that action to limit the supply of credit will lead to a rise in interest rates and let money supply respond naturally to the change.

Action to influence the level of interest rates takes place mainly in the market for short-term funds since changes in short-term rates will cause long-term rates to change and affect the cost of new investment funds. Central to the Bank of England's activities in the money markets is the role of the discount houses. These institutions operate on very tight margins and must balance their books daily so that a shortage of funds will force them to exercise the 'lender of last resort' facility they enjoy from the Bank of England.

The funds raised in this way are expensive and erode their profits so that they will wish both to raise the interest rates they themselves charge and contract their lending so that they can release their debt with the Bank of England. Until 1981 the Bank published the rate it charged for this facility – 'minimum lending rate' – and did lend directly to the discount houses. Since then the facility has been exercised mainly through the rediscounting of bills of exchange at a rate undisclosed in advance. Despite these changes the tendency is still for money market, and therefore other, rates to follow changes initiated by the Bank. The monetary authorities can also influence long-term rates directly by offering higher interest coupons on new issues of stock and thus making lower-interest-bearing stocks less attractive.

While higher interest rates should lead to a reduced demand for credit and thus to a multiplied contraction in the money supply the situation is complicated by the interaction with funds from external sources. Higher interest rates will attract foreign funds both into the banking system and into the euro-currency markets and these will tend to generate money supply growth, particularly where demand for funds is inelastic.

LIQUIDITY REQUIREMENTS

In theory the absence of any requirement to keep back part of each new deposit as reserves would allow the credit creation multiplier to produce an infinite increase in new deposits from one extra pound placed on deposit. In practice the prudence of the banks in wishing to keep some assets in liquid form and in avoiding loans entailing an unreasonable risk means that there are leakages from the circular flow of credit. None the less the monetary authorities could impose the additional constraint of a liquidity requirement and until 1971 the clearing banks undertook to keep 8 per cent of their assets in cash and over a quarter of their assets in liquid or semi-liquid form. The system which operated between 1971 and 1981 exposed the problems inherent in a system of liquidity requirements based on assets other than cash. The 12½ per cent reserve asset ratio maintained by the banks included items such as money at call with the discount houses and Treasury bills – items which could eventually find their way back into the banking systems. The ineffectiveness of the system was further illustrated by the tendency for the banks to maintain liquidity ratios higher than those required so that any attempt to impose a stricter ratio had little impact. Since 1981 the banks have been expected merely to deposit ½ per cent of all new deposits with the Bank of England though obviously they continue to have a higher reserve ratio than this as they continue to keep around 5 per cent of assets with the money market, around 6 per cent in cash in their tills and they still operate working balances at the Bank of England to settle their Clearing House debts and so on.

SPECIAL DEPOSITS

One way of reducing surplus liquidity is to make use of special deposits. These were introduced in 1960 and require the banks depositing a specified proportion of their total deposits with the Bank of England, on which they receive the prevailing Treasury Bill rate of interest. Such deposits are financed by the liquidation of semi-liquid assets and the effect is thus to make the banks lower on liquid funds than they would wish. In taking measures to rectify this position they will bid more actively for deposits, thereby pushing up interest rates while cutting back advances. Under the new arrangements for monetary control announced in 1981 special deposits occupy a key position in the control of credit creation.

QUANTITATIVE AND QUALITATIVE CONTROLS

Instead of reducing the banks' liquidity the authorities may limit the level of total bank advances. Periodically through the 1950s and 1960s the Bank of England gave instructions to restrict the level of total advances to the private sector. These quantitative controls were often accompanied by qualitative directions which instructed the banks to give priority to certain classes of borrower during the period of restriction, notably industrial firms with export potential. Quantitative controls were 'abolished' under Competition and Credit Control in 1971 but reappeared in 1974 with the 'corset'. The corset placed a limit on the growth of interest-bearing eligible liabilities (IBELs) in that if IBELs grew by more than a given 1 per cent per month the banks would in effect be fined as they would have to place a proportion of the excess on interest-free deposit with the Bank of England, this proportion rising with the size of the excess. Though lifted for a short time in 1975 the corset was soon restored and was finally abolished in 1980, by which time it had become clear that the banks had found various ways of avoiding the constraints imposed by the corset. Qualitative controls remain in force with priority being given to export finances – though in practice the banks are more willing to lend to personal customers on salaried incomes than small firms seeking help to expand their markets overseas.

DIRECT CONTROLS

Monetary policy can be used directly on the individual through hire-purchase and other personal credit controls. In the 1960s such controls were frequently in use with changes being made in the initial deposit required and the permitted repayment periods. However, their effectiveness has been reduced in recent years with the growth of other forms of consumer credit less subject to control, such as credit cards and the new range of loans provided by the clearing banks and finance companies. In 1982 even the long-standing controls on car purchase were sufficiently relaxed as to be of no great significance.

THE EFFECTIVENESS OF MONETARY POLICY

Monetary policy originated to enable the government to deal with problems arising out of the gold standard. Thus monetary measures were aimed either at supporting the exchange rate or at ensuring that the domestic money supply moved in line with the requirements of the current balance of payments. After Britain left the gold standard in 1931 the government was free to use monetary policy in line with the requirements of the domestic position and during the Great Depression a cheap money policy was adopted in an attempt to stimulate economic activity. The lack of success can be attributed to the fact that low interest rates and easy credit appear to make little impact if business confidence is low and firms are unwilling to invest. Furthermore with prices falling and the value of money rising the real interest rates are actually higher than the nominal figures quoted.

In the post-war period the adoption of Keynesian demand management theories by successive governments led to monetary policy being largely ignored and bank rate remained unchanged at 2 per cent from 1932 until 1951. In 1958 the Radcliffe Committee argued that monetary policy was largely ineffective although interest rates were accorded some influence over the investment decision if they change frequently. Throughout the 1950s and 1960s monetary policy was essentially seen as an adjunct to fiscal policy. It consisted primarily of hire-purchase controls and quantitative controls with little emphasis on controlling the money supply. Interest rate changes were employed to deal with the external position of sterling rather than demand in the economy. In any case the consensus view at this time was that just as cheap money policies were ineffectual in dealing with a slump, dear money policies were inadequate to stop inflation since they could neither deter spending nor encourage saving while if the economy were doing well firms would be willing to invest even if the cost of borrowing were high.

In the 1970s renewed interest in monetary policy followed the apparent failure of fiscal and other measures to deal with inflation. In addition monetarist economists like Milton Friedman accused governments of being the biggest contributors to inflation through excessive public expenditure financed by the printing of money and accompanied by a cheap money policy in order to keep its own borrowing costs down. The Labour government of 1974–79 was forced into a more monetarist position, particularly after it had to seek assistance from the International Monetary Fund, while the Conservative government elected in 1979 adopted an openly monetarist stance. Thus instead of monetary policy being an adjunct to fiscal policy it became once again the key government policy in the management of the economy. However, the same question marks have once again, as in the past, hung over the effectiveness of monetary policy. Firstly, monetary measures are unwieldy instruments difficult to apply specifically so that higher interest rates affect depressed areas as well as overheated sectors of the economy. Secondly, monetary measures have historically had little effect in promoting economic activity though they certainly can dampen business activity if only because of the disruptive effects on cash flow and business confidence. Thirdly, there is an inevitable time-lag between the implementation and the result of policies and if the government's nerve fails during the disruptive time-lag period it will undo all the work done on controlling the money supply – the Reagan administration in the United States reversed many of its monetarist measures during the latter

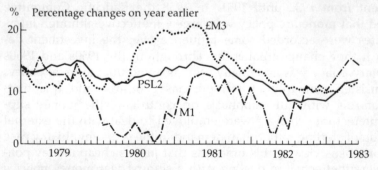

Source: *Economic Progress Report*

Fig. 18.3   Monetary growth

part of its first term. However monetarist policies must not be confused with monetary policies. The biggest criticism of monetarism is that it confines itself almost exclusively to monetary policy to achieve its ends rather than regarding monetary policy as having a positive role to play as part of the overall economic strategy.

Fiscal policy

The traditional view of fiscal policy, and one which survived until the late 1930s, is that it is concerned with the most effective ways of raising the revenue necessary to finance government expenditure. As a result the government would seek always to balance its budget so that during a depression, with unemployment rising and tax revenues falling, the government would endeavour to cut its expenditure to match its contracting income. From the analysis of a deflationary gap it can be predicted that such a move will make the depression deeper. Keynes argued instead that the government should increase its expenditure in an attempt to stimulate the economy for there is no guarantee that on its own the economy will break out of its deflationary gap equilibrium. This *discretionary* fiscal policy involves the active manipulation of government expenditure and taxation to counter the prevailing tendencies of the economy, whether inflationary or deflationary.

Even in the absence of government intervention the fiscal system tends to compensate naturally, in part at least, for the fluctuations of the trade cycle. Thus in a recession rising unemployment and falling consumer demand will lead automatically to a fall in the level of tax receipts and government expenditure will rise as increased payments are made in unemployment and social security payments. During boom conditions inflation will force up tax payments and cut social security payments. However, these natural forces will only operate provided the government is willing to accept that they will lead to the budget being in deficit or surplus and not in balance. In any case these built-in stabilisers are not sufficient to eliminate fluctuations in economic activity and must normally be reinforced by positive fiscal measures. Thus if there is a deflationary gap the government can cause an upward shift in $C+I+G+X$ by increasing its own expenditure (G) or cutting taxes and encouraging expenditure by the private sector (C and I). The increase in government expenditure or cut in taxes need not be as great as the size of the deflationary gap since the multiplier will operate to exaggerate the effect of any action taken. Thus if there is a deflationary gap of £100 million between current expenditure and full employment income and the Government Expenditure multiplier is 2 an increase in Government Expenditure of £50 million will close the gap, the remainder coming through regenerated expenditure in other sectors of the economy. A similar effect could be achieved through tax cuts but to achieve a given increase in national income the tax cuts will have to be greater because of the lower taxation multiplier effect. To reduce an inflationary gap the Government can budget for a surplus by cutting its expenditure or raising taxes – again the former carries a larger downward multiplier effect.

While monetary and fiscal measures have been considered separately here, they are usually operated in conjunction. An increase in government expenditure will lead to the creation of new incomes and this in turn will generate a growth in bank deposits and a multiplied creation of credit. Thus increases in private investment and consumer expenditure will close more of the deflationary gap than the original government injection. Furthermore the way in which a government finances a budget deficit or disposes of a surplus will also affect the conduct of its monetary policy – a subject dealt with in more detail in the next chapter.

THE LIMITATIONS OF FISCAL POLICY

The use of a positive fiscal policy originated at a time when all economic ills were associated with the problems of the trade cycle. Even here there were two limiting factors. On the one hand such fine tuning required the government taking action at the right time otherwise it might introduce expansionary measures when the economy was naturally about to come out of recession or drive a depression deeper by cutting expenditure when a boom had already peaked. There is evidence to suggest that such circumstances sometimes occurred. Secondly the frequent sterling and balance of payments crises of the post-war period forced the government to take short-term measures to deal with the external problem and abandon, temporarily, the demands of the domestic situation. The result was the stop-go cycle of the years up to the late 1970s when little progress was made in solving the long-term problems underlying the need for such regular government intervention. Thus the government's main concerns were to maintain full employment and a reasonable balance of payments position and these necessitated an alternation between expansion and restriction. Largely ignored in the uncertain situation created was the need to modernise British industry and increase capital investment to sustain economic growth and rising living standards. Furthermore inflation was allowed to get increasingly serious before it was tackled – despite the implications it had for other government objectives.

Apart from the strains imposed on the use of fiscal policy by the general economic situation and the conflicting requirements of different economic objectives an additional difficulty arises from the need to deal with those unemployment and inflationary problems which exist independently of the trade cycle. Thus an expansionary fiscal policy will not eradicate regional unemployment nor necessarily solve the problems posed by technological unemployment; both require specific remedies of the type discussed in Chapter 13 rather than general policy measures. Another difficult challenge to the effectiveness of fiscal policy arises from cost-push inflation which may occur both during periods of full employment and ones of depression. If the economy is operating below the full employment level, deflationary fiscal (or monetary) policies will drive the economy deeper into depression without necessarily removing the inflation in the economy. Indeed such policies are likely to make cost-push inflation worse since higher taxes will lead to calls for higher compensatory factor rewards while tighter credit will force up interest charges, and thus capital costs, paid by firms leading to their pushing up prices. Thus the government may find itself caught between tighter fiscal and monetary measures to reduce demand-pull inflation and raise cost-push or a relaxation of these measures to reduce cost-push and increase the risk of de-

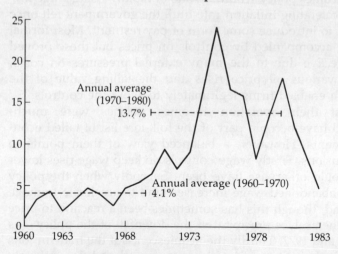

Source: *Economic Progress Report*

Fig. 18.4   Retail price inflation (1960–1983) % change p.a.

mand-pull. The tendency for inflation to become ingrained in the economic fabric enables prices to rise even when unemployment is on the increase so that 'stagflation' occurs with high inflation and a deflationary gap and the Phillips curve moves upwards with higher and higher levels of unemployment required to cure a given rate of inflation.

Prices and incomes policy

The apparent inadequacy of traditional policies to deal with the high inflation rates of the late 1960s and early 1970s led to a series of experiments involving controls over prices or incomes or both. Each was introduced on roughly the same grounds; that an inflationary spiral of prices and wages had become established and some form of voluntary or statutory control was necessary to remove the pressures for this upward spiral to continue. Each policy, again, aimed to set targets for inflation and thus for permitted rises in wages, ranging from the total freeze imposed in 1966 by the Labour government to the complex index-linked formula of the early 1970s, introduced by the Heath government. Whether introduced by a Labour or a Conservative government the pattern of successive incomes policies was similar. The policy would be accepted at first, if grudgingly, but would encounter growing opposition from the unions until finally abandoned. The period following the incomes policy would be one of rapidly-rising wage levels and an accelerating inflation rate until the government felt once more obliged to introduce some form of pay restraint. Most formal policies were accompanied by controls on prices but these proved even less effective due to the many external pressures on costs, such as the various oil price rises and the falling value of the pound, which enabled firms legitimately to avoid the controls.

Throughout their operation incomes policies were much-maligned and have become part of the folk-lore list of failed economic experiments. However, a balanced view of them points to certain conclusions. Firstly wage controls do keep wage rises lower than they would otherwise have been. Secondly when the policy is relaxed or abandoned wage increases tend to accelerate to make up lost ground, though this has sometimes been a reaction to price rises which themselves precipitated the downfall of the policy – as in 1949, 1973 and 1977. Thirdly the acquiescence of the trade unions is vital to a prolonged period of income control and this can only be achieved if the main political parties are willing to adopt a bipartisan approach to incomes policies. Instead each party when in opposition attacked the incomes policy of the other and encouraged the unions to believe that it would not reimpose income restraint when returned to office. Fourthly public sector workers fared worse than private sector workers under the policies since the government had more influence over their pay negotiations and wished to present them as an example to the rest of the economy. As a result public sector workers would lead the chase to 'catch up' when controls were abandoned. Fifthly pay differentials get distorted by incomes policies and skilled workers in particular may suffer excessively in this context. Finally some groups find it easier to evade the controls than others especially where fringe benefits can be more easily increased instead of monetary remuneration.

Incomes policies had been in operation in one form or another for so long that when the Conservative government elected in 1979 stated its intention to dispense with this policy option (to the delight of the trade unions) even they appear to have forgotten what the absence of an incomes policy actually means. Thus the government has each year announced a pay-norm for the public sector to allow for strict controls on the growth of public expenditure. The rest of the economy has supposedly reverted to a system of free collective bargaining and market forces though the familiar old problems have re-emerged of successful pay negotiations depending for a group of workers not just on their efficiency or the profitability of their industry but just as much on their muscle power – proving once again that market forces and efficiency are not necessarily synonymous. None the less the government's abandonment of incomes policy was in conformity with their monetarist view that all inflation is at root demand-pull and fuelled by government-led money-supply growth. In such circumstances they could do nothing else than base their counter-inflationary policies on control of the money supply and of government expenditure.

Questions for analysis

1. 'Full employment and stable prices are incompatible.'
   'Inflation causes unemployment.'
   Examine these statements, explain what is meant by each and attempt to reconcile the contradictions in them.
2. Consider the view that incomes policies prevent the efficient allocation of resources. Why are they disliked by both highly profitable and very weak firms?

Chapter 19

PUBLIC FINANCE

The subject of public finance has turned full circle in the twentieth century. Until the 1930s fiscal policy was concerned with maximising the efficiency of the tax system in order to finance essential public expenditure. For the next thirty or forty years fiscal policy was regarded as a macro-economic instrument of government – the size of the budget being less important than the attainment of the government's economic objectives. In the 1980s attention has swung back to attempts to severely control the level of public expenditure – both because of its possible strong correlation with inflation and because of the rapid growth of public expenditure as a proportion of total national income. While the government has not abandoned the right to use discretionary fiscal policy there is none the less a greater emphasis on the financial rather than the economic efficiency of particular forms of taxation and expenditure.

The principles of taxation

These were first outlined by Adam Smith in *The Wealth of Nations*:

(a) Certainty: it should be clear to taxpayers how much tax they have to pay and when they have to pay it.
(b) Cost: the cost of assessing and raising taxation should be kept to a minimum.
(c) Convenience: within reason taxes should be payable at times most convenient to the taxpayer.
(d) Equality: members of the community should pay taxes in proportion to their income.

The first three of these principles are not contentious and by and large the British tax system complies with them. It is open to the public to find out their liability for tax even if they do not know in advance and the system for payment of taxes is sufficiently flexible to allow for convenience in the timing of tax payments. Some question marks do, however, hang over the costs of tax collection. The tax system has become so complex that whole armies of experts are employed by taxpayers to find loopholes and by the Inland Revenue to close them so that the costs of compliance and of minimising liability must inevitably increase. It is also of course not unknown for some taxes to cost more to collect than the tax actually yields – as in the case of dog licences.

The principle over which there is the greatest dispute is that of equality. Although Smith argued for equality in terms of proportion of income it is possible to argue also either for equality of tax liability, irrespective of income, so that everybody pays the same tax, or for equality of burden so that the impact felt by each taxpayer is the same, whatever the income. These three views of equality give rise to the classification of taxes on the basis of whether they are regressive, proportional or progressive.

1. *Regressive taxes.* A regressive tax is one which takes a higher proportion of income the lower the taxpayer's income. The ultimate in regressive taxation is thus the poll tax where every taxpayer pays the same amount in tax, whatever his income. Regressive taxes are clearly a greater burden for the lower paid and at first sight might appear unjustifiable but there are arguments in favour of their being levied in certain cases. Taxes on luxury items are regressive but people have some choice over whether they buy the item; if regressive taxes were abolished it would be difficult to tax expenditure, even on luxuries. In certain cases the tax is directly linked to the service provided, as with television licences. Again when the welfare state was established it was intended that national insurance contributions should be the same for everybody as would be health care and pensions so that there would be no discrimination between different sections of society.

2. *Proportional taxes.* Here every taxpayers pays the same percentage of income in tax so that the rich pay more taxes than the poor, in absolute though not relative terms. Instinctively this system seems fair but it cannot be argued that each taxpayer feels the 'pain' of taxation equally. If a proportional tax were fixed at 20 per cent it would mean that a person receiving income of £100 per week would pay £20 in tax and another receiving £1,000 per week would pay £200, but though the latter is paying far more tax it is the amount which remains which determines whether the tax is felt

equally. In this case the poorer person may have to go without some necessities – the latter clearly will not. Few taxes are truly proportional in practice since very low-earners are usually exempt from tax on income but national insurance contributions are proportional over income ranges between the low-paid and those on twice average earnings.

3. *Progressive taxes.* Here those on higher incomes pay a greater proportion of their income on taxes than the low-paid. The aim is to achieve 'vertical equality' in that the burden of taxation is felt equally despite variations in the proportion of income paid in tax. It is also desirable to achieve 'horizontal equality' in that individuals with similar incomes and similar commitments should pay similar amounts of tax. This concept further requires that if one economic activity is taxed all similar activities should be taxed at the same rate.

The British system of the taxation of individuals is progressive, notably income tax and capital transfer tax; indeed before the tax reforms carried out by the Conservative government of the early 1980s the system was very steeply progressive. The justification for a system of progressive taxation rests on three main arguments.

Table 19.1   Progressive Tax Rates (1984–85)

1. Income Tax

Taxable Income (£)	Band (%)
0–15,400	30
15,401–18,200	40
18,201–23,100	45
23,101–30,600	50
30,601–38,100	55
over 38,00	60

2. Capital Transfer Tax

Band of chargeable value (£000s)	Rate on death (%)	Lifetime rate (%)
0–64	Nil	Nil
64–85	30	15
85–116	35	17½
116–148	40	20
148–185	45	22½
185–232	50	25
232–285	55	27½
over 285	60	30

Firstly the tax paid is related to the ability to pay. This argument stresses the fact that marginal income has a declining utility so that the more a person earns the less economic satisfaction is derived from each extra pound of income – or lost if that pound is paid in tax. Secondly it enables income to be redistributed from the wealthy to the poor and in so doing benefits the well-off by providing a broad base of consumer demand which is necessary for the promotion of economic growth and the advancement of society. In relation to this it might be added that the relatively wealthy have a more than proportionate stake in ensuring that such public services as defence, law and order are maintained as they have more to lose if society breaks down. Thirdly the system is the only way of reducing the large economic rent payments that the economic system generates for certain groups such as highly paid entertainers. It is also necessary to stop wealth and income becoming excessively concentrated in the hands of a relative few.

Despite the very strong arguments in favour of a progressive tax system there are many criticisms concerning the degree of progression and the distortional effects this has on the efficiency of the economy. The main criticisms are:

1. The disincentive effects. The complex interaction of tax thresholds and social security benefits mean that higher incomes yield no net gain to the recipient for those caught in the poverty trap. Certainly there is a strong case for tax thresholds to be much higher – comparable in real terms to what they were in the 1960s. The other disincentive argument that it is not worth able top managers seeking promotion or new responsibilities presupposes that income is the only factor in career advancement and in any case the highest tax band is now, at 60 per cent, much less of a disincentive than the 83 per cent once levied on higher incomes.
2. There is an inducement for higher earners to seek non-taxable forms of income such as 'perks' and this leads to inequalities between those who receive such perks and those who receive only salaries subject to direct taxation.
3. Considerable scarce resources are allocated to the avoidance of taxation through taxpayers seeking loopholes in the system and the government then having to close them. If the tax is high enough some taxpayers may seek to evade it by non-declaration of income.
4. The system of allowances is arbitrary and if not seen as fair will cause resentment among those sections who feel most penal-

ised. It is very important that the tax system be seen as fair by the taxpayers since the system relies on the majority of the population being honest and accepting a duty to pay taxes. If the system is seen as excessively harsh many taxpayers will do all they can to evade it.

INDIRECT TAXES

Given the strong argument for progressive taxes is there a case for indirect taxes at all – as they all tend to be regressive in their effect? The strongest argument in favour of indirect taxes is that they do confer some element of choice. If there were no indirect taxes some 50 per cent of government revenue would be lost and would have to be made up by increasing direct taxes and further reducing the proportion of income over which the individual has control. While it is true that initially everything he buys will carry either value added tax (VAT) and/or customs or excise duties at least he can choose between the various goods and services involved. Furthermore many of these goods are luxuries or potentially harmful or both so taxation may deter too many economic resources being directed to their production and consumption. A final advantage of indirect taxation is that it is an extremely simple system to operate, there being no exceptions and it being relatively cheap to collect – much of the work being done by retailers in the case of VAT. Despite this the British system of taxation has tended to be far more based on direct taxes than its European neighbours and this was especially the case in the 1970s. The fact that indirect taxes are regressive need not be a deterrent to their use since higher tax thresholds can be the main means by which direct taxes are reduced while welfare benefits can be raised to compensate the lower paid. On the other hand it must be remembered that in purely financial terms the aim of a tax is to raise revenue for the government so the imposition of indirect taxes on a product to the point where demand becomes elastic would clearly be counterproductive.

The budget

The annual budget statement originated as an outline of the government's expenditure plans for the forthcoming year and the proposed means by which revenue would be raised to meet this expenditure. The principle aim of the Chancellor of the Exchequer would be to balance his budget or even achieve a surplus; only during a war would the government accept the need for a deficit.

The role of the budget was revolutionised by the advent of Keynesian economic theory and the acceptance by the government of a central role in influencing the economy and also by the growth in public expenditure which followed the Second World War and the emergence of the welfare state. Reference will continue to be made here to *the* budget but in fact most Chancellors in modern times have resorted where necessary to a mini-budget or two during the course of the year. These two reasons for the changing role of the budget are interrelated. If the government is to take responsibility for the management of aggregate demand it is inevitable that it should seek to increase its direct control over the economy to facilitate the implementation of its policies. At the same time the greater the degree of state involvement in the economy the more significant the effect of changes in the public sector on other parts of the economy.

The modern budget thus combines two functions. Firstly it continues to outline the government's revenue and expenditure plans to meet its political and financial objectives over the coming year. Thus there may be changes in the importance given to different classes of expenditure, changes in the structure of taxation – either to improve its efficiency or to effect a redistribution of income – and changes in the size of the budget to compensate for inflationary effects. Secondly the net effect of such changes in revenue and expenditure can be calculated as having an expansionary, a neutral or a deflationary effect on the economy as a whole and thus the government can exercise its function of managing the level of aggregate demand in the economy through the use of discretionary fiscal measures. At first sight it might seem that a balanced budget is synonymous with a neutral one and that a budget deficit is necessary to achieve an expansionary influence. In fact there is scope, even within a balanced budget, to influence the level of economic activity so the balanced budget is examined first.

THE BALANCED BUDGET

The equalisation of revenue and expenditure for the forthcoming financial year means that there is no change in the total national debt and no public sector borrowing requirement (PSBR) for the year. Budgets of the 1930s were of this pattern yet they continued also to be mildly expansionary in their effect by means of redistributive taxation. This was achieved through making the taxation system more progressive and the subsidisation by the government of services which chiefly benefited the poor. This system worked because the downward multiplier of the higher taxes imposed on

Table 19.2 How public spending is paid for £ billion

Income	1983–84 Budget Forecast	Latest estimate	1984–85 Forecast
Central government taxation			
Income tax	31.4	31.3	33.8
Value added tax	15.5	15.3	18.0
Corporation tax	6.2	6.0	8.4
Oil duties	5.7	5.6	6.1
Petroleum revenue tax	5.2	6.1	6.0
Spirits, beer, wine, cider and perry	3.9	3.9	4.0
Tobacco	3.7	3.8	4.1
Vehicle excise duty	1.9	2.0	2.1
National insurance surcharge	1.7	1.7	0.9
Taxes on capital	1.5	1.6	1.7
European Community duties	1.4	1.3	1.4
Other (including accruals adjustments)	3.3	3.9	2.9
Total	**81.5**	**82.5**	**89.4**
National insurance, etc. contributions	21.2	21.4	23.0
Local authorities rates	13.0	12.1	12.9
North Sea oil royalties, etc.	1.6	1.9	2.0
General government trading surplus and rent	3.3	3.1	3.0
General government interest and dividend receipts	2.3	2.2	2.4
Adjustments			
Accruals	—	-0.2	0.6
Other†	3.4	3.7	3.5
Public corporations transactions*	-0.5	-0.8	-1.8
Total receipts	**125.9**	**126.1**	**135.1**
Public sector borrowing requirement	8.2	10.0	7.2
Total receipts and borrowing	**134.1**	**136.0**	**142.3**

Expenditure	1983–84 Budget forecast	Latest estimate	1984–85 Forecast
Social security	34.6	35.3	37.2
Defence	16.0	15.7	17.0
Health and personal social services	14.6	14.7	15.4
Education and science	12.6	13.4	13.1
Scotland	6.7	6.8	6.9
Industry, energy, trade and employment	6.2	6.1	5.6
Law, order and protective services	4.6	4.7	4.9
Transport	4.4	4.6	4.4
Northern Ireland	3.8	3.8	4.0
Other environmental services	3.5	3.8	3.5
Housing	2.8	2.8	2.5
Wales	2.5	2.6	2.6
Overseas services	2.0	2.3	2.3
Agriculture, fisheries, food and forestry	1.8	2.1	2.0
Other public services	1.7	1.7	1.8
Common services	1.0	1.0	1.1
Arts and libraries	0.6	0.6	0.6
Local authority current expenditure not allocated to programmes (England)	0.9	—	0.7
Adjustments			
Special sales of assets	-0.8	-1.2	-1.9
Reserve	1.1	0.1	2.8
General allowance for shortfall	-1.2	-0.3	—
Planning total in Cmnd 9143§	**119.3**	**120.3**	**126.4**
Revisions since Cmnd 9143	—	—	-0.1
Revised planning total	**119.3**	**120.3**	**126.2**
Gross debt interest	14.8	15.7	16.0
Planning total plus gross debt interest	**134.1**	**136.0**	**142.3**

* Comprises total interest payments by nationalised industries (and other public corporations treated similarly for public expenditure planning) and the trading income of the remaining corporations.

† Comprises other miscellaneous receipts and adjustments from the definition of public expenditure used in the national income accounts to that used in Cmnd. 9143.

§ Figures in the first column are from table 5.5 in the *Financial Statement and Budget Report 1983–84* translated from Cmnd. 8789 to Cmnd. 9143 definitions.

Source: *Economic Progress Report*

the better-off was smaller than the upward multiplier effect of increased expenditure on the provision of public services because some of the extra tax raised would have been withdrawn from the circular flow anyway, either as savings or as import expenditure. While a mildly successful policy this did not cure the depression of the 1930s and it is unlikely that a severe depression could be cured by redistributive taxation alone since eventually tax rates would become prohibitive.

In modern times the balanced budget is more likely to be effective in an expansionary context by an increase in the size of both sides of the budget because there are so many areas of the economy in which the government has a direct involvement. Again the expansion would be the result of the upward multiplier of increased government expenditure outweighing the increased taxation downward multiplier. It is also worth making the point that a government wishing to reduce its involvement in the economy by a reduction in both sides of the budget will cause national income to contract.

THE BUDGET DEFICIT

A budget deficit, where public expenditure exceeds taxation, is likely to be far more expansionary than a balanced budget. This can be achieved either by increasing public expenditure or by cutting taxes or a combination of the two. Again it must be remembered that the taxation multiplier is smaller than the government expenditure multiplier so that greater tax cuts than increases in expenditure will be necessary to close a given deflationary gap. Deficit spending generates incomes and so increases expenditure on consumption in the following way. The government undertakes public investment which does not compete with private investment by building hospitals, schools, roads and so on. This investment expenditure is financed by borrowing and so it does not involve reducing private investment unless the borrowing draws funds away from the private sector. It may be asked, however, whether there is a downward multiplier effect from the government attracting funds which would otherwise have been used for consumption. In fact the funds attracted for public investment would very often have been withdrawn from the national income flow anyway so once again any downward multiplier effect will be outweighed by the upward multiplier. In addition the source of the government's borrowed funds will be very important in determining both the size of the multiplier and the impact on the money supply. This topic will be discussed a little later.

THE BUDGET SURPLUS

A budget surplus, where government revenue exceeds public expenditure, is appropriate where there is an inflationary gap and aggregate expenditure is above that required to maintain full employment. This surplus may be achieved either through increases in taxes, especially those on expenditure, or cuts in government expenditure. The resultant surplus revenue can be used to redeem part of the national debt as there will, for the current year, be a negative PSBR. The redeemed debt will have an expansionary effect on the money supply but this will be outweighed by the downward multiplier effect of the surplus. As Britain had inflationary pressures in the economy throughout the 1950s and 1960s it might be expected that there was a string of budget surpluses. That there was not is due to the fact that a persistent balance of payments deficit led the government to make up the shortfall in aggregate expenditure left by a deficiency in export earnings.

THE FINANCING OF THE PSBR

The size of the PSBR has become a key issue in recent years because of its relationship to both public expenditure and the money supply – two areas in which the government is committed to exerting greater control. The precise impact of a given PSBR depends mainly on the way it is financed. Firstly the government can borrow from the UK private sector by selling stock to individuals and firms. The effect of this is to reduce on the one hand private sector liquidity and potential expenditure but more than compensate for this by increased expenditure by the government in areas where the multiplier effect will be greatest. The disadvantage of financing the PSBR in this way is that the government may draw resources away from the expansionary areas of the private sector and, if its borrowing is large enough, push up interest rates generally and deter natural recovery in the economy. Secondly the borrowing requirement may be financed by overseas lenders through their purchasing sales of government stock. Since there is no reduction in bank deposits to finance this deficit the effect will be more expansionary than a PSBR financed by the UK private sector. Thirdly the deficit can be financed by the UK banking sector, either through the purchase of government stocks or of Treasury bills. Where a bank buys government securities there is no reduction in bank deposits or the money supply to counter the expansion occurring from the government's own increased expenditure. Furthermore if the securities in question are Treasury bills this will increase the liquidity of the banks and enable an expansion of the money supply through the credit creation multiplier. The higher the proportion of a given deficit financed by the issue of Treasury bills, the more expansionary that deficit tends to be. It was the tendency, of governments in the 1970s to finance their deficits via sales of securities to the banking sector – in particular to the Bank of England – which led to changes of deficit financing through the printing of money.

THE LONG-TERM NATIONAL DEBT

The PSBR of the current year adds to the national debt which has accumulated over the years through Government borrowing in the past from residents or institutions in this country or overseas.

Table 19.3   The National debt

	National debt		Debt interest	
	£ billion	% GNP	£ million	% GNP
1900	0.6	31.9	20	1.0
1914	0.7	25.6	19	0.8
1921	7.6	147.7	337	6.8
1938	7.8	150.6	265	5.1
1946	23.0	259.9	532	6.0
1975	46.4	49.0	4,210	4.4
1982	118.6	52.4	14,500	6.4

Source: NIESR

Apart from the last thirty years the debt has always grown most rapidly during time of war and much of the accrued total consists of past war borrowings for which there are no tangible assets today. Much of the additional debt in the post-war period has been to enable investment by the local authorities and nationalised industries. Until recent times there was a widely-held view that when circumstances permit the national debt should be repaid and in the eighteenth and nineteenth centuries there were several attempts to clear it. This view was held partly because of the dislike for 'deadweight' debt which could no longer be related to existing assets and partly for fear that the rising value of money in the nineteenth century would make the cost of the debt in terms of interest payments increasingly difficult to bear. In modern times, however, a large proportion of the new debt has arisen from the provision of new capital assets, especially for local authorities and the nationalised industries. The demands made on modern governments for new resources make it likely that only in years of severe restraint will taxation be sufficient on its own to finance government expenditure. Repayment of the debt, which in any case is largely serviced by the stockholders themselves through taxation on their interest and capital gains, could only be achieved by a series of huge budget surpluses which would have an extremely depressing effect on the economy. Indeed the deflationary effects of such a move would far outweigh any inflationary effects of the release of funds for the private investment sector.

None the less the view persists that the debt represents a burden on the nation as a whole, but particularly on the taxpayers, and that the debt is passed on to be borne by future generations. In fact at the time the debt is incurred there is a subsidisation of taxpayers by stockholders which in a later generation requires taxpayers to subsidise stockholders. However, there are a number of factors which may lead to the debt being a current burden. If, as was feared in the nineteenth century, the value of money rose, both the debt itself and the interest costs of supporting it could become a severe burden. In practice the high inflation rates of recent times have worked to reduce considerably the real value of the national debt. Whereas internal debt is not a burden, that held externally is, since the interest payments on such debt may pose difficulties for the balance of payments. If, as is usual, the debt is in the currency of the lender, the burden cannot be reduced by inflation or any depreciation of the borrower's currency and devaluation will increase substantially the burden of such debts. Another problem concerns the diversion of investment funds from the private sector to the government; if the private sector investment lost would have contributed more to economic growth such public investment is adversely affecting the development of the economy. Finally there is the effect of the debt on the conduct of monetary policy. Any reduction in the debt creates difficulty in the conduct of monetary policy which relies on the existence of a large marketable debt for the conduct of open market operations. On the other hand the larger the debt the greater the continuing flow of maturities and the need to refinance maturing debt may induce the Bank of England to support the market for government securities almost continuously to make it receptive to funding operations. On the whole the Bank believes that a large national debt has been a hindrance in its monetary policy operations. Of course if there were no national debt the government would no longer be able to use budgetary policy to control or stimulate the economy.

PUBLIC EXPENDITURE AND THE NATIONAL INCOME

Irrespective of the use of the budget as an economic policy instrument the late 1960s and early 1970s witnessed a rapid growth in

Table 19.4   Ratio of public expenditure to GDP

Year	%
1914	9
1928	18
1938	18
1945	63
1958	33
1984	44

the level of public expenditure both in real terms and as a proportion of total expenditure.

This growth in public expenditure aroused concern that it might have grown so much as to create various economic problems. Thus if the high expenditure led to taxes being pushed to very high levels this may have disincentive effects or set off a cost-push inflation spiral. Furthermore the increased public expenditure could lead to too high a proportion of resources being absorbed by the public sector to the detriment of the needs of the private sector. Awareness of these problems led to the last Labour government issuing a white paper in 1977 to outline its plans for reversing the upward trend in the share of resources and total expenditure accounted for by the public sector. Such control over public sector expenditure was seen as an essential prerequisite for stricter control of the money supply.

The new Conservative government elected in 1979 was even more firmly committed to controls over public expenditure as part of its strategy to reduce the involvement of the government in the economy and thus enable substantial reductions in personal taxation. Five years later the proportion of total expenditure undertaken by the government and the ratio of personal taxation (including national insurance) to total expenditure were both the highest in history and the PSBR continued to prove difficult to reduce. The reasons for this strangely opposite effect to the policy undertaken were several.

1. The policy of firm control over the money supply to reduce inflation led to a deepening of the recession and higher unemployment. This in turn involved lower tax receipts and higher government expenditure.
2. The scale of services offered under the long-established welfare state means that public expenditure will grow even when total expenditure is falling.
3. A downward balanced budget will have a deflationary effect on

the economy and thus public expenditure is not reduced as much as taxation.

4. Unforeseen or ultimately irreducible expenditure has been forced on the government as with the Falklands conflict and the EEC budget contribution.

Part of the shortfall in public expenditure requirements has been met by the sale of public assets through the privatisation programme. While this provides a short-term solution it does mean that in the future there will be smaller revenues from profit-making government enterprises to offset necessary expenditure so posing a threat of higher taxation or a reduction in services. However natural it is for most people to wish there to be reductions in the level of taxation – even if this involves some reduction in services – it must be remembered that a downward budget will not only reduce services faster than taxation, it will also serve to redistribute income towards the wealthy. In 1984 most reliable sources estimated that only those people on incomes of well over £20,000 were paying less tax than in 1979 while the lower paid were both paying more taxes and receiving less services.

Questions for analysis

1. Examine the effect on a British manufacturer of consumer durables of the action taken by a British government in the following situations:

    (a) A major aid programme for the engineering industry to assist its modernisation and to stimulate technological innovation.

    (b) A reform of the tax system to shift the burden of taxation from direct to indirect taxes and from the higher-paid to a more even spread over all income ranges.

    (c) An attempt to deal with inflation by tight monetary controls.

    (d) The reintroduction of exchange control regulations to prevent British institutions and companies increasing their overseas investments.

2. Account for the growth in the relative importance of public expenditure as indicated by Table 19.4 earlier in this chapter.

Chapter 20

INTERNATIONAL TRADE

It is possible for economies to function independently of the rest of the world and throughout history countries have sought to achieve self-sufficiency to reduce their economic, and therefore their political, dependence on other nations. However, the price of self-sufficiency is the sacrifice of access to those goods and services which the country cannot produce itself. As societies become more and more sophisticated and demanding in their tastes doubts grow concerning the ability of a modern advanced society to provide independently all the resources it needs to develop its full economic potential, and satisfy all the needs of its people. Even if a national economy could produce limited quantities of all the goods required by society this situation would result in high costs in terms of resource usage. International trade, on the other hand, permits countries to specialise in the production of those goods and services in which it is economically efficient and to trade some of these for goods and services which it cannot produce so efficiently. Thus trade enables countries to raise their living standards by making more goods available, both in terms of variety and quantity, and through lowering prices as international specialisation enables the development of economies of scale and the greater optimisation of resource allocation.

Absolute advantage and comparative advantage

When examining the question of international specialisation a country may benefit from specialisation either on the basis of absolute advantage or because it enjoys a comparative advantage in the production of one type of goods or a variety of goods. These two principles are illustrated in Table 20.1.

In Table 20.1(a) it is clear that Country X should specialise in the

Table 20.1   Output of two goods from 10 factor units of input

	(a)		(b)	
	Country X	Country Y	Country X	Country Y
Wheat	50	60	60	110
Iron	30	10	50	60

production of iron and Country Y in the production of wheat since this will result in total wheat production of 120 units and total iron production of 60 units. So if the two countries engage in trade with each other both will be able to enjoy more of both goods with the same resource allocation as if they did not trade. The advantage derived from trade in this case is obvious as each country has an absolute advantage in the production of one of the goods. In Table 20.1(b) Country Y has an absolute advantage in the production of both wheat and iron and thus would derive, apparently, no advantage from trading with Country X. However, there will be a benefit from trade because each country has a comparative advantage in one product. The term comparative advantage refers to the fact that, even if one country is more efficient at producing all goods than another, the latter will be relatively less inefficient at producing some goods and thus have a comparative advantage in producing these. Just as not every person who could do a particular job chooses to do so but prefers to earn higher rewards in another occupation, so Country Y should specialise in wheat production at which it is vastly superior and lease iron production to Country X where the gap in efficiency is marginal. By specialising in this way each country should enjoy higher living standards, not necessarily through having more of all goods for consumption but by expending less resources for each unit of output received. Thus in Table 20.1(b) it costs Country Y, without specialisation, 0.54 (60/100) units of iron to produce one unit of wheat while in Country X it costs 0.83 (50/60) units of iron to produce one unit of wheat. The opportunity cost of producing wheat in Country X is higher than in Country Y while the reverse is true in the case of iron. If both countries specialise in the product they are relatively

Table 20.2   Output using 10 factor units of input

	Country X	Country Y
Wheat	—	220
Iron	100	—

better at, the data from Table 20.1(b) can be redrawn as in Table 20.2.

The rate of exchange between the two countries is determined by the opportunity cost in each so that Country Y will benefit provided it receives at least six units of iron for every eleven of wheat while Country X will need to receive at least six units of wheat for every five of iron. If the rate of exchange of six units of iron for ten of wheat is adopted trade between the two countries will result in the following situation.

Table 20.3

	Country X	Country Y
Wheat	100	120
Iron	40	60

Country Y has clearly benefited since by using the same resources it has the same level of iron consumption as before but an extra ten units of wheat. Country X has also gained, though not so obviously, since despite having less iron than before specialisation took place it does have about twice as much wheat. Whereas ten units of input could produce sixty units of wheat and fifty of iron without trade, Country X now receives the equivalent of $12\frac{1}{3}$ units of production from the same ten units of input. Clearly there are various other rates of exchange between the two countries which would enable both of them to benefit from trade and the actual rate which operates will depend on the bargaining power of the two products. While it is possible to see the benefits deriving from the law of comparative advantage in bilateral trade the law applies more fully to multilateral trade and thus provides a stimulus to the attainment of free trade.

Despite the obvious advantages of the application of this theory there are several qualifications which must be made. Firstly there is an assumption that free trade in goods prevails. In practice the trade in commodities and manufactured goods is restricted by customs duties, tariffs and quotas, while many countries have trading agreements favouring the parties to the agreement at the expense of other countries, e.g. the Common Market. Secondly the theory ignores transport costs and other impediments to the free flow of goods, such as different currency and banking systems and restrictions on the movement of capital and labour. Thirdly the theory neglects the law of diminishing returns and the problems of over-specialisation and one-crop economies. Finally, and most important of all, political factors determine to a large extent which industries shall be fostered and promoted in a country and for reasons of strategy or self-sufficiency countries will not wish to abandon some industries entirely in order to obtain the benefits deriving from the law of comparative advantage. The theory came closest to being put into practice during the last century when economies could be held static in terms of the variety of economic activities undertaken so that the colonial territories were often not allowed, and certainly not encouraged, to industrialise. Instead they specialised in one or two crops and this allowed the 'mother' country to expand rapidly her own industries. In the modern era with countries seeking to alter the balance of their economies and increase the supply of factors of production the application of comparative advantage is more difficult to initiate.

The terms of trade

The terms of trade relate to the physical rate of exchange of the goods a country sells for the goods it buys and thus is connected to the principle of comparative advantage. In the example of comparative advantage discussed above the exchange rate was established as 6 units iron = 10 units wheat. Both countries would still benefit, however, provided the exchange rate is between the two extremes 6 units iron = 11 units wheat and 6 units iron = 7.2 units wheat. If the exchange rate between Country X and Country Y changes from 6 units iron = 10 units wheat to 6 units iron = 8 units wheat then Country X will receive less wheat for each unit of iron it exports than previously so that its terms of trade have worsened while those of Country Y have improved. Thus the terms of trade of a country relate the prices of its exports to those of its imports so that if a given volume of exports exchanges for a smaller volume of imports than previously the terms of trade have become less favourable and vice versa. The terms of trade are therefore the export-price of imports and this relationship can be expressed as an index number:

$$\text{Terms of trade index} = \frac{\text{Index of export prices}}{\text{Index of import prices}} \times 100$$

An improvement in the terms of trade resulting from a rise in the index means that fewer exports need be sold to pay for a fixed quantity of imports. Unfortunately such an improvement in the terms of trade does not necessarily benefit the country since as export prices have risen relative to import prices there may well be a fall in overseas demand for the country's goods outweighing the rise in the value of goods actually sold. The effect of a change in the terms of trade depends on the price elasticity of demand of the country's exports and imports. Thus countries with high inflation rates and exports with highly elastic demand will find that an improving terms of trade is accompanied by a deterioration in the level of export earnings. Similarly if there is a fall in the terms of trade due to a rise in the prices of essential imports then while export earnings stay constant the import bill will rise. The UK terms of trade has fluctuated wildly over the last forty years. In the 1940s and early 1950s the terms of trade deteriorated because of the rapid rise in commodity prices but in the period after 1952 a fall in commodity prices led to an improvement. Until 1967 the terms of trade were fairly stable but the devaluation of sterling in that year led to another deterioration. The very rapid rise in oil prices in the early 1970s followed by the fall in the value of sterling in 1975–76 caused a further sharp decline though this was largely reversed in the late 1970s by the recovery of sterling and the high rate of inflation. In the 1980s the slowing down of inflation and the changing structure of Britain's export earnings made the terms of trade increasingly unpredictable.

Table 20.4   UK terms of trade measures 1975 = 100

Year	Total goods	Non oil
1975	100	100
1977	100	102
1978	106	106
1979	106	108
1980	104	112
1981	102	115
1982	101	115

The balance of payments

All countries now keep some kind of official record of the receipts and payments which occur over the year in respect of the trade in goods and services and other currency movements. Although these balance of payments figures are published in considerable detail and are adjusted to take account of seasonal variations they do not present accurate figures due to the many inaccuracies which arise out of such problems as double-counting or under-counting of goods, difficulties in identifying many of the international trade transactions which take place and delays in the recording of exports and imports. Furthermore as the balance of payments represents a moment in time it is extremely unlikely that both sides of the balance sheet will match without some adjustment. However, the published figures do represent a useful guide to trends in the structure of trade and its payments. The balance of payments accounts are divided into a number of sections.

THE CURRENT ACCOUNT

This is the record of trade in goods and services. It consists firstly of the balance of trade made up of the export value of goods minus the value of imported goods. Secondly there is the balance of invisibles which is made up of several parts. Firstly there are those payments involving the export and import of services such as banking, insurance, shipping and tourism. Secondly the receipt of earnings by British residents arising out of interest, dividend and rent payments on capital and property holdings overseas is included, as are the payments to overseas residents of income from similar holdings in Britain. Thirdly there is the transfer of gifts, pensions and similar payments between British and overseas residents. A final item on the current account consists of government expenditure overseas including payment for military equipment and for the maintenance of representation abroad.

INVESTMENT AND OTHER CAPITAL FLOWS

This section includes all movements of capital to and from the country. Firstly there is the purchase of stocks and shares by individuals and institutions. Secondly there is the provision of long-term loans by one government to another. Thirdly is the short-term capital account consisting of additions to or withdrawals from balances in British banks from overseas and the dealings of these banks in foreign currencies, trade credit given on exports and imports and the borrowing of eurocurrencies in London for overseas investment. Many of the short-term movements in capital account reflect currency speculation, changes in interest rates and overseas confidence in the economic and political situation and are termed 'hot money' movements.

THE TOTAL CURRENCY FLOW

The two sections above when added together should result in a figure equal to the net receipt or loss of foreign currency over the year in question. As in the case of the national income accounts there is, however, a residual error to take account of omissions and errors termed the 'balancing item'. When this item is added in (or subtracted) and account has been taken of any changes during the course of the year in special drawing right (SDR) allocations and international monetary fund (IMF) subscriptions the total currency flow can be calculated.

OFFICIAL FINANCING

This section is on the other side of the balance sheet to the total currency flow and shows how a surplus or deficit is settled. The main items are thus changes in the level of UK gold and foreign currency holdings, reflecting payment for an overall deficit or earnings from an overall surplus, and changes in the level of borrowing from the IMF and other international monetary authorities. Thus a deficit could be financed either by the depletion of gold and foreign currency reserves or through borrowing from the IMF. Net increases in reserves are shown as a (−) while net decreases are shown as a (+) so that if the total currency flow shows a deficit (−) the balance on official financing will show a (+) total of an equal amount so that the two sides cancel out.

From the above analysis of the balance of payments it is apparent that a deficit on current and capital accounts constitutes an outflow of funds while a surplus represents an inflow. A surplus does not necessarily signify that the country has had a successful trading year since the surplus could well be the result of a large inflow of capital funds which could be withdrawn at a later date and in the meantime will earn interest and dividend payments which will result in an outflow on the invisibles balance in future years. The balance of payments will only be in balance in the sense that the total currency flow will be exactly equal to the official financing. A balance of payments equilibrium refers not to a balance but to a situation in which deficits and surpluses are relatively small and average out over a few years. In practice countries tend to be permanently in surplus or in deficit for long periods according to the structure of their economy. Thus developing countries usually have a deficit on current account and depend on investment from overseas to achieve equilibrium. Newly developed countries with competitive industries frequently enjoy a balance of trade surplus which can be used to build up overseas investments for future invisible earnings. For many advanced countries these invisible earnings became vital to offset a balance of trade deficit as the country loses its competitive edge to newer industrial countries. Finally a deficit on the balance of trade may become so great that invisible earnings

Table 20.5   UK balance of payments (1982)

Current Account	£ million
Exports	55,546
Imports	53,427
Balance of trade	+2,119
Services	+3,844
Interest, profits and dividends	+1,577
Transfers	−2,112
Invisible balance	+3,309
Current balance	+5,428

Capital Account	
Overseas investment in the UK	+3,459
UK private investment overseas	−10,768
Official long-term capital	−337
Import credit	−224*
Export credit	−1,165
Foreign currency borrowing	+4,173
Exchange reserves in sterling	+408
Overseas sterling balances	+4,164
External lending by UK banks	−3,243
Other transactions	+682
Capital balance	−2,851

Official Financing	
Net transactions with overseas monetary authorities	−163
Foreign currency borrowing	+26
Official reserves	+1,421
Total official financing	+1,284
Balancing item	3,861

* Normally a (+) figure

Source: *Annual Abstract of Statistics*

are not sufficient to offset it; a situation faced by Britain in the past
and a likely future threat once the North Sea oil reserves begin to
run down. Once a country's current account is persistently in surplus or in deficit its balance of payments is in disequilibrium and
the government will be forced to take steps to remedy the situation.

Balance of payments correction

Where a country suffers from a chronic deficit it will find that either it must continuously run down its gold and foreign currency reserves or pay for the deficit by borrowing. Eventually the reserves will be exhausted and foreign confidence will collapse and make further borrowing difficult and, ultimately, impossible. In attempting to avert this crisis and cure a deficit a country has recourse to three possible policy strategies.

Direct controls.   These are policies aimed at artificially limiting imports or stimulating exports. The two main forms of direct control are tariffs and quotas. Tariffs are taxes imposed on imported goods thus raising their prices and making them less competitive against domestic goods, while quotas are physical limits on the quantities of particular imports into the country. Tariffs tend to be more effective when applied to goods whose prices are already close to their UK counterparts while quotas are best applied to very cheap goods where even a large tariff would still leave them highly price-competitive. Other direct controls include exchange control to limit the amount of domestic and foreign currency leaving the country and restrictions on investment overseas. However, as import controls could run counter to existing international agreements, they would only be accepted by other countries as a short-term measure. Were other countries to retaliate there would be no gain and the contraction in world trade which resulted would do considerable harm to all trading nations. An alternative to import controls is some form of export incentive such as tax concessions, subsidies and cheap credit and while these are generally acceptable they still rely on the willingness of firms to go out and seek overseas markets.

Deflationary measures.   Since these will tend to slow the growth of domestic demand or even reverse it the effect will be to reduce inflationary pressures in the economy thus making domestically produced goods more competitive both at home and overseas. Further the contraction of domestic demand should stimulate companies into seeking overseas markets for their goods. Finally a drop in consumer expenditure should reduce the demand not only for domestic goods but also for imports. A deflationary package could include monetary measures to raise interest rates and reduce the availability of credit which will not only reduce demand but attract foreign funds into the country and thus assist the capital account. Domestic demand could also be reduced by fiscal measures involving higher taxes and cuts in government expenditure. For the purposes of dealing with a balance of payments deficit the most appropriate fiscal measures would be increases in indirect taxes and cuts in government expenditure overseas. The main problem with using a deflationary policy to assist the balance of payments is that the rate of economic activity slows and a deflationary gap opens, bringing with it higher unemployment and falling living standards. It also introduces the threat of cost-push inflation as the cost of living rises and pay claims respond accordingly, cancelling out any benefits of the deflationary package in making domestic goods more competitive.

Devaluation. This is a downward alteration of the value of the currency in terms of other currencies. An official devaluation is only possible when a system of fixed exchange rates operates but countries can allow their currencies to float downwards to achieve the same effect. If exchange rates are freely floating the exchange rate should reflect the purchasing power of the currency against other currencies thus reducing the likelihood of a large permanent deficit. Devaluation itself is normally regarded as a last resort because though exports become cheaper and imports dearer there is an accompanying fall in living standards and only if exports respond sufficiently to provide a substantial injection into the national income will this loss be recouped. A simple example will illustrate the effect of devaluation on the prices of exports and imports.

Table 20.6   1967 devaluation of sterling

Before devaluation £1 = $2.80		After devaluation £1 = $2.40	
British goods costing	£100 = $280	British goods costing	£100 = $240
US goods costing	$280 = £100	US goods costing	$280 = £117

While devaluation has clearly made the price of British exports more competitive and American exports less so these figures do not indicate the effect on the volume of trade and ultimately on the balance of payments. Thus those goods which are produced in Britain but are made from imported raw materials will not fall in price by as great a percentage as the nominal devaluation. Furthermore it is the elasticity of demand for exports and imports which will determine whether, and by how much, devaluation improves the balance of payments position. If the average of the elasticity of demand for exports and that of imports exceeds unity, devaluation will reduce the deficit while if the average is less than unity the deficit will actually get worse. If a country devalues by

10 per cent and the price elasticity of demand for its exports is 1.5 while that for its imports is 0.8 the results, based on all prices changing by 10 per cent would be as follows:

Before devaluation: Exports = 420 Imports = 480 Deficit = 60
After devaluation: Exports = 434.7 Imports = 485.8 Deficit = 51

Exports have increased by 15 per cent but lost 10 per cent in value while imports have decreased by 8 per cent but gone up 10 per cent in value so the deficit is reduced by 15 per cent which is not enough to eradicate it – an indication of how dependent is devaluation as a policy on favourable elasticities. A country which has inelastic demand for both exports and imports would actually improve the balance of payments by revaluing, i.e. increasing the value of its currency in terms of other currencies.

Devaluation carries with it the dangerous side-effects that as living standards immediately fall, if only temporarily, wage demands are likely to increase to try to restore real incomes and this will set off a wave of cost-push inflation eroding the benefits of devaluation. Devaluation also puts pressure on domestic industries to take up the increased demand for exports and to replace imports so that if firms are unable to expand output sufficiently there may also be demand-pull inflationary pressures. It is essential, therefore, to accompany devaluation by deflationary measures to counter the threat of inflation and perhaps a prices and incomes policy where higher import prices may trigger a wages-prices spiral.

Solving the problem of a chronic surplus is not so difficult but why should countries wish to solve this particular 'problem' anyway? To begin with a country in permanent surplus is building up large reserves of gold and foreign currency at the expense of deficit countries and eventually those countries will be unable to continue to buy goods and services from the surplus country as they strive to restore balance of payments equilibrium. In addition the permanent surplus country may find inflationary pressures occurring through excess demand while with the permanent net flow of goods out of the country the people are not enjoying the standard of living the country can afford. In the most extreme case it would become a 'miser' nation with enormous gold and currency reserves but while living on a minimum of goods and services. Apart from using the surplus to finance the country's investments overseas the practical solution would be to introduce expansionary monetary and fiscal policies which will increase import demand and raise living standards. More drastic measures would include policies to encourage imports and discourage exports or, as a final solution, revalue the currency.

The British balance of payments

In the mid-nineteenth century the British economy abandoned any further attempts at self-sufficiency and based its future on the ability of export earnings from manufactured goods, supplemented later by property and investment income from overseas, to finance the importation of food and necessary raw materials. The success of this period was assisted by the fact that Britain had a head start in industrial development and also had a large overseas empire in which colonial economies could be tailored to the mother country's requirements. By 1914, however, Britain was rapidly being overhauled by Germany and the United States in manufacturing output. The First World War established the pre-eminence of the United States while Britain was forced to sell off many of its overseas investments to help finance the war, a process which was repeated in the Second World War. Between the wars many of the older industries such as textiles and coal declined as earners of foreign currency but were replaced by newer industries like chemicals, automobile manufacture and electrical industries, all of which did relatively well during the 1930s. After the Second World War the success of the balance of payments depended on a strong manufacturing export position to pay for essential imports and in the late 1940s, while the rest of Europe was going through the reconstruction period, the situation was fairly healthy – though a surplus on invisibles was necessary to counter a balance of trade deficit. However, as competition in world trade grew, the relative decline of Britain's trading position accelerated; in 1950 Britain's share of the world trade in manufactures was 25 per cent while thirty years later it was only 6 per cent. The frequent balance of payments crises of the 1950s and 1960s led to a 'stop-go' cycle with alternating periods of economic expansion and an external deficit followed by stagnation at home but an external surplus. By 1967 the situation had deteriorated to such an extent that another sterling crisis precipitated a 14 per cent devaluation, though only after deflationary measures were introduced was a surplus achieved by 1970. A further crisis followed an attempt at rapid expansion of the economy in 1971 and another the rise in oil prices in 1973. It was at this time that government figures published the oil deficit separately to show that the balance of payments would be in healthy surplus but for the oil deficit and that all would be well once North

Sea oil was on flow. Certainly in the early 1980s the balance of payments was in surplus as Britain became a major oil producer but there was a continuing decline in the export of manufactured goods and in 1983 there was a surplus of manufactured imports over exports – for the first time in 200 years. As oil production begins to fall in the late 1980s the balance of payments will once again depend on the ability to sell overseas and in such circumstances one wonders how Britain could have allowed its manufacturing export position to decline so emphatically as to threaten its future economic well-being. There is no simple answer and in fact many influences have acted and interacted to promote decline and to hinder remedies being found and implemented.

The single most important factor in British overseas trade since the Second World War has been a lack of competitiveness. This inability to compete on pricing with overseas rivals stems from various causes. Firstly came the failure of British industry to invest sufficiently. While other countries in Western Europe were still undergoing reconstruction during the post-war boom British industry was able to operate successfully in overseas markets, despite using ageing equipment. Unfortunately the profits from this boom were not poured back into new capitalisation and by the early 1950s the advantage was lost. Secondly, and stemming partly from this low investment, was low productivity per worker. Yet even where new investment had taken place comparable to that in Europe productivity continued to be lower. The blame for this must be attached to Britain's system of industrial relations, whether it be management's inability to motivate and lead the workforce or the unwillingness of the workers to co-operate in the achievement of company objectives or a mixture of the two. Whatever the precise cause of the problem the roots must lie somewhere in Britain's strongly class-conscious industrial culture. Thirdly a high rate of inflation and overvalued currency combined to price Britain's products out of world markets in the 1960s and continued to be a problem in the 1980s when Britain's position as an oil-producer pushed up sterling's exchange rate. Fourthly was the failure of British overseas marketing techniques. In the 1950s too much emphasis had been placed on the slow-growth markets of the Commonwealth where however, it was relatively easier to market products due to common cultural and commercial ties. British exporters found it more difficult to go out and sell their products in the more competitive markets of Europe and North America and this competition was not based solely on price. British goods fell down on reliability, quality, delivery dates and after-sales service too. The other main

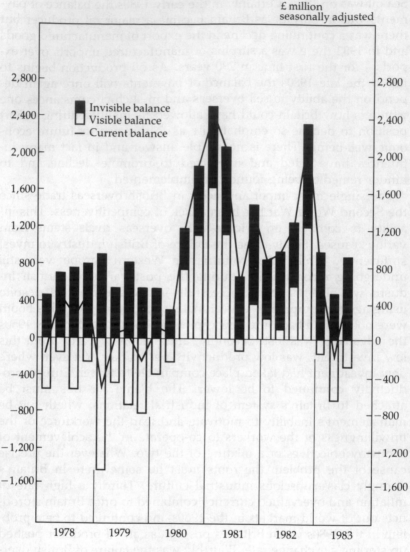

£ million
seasonally adjusted

■ Invisible balance
□ Visible balance
— Current balance

Source: *CSO Economic Trends*

Fig. 20.1   Balance of payments: current account

factor militating against a good export record was the poor performance of the UK economy, a performance which both springs from and reinforces the lack of overseas competitiveness. This lack of competitiveness leads to a decline in exports and a growth in imports and thus a balance of payments crisis which in turn leads to government action to reduce demand. A slowing of domestic demand growth deters investment and holds back the growth of productive capacity and product development so that manufacturers fall further behind their international rivals. When economic activity increases again industry is unable to cope with the demand and imports rush in to fill the gap, resulting in another balance of payments crisis. At the same time a slow overall growth rate leads to wage-earners seeking higher pay increases than the growth rate will support and results in further inflationary pressure and reduced competitiveness for domestic producers. It had been hoped that the bonanza of North Sea oil would provide the funds for remodernisation of British industry and a balance of payments surplus sufficient to enable governments to pursue policies of growth and development to prepare the economy for effective competition when the oil ran out. Unfortunately the deep and prolonged recession has meant that most of the oil revenue has gone on financing unemployment.

Questions for analysis

Table 20.7

Exports	600
Imports	700
Net property income from abroad	100
Banking, shipping and other services	+200
Tourism	−350
Public and private investment abroad	150
Overseas investment in the UK	100
Export credit	60
Import credit	140

1. From the figures in the above table calculate:

(a) The balance of trade
(b) The balance on invisibles
(c) The balance on current account
(d) The balance on investment and other capital flows.
(e) Given a repayment to the IMF of £100 million the total change in gold and foreign currency reserves.
(f) Given that the elasticity of demand for exports is 1.4 and that for imports is 1.2 what will be the effect on the balance of trade of a 10 per cent devaluation?
(g) What are the likely effects on the internal economy of such a devaluation?

2. Your company is a leading manufacturer of electrical goods in the UK. The Industry is highly competitive and in recent years the market has become increasingly infiltrated by goods from overseas manufacturers, notably Third World countries. At the same time your exports have been decreasing due to higher export prices, resulting both from the high external value of sterling and the high labour costs caused by poor productivity.

Analyse the likely effects on your home and overseas markets in each case of the following actions being taken by government authorities.

(a) The introduction of a 20 per cent VAT rate on all luxury goods by the British government.

(b) Subsidies granted by Far East Asian governments to industries producing electrical goods within their countries.

(c) The adoption of a policy of price controls by the British government.

What remedies are open to your company to deal with any problems so created?

Chapter 21

THE FINANCIAL STRUCTURE OF INTERNATIONAL TRADE

In the last chapter, the section on the terms of trade illustrated that, certainly so far as bilateral trade is concerned, it is possible to conduct trade on a barter basis, the rate of exchange between the two countries depending on the relative bargaining power of the two commodities. While such a system of barter could, with difficulty, be extended to multilateral trade, in the modern world economy it has given way to a system of trade based on the rate of exchange between the currencies of the various trading countries rather than on the rate of exchange between the actual goods traded. None the less barter trade is still quite common where one of the countries is short of foreign currency.

Exchange rates

The exchange rate between two currencies can be determined either by the purchasing power of one currency in relation to the other, i.e. by market forces, or by reference to some external standard of value recognised by all trading nations. Historically the most important external standard was the gold standard whereby countries kept the value of their principal monetary unit equal to the value of a defined weight of gold. During the late nineteenth century all the major trading nations were on the gold standard which meant that their currencies were freely convertible into gold, both domestically and externally, and also that the exchange rate between two currencies was closely related to the gold content of their respective monetary unit. Thus if the pound sterling weighed four times the American dollar and both contained the same purity of gold then £1 = \$4. There would, however, be some movement in exchange rates since the rate of one currency against another could fall marginally on the foreign exchange market before it became cheaper for an importer to pay the transport costs of shipping gold abroad rather than paying a debt by purchasing the necessary foreign currency.

The gold standard

The great advantage always claimed on behalf of the gold standard is that it is self-adjusting and thus acts to maintain the stability of exchange rates, restore balance of payments equilibrium and control movements in the domestic money supply. Exchange rates must reflect the relative gold content of the two currencies and thus can only move between fairly narrow limits but if a country experiences a serious drain on its gold and foreign currency reserves it would have to consider devaluing its currency by reducing the gold content of its monetary unit. A drain on the gold reserves would also affect the money supply since the majority of banknotes would be backed by gold and a reduction in the gold stock would thus lead to a contraction in the level of cash. At the same time the central bank would conduct open market operations to contract bank deposits. Under the gold standard the balance of payments would always return to equilibrium since if a country suffers a deficit the export of gold will lead to the monetary authorities introducing deflationary measures to contract the money supply and this in turn will result in lower prices as demand for goods and services drops. As lower prices will make exports more attractive it is to be expected that export receipts will rise and balance of payments equilibrium restored. Where a country had a balance of payments surplus an opposite sequence of events could be expected to occur.

In practice the gold standard never worked as well in operation as the theory suggested. It is true that while world trade was expanding and the world economy was buoyant the system appeared to work well but it was unable to cope with the strains placed upon it after the First World War. To begin with its greatest attribute – that of stability – depended on the world supply of gold growing at a steady rate and roughly in line with the growth of world trade. If it grew too quickly, as in the 1850s, world-wide inflation would result while if it grew too slowly this could have a depressing effect on the level of world trade. A second major difficulty arose over the conduct of monetary policy since the external situation would dictate the monetary measures to be pursued regardless of the state of the domestic economic situation. Thus if the economy is depressed and confidence low gold will leave the country and force the government to adopt deflationary measures and so worsen the depression. Yet the greatest failing of the gold standard, and the one which was ultimately to bring about its downfall, was its inability to function adequately in a crisis like that of the inter-war period. In order that the gold standard could work effectively gold movements had to be allowed to work freely on each country's price level so that an inflow of gold raised, and an outflow of gold lowered, the price level. In fact many countries, when faced with a serious depression, resorted to managing the gold standard to avoid the worst effects of the slump. Even where countries were prepared to 'obey the rules' circumstances were against them. Britain attempted to keep sterling at its pre-1914 international exchange rate and this entailed a policy of severe deflation to raise the internal purchasing power of the pound. Unfortunately while prices fell factor earnings, particularly wages, proved resilient to downward pressure so that dear-money deflationary measures had to be pursued with greater vigour even though there was high unemployment after 1920. The cumulative effect of all these factors, together with the international crisis sparked off by the 1929 Wall Street crash, led to the abandonment of the gold standard by most countries during the 1930s and years of international financial chaos.

Floating exchange rates

In the absence of an external standard exchange rates are determined by the interaction of the supply and demand for the currency in question priced in terms of another currency. The demand for a currency comes from those wishing to purchase goods in that currency and to invest in the currency. The supply of a currency comes from those who wish to exchange that currency for another in order to buy goods or to invest funds in that other currency.

In Fig. 21.1 the initial exchange rate for dollars is P_1 with the quantity of dollars traded at Q_1. An increase in demand for dollars by those holding sterling leads to a shift in demand from D_1 to D_2 and a new equilibrium exchange rate of P_2 with a new quantity of dollars traded at Q_2. This increase in the demand for dollars may stem from one of two main causes. Firstly British prices may have risen relative to American prices thus making American goods and

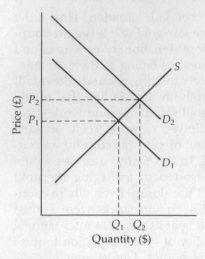

Fig. 21.1

services more attractive and shifting the balance of trade in
America's favour. The extent to which this is likely to happen depends on the elasticity of demand of the exports of the two countries. Thus Britain's terms of trade will have improved and if the
price elasticity of demand for her exports is less than one export
revenue will rise and American demand for sterling would rise too,
at least partially compensating for the increased demand for dollars
from British buyers. Relative inflation rates, therefore, must influence the exchange rate between two currencies. Secondly there is
the importance of interest rates since international investment
funds can be moved easily to the financial centres offering the highest rates; among the advanced countries at least higher interest
rates will increase demand for and strengthen a currency. Such
rises in exchange rates offer prospects of a profit on the rate of exchange itself and thus speculative demand for a currency is another
important cause of exchange rate fluctuations. Finally there is the
impact of economic and political events within countries. Thus
domestic economic or political difficulties or even uncertainty may
lead to a switch from sterling to dollars or vice versa. Furthermore
a depletion of official reserves which threatens the exchange rate
may lead to a switch out of a currency to avoid a loss in the value
of currency holdings. This presents a particular problem if there are
large holdings of the currency overseas as was the case when sterling was a reserve currency and was used by most Commonwealth
countries for the settlement of debts.

The main advantage of floating exchange rates is that they allow internal policy-making to be detached from the external economic position. Unlike the gold standard floating exchange rates permit a government to pursue expansionary domestic economic policies even when there is a deficit on the balance of payments since the deficit should lead to a fall in the exchange rate sufficient for export prices to fall enough to restore equilibrium on the balance of payments. In theory, therefore, there is less need for substantial gold and foreign currency reserves since a deficit should not last long enough for the drain on reserves to become serious. The other key advantage of floating exchange rates is that as rates can move up or down in response to market forces there is little danger of the currency becoming either greatly undervalued or greatly over-valued, and thus prone to the activities of speculators. On the other hand floating exchange rates do have their disadvantages. They tend to be more volatile and this may weaken the confidence of trading nations. Uncertainty about the future value of a currency may lead importers to buy foreign currency in advance of their needing it if they think the currency will become more expensive (a lead) and this will indeed push up the price of that currency. Similarly exporters may delay converting foreign currency earnings into their own currency if they feel that the foreign currency will appreciate and yield them a profit (a lag). This action will tend to make expectations come true as well as the artificial shortage of the foreign currency in question pushes up its exchange rate. Nor is there any guarantee that a floating exchange rate will cure a balance of payments problem. A falling exchange rate may lead investors to withdraw their funds and damage the position on capital account while neither exports nor imports may be sufficiently elastic in demand to compensate for the depreciation of the exchange rate. While the forward exchange market enables both exporters and importers to avoid the problems of uncertain future exchange rates, floating rates themselves add to the uncertainties of world trade and thus tend to be unsatisfactory during periods of instability in world trade like the 1930s.

Fixed exchange rates

The collapse of world trade and the uncertainties of floating exchange rates exposed by the experiences of the 1930s prompted a search for a compromise between the rigidity of the gold standard and the uncertainty of floating rates and culminated in the system of managed currencies which dominated the post-war period until the early 1970s. Clearly it is not possible to suspend market forces entirely and even with a regime of fixed exchange rates there must be marginal movements in the relative values of currencies. Where the system differs from that of floating rates is that countries undertake not to permit their currencies to deviate more than a certain percentage from the par rate of exchange against other currencies. Thus if the permitted deviation is 1 per cent either side of par the monetary authorities will intervene to prevent a breach of either the upper or the lower 1 per cent variation. If the rate threatened to rise above the upper peg the authorities would intervene to sell more of the country's currency, thereby increasing supply and pushing the exchange rate down. If the rate were in danger of breaching the lower peg the authorities would buy their own currency on the market to increase demand and push up the exchange rate. This is shown in Fig. 21.2 where an increase in the demand for sterling to D^1 threatens to force the exchange rate above the upper peg and leads the Bank of England to increase the supply of pounds and reduce upward pressure on the exchange rate.

Fixed exchange rates have the advantage that stable currencies are more conducive to the development of international trade than are floating currencies. However, as with the gold standard, governments must subordinate their domestic economic policies to

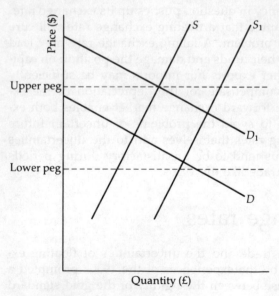

Fig. 21.2

the need to maintain an adequate balance of payments position and thus protect the exchange rate, resulting in Britain in the stop-go cycle of the 1950s and 1960s. This necessitates the holding of substantial gold and foreign currency reserves in order to be able to support the currency if necessary. At the same time there is always the danger that currency speculators may mount a concerted campaign to force either revaluation or devaluation on a currency and thus give themselves a substantial profit.

The International Monetary Fund

This agency was established at the end of the Second World War in response to the call at the Bretton Woods conference in 1944 for international co-operation to provide a strong framework for the promotion of world trade and international confidence following the disastrous experiences of the 1930s. The primary function of the IMF was to act as a bank to provide funds to countries which experienced balance of payments or other international liquidity difficulties and thus prevent excessive pressure on the gold and foreign currency reserves of individual countries. Indeed the very existence of this facility was seen as reducing the risk of pressure building up on a currency should it encounter temporary difficulties. Most of the independent countries of the world are now members of the IMF with the notable exception of the Soviet Union and some of her satellites. A keystone of the IMF system was, at the time of its foundation, an insistence on fixed exchange rates to help promote stability. Member countries would fix the value of their currencies in terms of gold or the US$, which itself was valued at the rate of $35 equals 1 oz. gold. There was thus still a watered down version of the gold standard with the dollar being internationally exchangeable for gold and other currencies indirectly linked to gold via the dollar. Each country was expected to take appropriate action to ensure that its exchange rate did not deviate by more than 1 per cent either side of its agreed par value. In order to maintain the stability of exchange rates the IMF opposed changes in the par values of currencies except where a persistent and incurable disequilibrium on the balance of payments showed that the currency in question was fundamentally out of line with its true international value. It was recognised that in such circumstances a deliberate and substantial revaluation or devaluation was preferable to continued speculation and uncertainty. Where difficulties were seen as temporary but none the less of serious concern for the member affected, the drawing (borrowing) facility was available.

The drawing rights of a member were determined by its quota or subscription to the Fund, the quota in turn being based on that country's importance as a trading nation. The first 25 per cent of the quota was to be in gold or $US and the remainder in the member country's own currency. The gold contribution to the quota was withdrawable as required while further drawings were to be available up to a maximum of twice the size of the original quota; though each successive drawing would be conditional on action being taken to deal with whatever crisis had precipitated the request for assistance. Thus the IMF facility to the UK in 1976 was made on the understanding that the British government would get the growth of the money supply under control and take steps to limit government expenditure. These principles still stand although in recent years the IMF has relaxed to some extent the stringency of its lending policy. Where pressure on a currency is the result of speculation rather than a real difficulty the IMF will grant a standby credit which can be drawn on if required and which itself is usually sufficient to lift the pressure.

The system of managed currencies came under increasing pressure itself in the 1960s. In part this was due to the growing weakness of the two reserve currencies, the dollar and the pound. A persistent balance of payments deficit in Britain and the steady deterioration in the United States' external position reduced confidence in both currencies and in the case of the dollar this was particularly worrying since that currency represented over 70 per cent of all official foreign exchange reserves. The strains placed on sterling led to its being phased out as a reserve currency in the early 1970s while by 1971 the rising market price of gold and the decision by France, in particular, to hold reserves in gold rather than dollars led to international confidence in the dollar weakening to such a point that its convertibility into gold could no longer be maintained, and the link with gold of the international monetary system was finally abandoned. The demonetisation of gold was now possible and both the IMF and the United States sold off large holdings of gold in the 1970s. The official unit of international liquidity used by the IMF was now the special drawing right unit. Special drawing rights (SDRs) had been introduced in 1970 to increase the world supply of liquidity and consist in effect of non-repayable credits given to IMF members, in proportion to their quotas, to be used to obtain required foreign currency by exchanging them with the appropriate country. Thus Britain can obtain Swedish krona by transferring some of its SDRs to Sweden in return for krona. The irregular expansion in the total SDR issue has enabled world liquidity

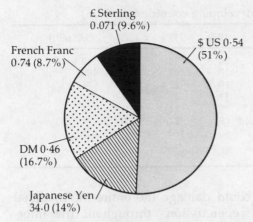

Fig. 21.3   Composition of the SDR unit

to grow more than would otherwise have been the case. The value of the SDR unit is expressed in a basket of currencies so that each member country's currency has an exchange rate against the SDR unit.

The end of the convertibility of the dollar also signalled a return to a system of floating exchange rates. In 1971 the growing instability of exchange rates led to a widening of the pegs within which currencies were allowed to move to 2¼ per cent either side of the par value but the growing instability of the system could not be halted and by 1973 all the major currencies of the world were floating. The new situation was recognised in 1978 when the IMF's rules were changed to charge it with the surveillance of the floating system. However, such surveillance is almost meaningless since most countries operate 'managed' or 'dirty' floating under which they keep the degree of the float within limits. Further problems for the IMF came after 1973 when the rise in oil prices led to a huge transfer of reserves to the oil-producing countries and created liquidity problems for the non-oil-producing developing countries. The world recession of the 1970s placed further strains on many countries and in the 1980s some Third World countries have come close to bankruptcy, such as Mexico and Nigeria. Even relatively advanced countries like Poland and Argentina have needed help in rescheduling their debts to the international banking community. Despite the increased assistance given to developing countries and the recycling of the oil-producers' reserves to the poorer nations via aid and the eurocurrency markets the international monetary system remains under threat of the collapse of one of the

Table 21.1   Total debts of the developing countries ($ billion)

Source of lending	1971	1975	1979	1982 (est.)
Official development assistance	24	34	53	63
Export credits	27	42	100	148
IMF, World Bank, etc.	10	22	47	76
Banks	11	49	131	210
Private borrowing and bond issues	9	11	31	55
Other including OECD countries' aid	9	22	43	74
Total	90	180	405	626

Source: OECD

poorer countries since this could damage the entire international banking system and have repercussions throughout the international community.

Questions for analysis

1. Consider the arguments for and against a return to the system of fixed exchange rates which prevailed until 1971.
2. 'With the demonetisation of gold international trade can be conducted on acceptability and trust in the various forms of international liquidity in much the same way as domestic trade.'
   (a) What are the main forms of international liquidity in use?
   (b) What weaknesses are present in the financing of international trade which are not present in domestic trade?

Chapter 22

INTERNATIONAL ECONOMIC ORGANISATIONS

The development of international trading associations and companies is a natural development of the principle of economies of scale. Firms benefit from economies of scale by expanding their scale of operations while countries benefit from international economies of scale by specialising in the goods and services where their proficiency is highest. These principles can be extended so that international companies can benefit from large-scale production spread over a number of countries while whole countries can form larger trading blocs so that they faciliate the development of internal specialisation. The need to assess the importance of multinational companies and international trading blocs separately arises from the tendency for them to develop individual characteristics peculiar to such institutions. Thus multinational companies behave differently to large national companies while economic units made up of several states do not behave like large nation-states.

International trade associations

It is important here to distinguish between associations formed and agreements made to promote freer trade between nations and an association formed to promote trade between the members to the exclusion, or at least disadvantage, of countries not party to the agreement. In the late nineteenth century this difference manifested itself in the different attitudes of those in favour of free trade and those who supported Imperial preference. Since the last war the two strains of development have been represented by the General Agreement on Tariffs and Trade (GATT) and the various economic trading blocs such as the European Economic Community (EEC) and Comecon. While GATT has strived to reduce the barriers to trade for the benefit of all trading nations the EEC and similar other bodies have tended to be inward-looking and more concerned with improving trade relations with each other rather than with the rest of the world.

GATT

Against the background of the collapse of international trading confidence of the 1930s and the wave of protectionism which had followed it the United Nations planned in 1947 the establishment of the Organisation for Trade Co-operation. Pending the formation of this body the General Agreement on Tariffs and Trade was established as an interim measure. Unfortunately disputes over terms of reference meant that the Organisation for Trade Co-operation never actually came into existence so GATT acquired a permanent position in world trade. The aim of GATT is to achieve a reduction in the barriers to world trade and to this end regular conferences have been held, resulting in member countries reducing tariffs on a reciprocal basis. The last major round of tariff cuts followed the Tokyo conference of 1973. Unfortunately the world recession of the 1970s led to a revival of interest in protective tariffs and at the GATT conference in 1983 most of the running was made by those countries wishing to increase tariffs. Ultimately a compromise resolution by Canada led to tariffs being held at current levels though, ominously, the matter remains subject to future review. Central to the working of GATT is the 'most favoured nation clause' which provides that every tariff concession agreed between any group of countries must be extended to all members of GATT so that countries may be unwilling to reduce tariffs with one country if this means extending the same concession to certain other countries. However GATT does allow developing countries more leeway in the imposition of trade restrictions and also permits members to establish customs unions and free trade areas although such associations do result in discrimination against countries which are not members of these associations.

Customs unions and free trade areas

A customs union is an arrangement between two or more countries whereby tariffs between the members are abolished and a common external tariff is established. Such customs unions as the German *Zollverein* of the nineteenth century and Benelux established after the Second World War are examples of this. Clearly such arrangements require a supra-national agency to control the workings of the union and members are thus bound by treaty obligations and acceptance of some loss of sovereignty – indeed they have often been forerunners to formal political unification. Free trade areas are weaker arrangements in that member states retain the right to determine their own external tariffs. The only agreement made is that of free trade between members and this requires neither a loss of sovereignty nor a supra-national institution. An example of this was the European Free Trade Association established in 1957 by the UK, Sweden, Denmark, Norway, Switzerland, Austria and Portugal and to which some other European states, like Finland and Iceland, later affiliated.

The European Economic Community

In the years of reconstruction after the Second World War there was considerable support for a movement towards European unity as evidenced by the formulation of the Organisation for European Economic Co-operation in 1948 and the Council of Europe in 1949, the former to foster economic co-operation and the latter a common acceptance of human rights and rule of law. While all the states of Western Europe became members of these two organisations closer co-operation was centred on the 'six' – Belgium. Netherlands and Luxemburg (who had formed Benelux already) together with Germany, France and Italy. For these countries economic and political co-operation offered the opportunity to reduce the antagonisms which had pervaded Western Europe for centuries and led to so many major conflicts between these nations. On the positive side closer alignment would restore and reanimate the close political links which the six had shared at various times in the past. When in 1951 the European Coal and Steel Community (ECSC) was established as a common market in coal and steel with no discrimination between the 'six' it was endowed with a supra-national institutional structure and an executive body having the power to make decisions binding on all the member countries. Those in Europe strongly committed to political unification hoped that the ECSC would lay the foundations for a European Defence Community and the integration of Europe's armed forces and defence structure under a unified command. It was the implication of future political and defence integration which deterred Britain from joining the ECSC until 1954 though in fact the European Defence Community never did materialise.

The economic co-operation stimulated by the ECSC was further extended by the formation in 1957 of the European Economic Community through the Treaty of Rome. The six now committed themselves to eventual economic and political union though as the member countries had steadily regained their national self-confidence and prosperity during the 1950s the latter objective was accorded little attention. The main aim was the creation of an economic unit of comparable size, wealth and influence to that of the United States in order to enable Europe to compete on equal terms and resist further Americanisation of the European economy. From a position of economic strength Europe would then be able to assert its freedom of political action from the American and Russian superpowers, even if it did not in the process result in one European state.

THE INSTITUTIONS OF THE COMMUNITY

The institutions established under the Treaty of Rome reflect the concern of the member countries to protect their national interest and this is shown by the extent to which each institution is composed of representatives of each country.

THE COMMISSION

This body has two members from each of the larger states and one each from the remainder. It heads the bureaucracy of the Community and is responsible for day-to-day administration, co-ordination of the policies of member states, the execution of policy and the enforcement of regulations. The commissioners are appointed for four-year terms, renewable for a further two years, and each is responsible for one or more of the various departments of the Commission which encompass the various activities of the community. From among the commissioners are chosen the prestigious offices of President and Vice-President – posts which are rotated among the member countries. Decisions of the Commission are taken by a simple majority but they must then be referred to the Council of Ministers for approval.

THE COUNCIL OF MINISTERS

The Council is formed from ministers from each of the member countries though the ministers at particular meetings of the Council vary depending on the issue under consideration – those most commonly attending tend to be Heads of Government, Foreign Ministers and Agricultural Ministers. The Presidency of the Council is rotated from one country to another on a six-monthly basis and the Presidents' role is a crucial one in that he or she is required to find conciliation and consensus from among the disputes which frequently rack ministerial meetings. The function of the Council is to consider proposals placed before it by the Commission and it may overrule any recommendations made. It is here that disputes over policies are fought out and progress in the Community's work is either made or retarded so that it is the Council of Ministers which takes the final decision on such matters as the budget, agricultural policy, foreign policy matters relating to the Community as a whole and so on. Though $\frac{2}{3}$ majority voting is in theory the procedure of the Council it is so difficult to impose a policy on a country which dissents that in practice all important votes tend to be unanimous. The voting system gives votes to each country according to its size but the smaller countries are given enough votes to ensure that they can block a decision supported only by the larger countries.

THE PARLIAMENT

The title of this body is something of a misnomer since although elected by universal suffrage it is not a parliament in the true sense of the word. Ministers are not responsible to it and it may not legislate on its own initiative. Thus the parliament is more like the English House of Commons of the sixteenth century or the French parlements of the eighteenth century – a place for debate, the airing of grievances and, in exceptional cases, the rejection of ministerial legislation. Its greatest strength lies in the area of the budget as it may approve the budget, amend it through an increase in certain areas of expenditure or reject it outright. If the last course is taken Parliament and ministers must seek to arrive at a compromise solution. In other matters the parliament has the right to criticise the laws introduced by the Commission but may not change them, the only sanction being the dismissal of the Commission through passing a censure motion having the support of two-thirds majority. Concerted action by Euro-MPs is frustrated by the fragmented structure of the parliament with ten different nationalities and only loose groupings of the various parties represented – indeed MPs are just as likely to vote on national as on party lines.

THE COURT OF JUSTICE

The Court is a supreme supra-national court of ten judges appointed by the member countries for a six-year term and assisted by four advocates-general. The Court deals with disputes between member states, disputes between member states and the institutions of the Community and disputes between individuals or corporate bodies and the institutions of the Community. Thus it frequently is called upon to settle disputes between the Commission and industrial countries refusing to accept the regulations of the Commission. Though in theory supreme it has no power to enforce its findings and depends upon the acceptance of its decisions by the parties to a dispute. The Court has no power to intervene in the internal civil or criminal proceedings of member states.

From the institutions outlined above have developed over seventy specialist agencies, many of them dealing with areas of economic policy and development and the work of some of these will be examined in subsequent sections.

THE MOVES TOWARDS ECONOMIC INTEGRATION

The Treaty of Rome specifically called for both economic and political unification of the signatory states. To date, however, it is primarily in the economic sphere that progress has been made and even here advances have been more significant in some areas than others.

1. *Customs union.* By July 1968 the six original members of the community had established a customs union. When the UK, Ireland and Denmark signed the Treaty of Accession in 1972 they were given until July 1977 to come into line with a common external tariff. This they did and in April 1979 the common external tariff was fixed at 7.5 per cent following the Tokyo round of tariff reductions. Greece became a full member in 1981 and similarly brought her external tariff into line. In theory the common external tariff could be expected to apply equally to all non-member countries but the situation has been complicated by the existence of past close trading relationships with non-member countries. Thus in 1957 France still had a large overseas empire while Belgium and the Netherlands also had overseas dependent territories. Similarly the UK had historical trading links with many Commonwealth countries as well as a long-standing free trade agreement with those members of the European Free Trade Association who had not joined the Community. The result has been a number of free trade and other agreements with non-member states, most notably the two Lomé Conventions with former dependent territories.

The Community has also worked towards the removal of such obstacles to trade as the imposition of rigid technical specifications on imports. Such obstacles are more difficult to outlaw by the regulations on free trade between members and, despite the Commission's efforts, have proved difficult to remove.

2. *Free movement of capital and labour.*   It has often been said that international trade substitutes the movement of goods for that of factors of production. For a community intent on economic integration, however, the free movement of factors of production is essential if progress is to be made beyond the establishment of a free trade area. Such interchange of resources is required in the development of larger multinational organisations which can achieve the economies of scale and the market size necessary to be able to rival the largest American companies. Furthermore the ability of firms to expand their operations without hindrance in overseas markets is likely to provide greater competition and choice which will be of benefit to the consumer. In this area progress has been promising and work permits are no longer required between member countries while companies have both expanded their overseas operations and increased the number of cross-nation mergers.

3. *Controls over cartels, restrictive practices and monopoly power.*   As well as encouraging the development of European multinational companies to increase competitiveness, the EEC has also sought through legislation to hinder the development of cartels and monopolies, whether national or international; indeed Articles 85 and 86 specifically forbid any restrictive practices or monopolies which restrict or distort trade between member countries. Most European countries already had some legislative codes dealing with these areas so only those EEC regulations which go beyond existing legislation in a particular country apply in that case. The role of administering the regulations falls on the Commission which may act on its own initiative or after receiving complaints from interested parties. In addition the Commission has shown increasing interest in the field of consumer protection, and in 1973 established the Consumers' Consultative Committee with representatives from major consumer groups. Resulting from recommendations by this Committee there have been issued regulations on health and safety standards, unfair sales practices, misleading advertising, consumer credit and opportunities for the redress of complaints. Many of the Commission's aims are embodied in the national legislation of member countries but it has been particularly active on its own account in the area of the supply of information. The legislation of the Commission regarding the behaviour of firms applies not only to companies domiciled within one of the countries of the Community but also the multinational companies operating within the Community.

4. *Agricultural self-sufficiency.* From its inception a key aim of the Community was the attainment of self-sufficiency in food production since the Community was the largest importer of agricultural produce in the world and this was thus an area in which the Community could suffer hardship if dependent excessively upon external supplies. Furthermore agriculture remained the single most important industry in the Community, employing as it did some 10 per cent of the working population. In order to stimulate output the Common Agricultural Policy (CAP) was formulated and brought into effect in 1968. Firstly it provides for a system of grants to enable farmers to modernise their methods through the introduction of modern machinery and technical expertise. Secondly it seeks to remove the uncertainties traditionally associated with the pricing of agricultural products which lead to resistance against increasing output – farmers tending to fare better when outputs are low and prices high than when a glut forces down market prices. The CAP seeks to avoid the problem of volatile prices by setting target prices for most agricultural products each year. An intervention price is then set at around 5 per cent below the target price and if the market price falls to this level the agricultural authorities undertake to buy up surplus production – this surplus production being intended to provide buffer stocks against periods of low production. While farmers within the Community receive a price somewhere between the intervention price and the target price and well above the world market price the risk of their being undercut by cheap foreign imports is countered by importers having to pay a levy to bring their prices up to the target prices.

5. *Regional and social development.* Like individual member states the Community has been keen to remove some of the worst inequalities of wealth between the various regions of the Community by provision of funds for new industrial development, the modernisation of long-established industries and the improvement of communications – such grants coming from the Regional Fund of the community. In addition loans for the modernisation of the coal and steel industries are available from the ECSC while the European Investment Bank also provides loans for new industrial development – particularly in development areas. Equally of importance to the UK is the Social Fund which makes grants to provide youth training and retraining for the unemployed.

6. *Monetary union.* Further economic integration eventually requires monetary co-operation among the member states and this

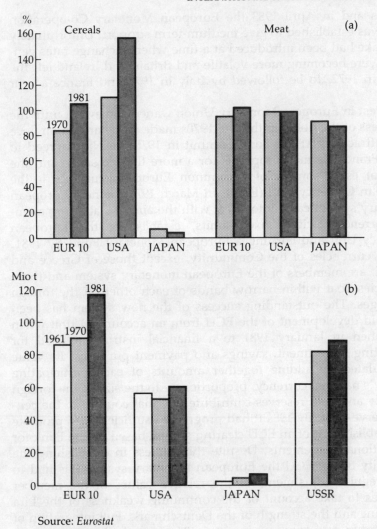

Source: *Eurostat*

Fig. 22.1(a) Degree of self-sufficiency of cereals and meat (b) Production of whole milk

fact was recognised in the decision of March 1971 to work towards European monetary union by 1981. In that year the 'Snake' was introduced whereby Common Market currencies were to move within narrower limits in their rates of exchange with each other than the limits prescribed by the IMF. To aid the new system member countries increased their subscriptions to the reserve pool established the previous year to assist countries in short-term difficulties and in April 1983 the European Monetary Co-operation Fund was established to give medium-term support. Unfortunately the Snake had been introduced at a time when exchange rates generally were becoming more volatile and Britain and Ireland left the Snake in 1972, to be followed by Italy in 1973 and France a year later.

Interest in European Monetary Union waned somewhat until the weakness of the dollar in the late 1970s made monetary union once more attractive. At the Bonn Summit in 1978 the Nine agreed to study Franco-German proposals for a more flexible snake and the eventual establishment of a common European currency – the European Currency Unit (ECU). In March 1979 the new European monetary system came into effect with the aim of stabilising member currencies within fixed limits, establishing the European Currency Unit and creating a European Monetary Fund by 1981. All the currencies of the Community, except those of Greece and the UK, are members of the European monetary system and these currencies float within narrow bands of each other on the foreign exchanges. The outstanding success of the new system has been the rapid development of the ECU from an accounting unit when established in January 1981 to a financial instrument used for accounting, investment, savings and payment purposes. Its value is calculated by adding together amounts of each participating country's national currency, proportionate to the size of the foreign currency and gold reserves contributed by that country to the central reserve pool. By 1984 it had progressed sufficiently to promote the establishment of an ECU clearing system based on the Bank for International Settlements. Despite this success in establishing the credibility of the ECU the European monetary system has had to make regular adjustments of the relative values of the member countries to take account of the continuing weakness of the Lira and Franc and the strength of the Deutschmark. Full integration of the member countries' currencies will require both a greater co-ordination of their economic and monetary policies and, eventually, a European central bank.

PROBLEMS OF THE EUROPEAN ECONOMIC COMMUNITY

Despite the undoubted successes achieved by the EEC over its thirty-year history it remains nearer to a group of nation-states joined together in a free trade area with other areas of common action than a confederation of states accepting supra-national integration, co-operation and direction of their economic and political affairs. Internal squabbles and rivalries and the adoption of nationalist stances have delayed progress in many key areas and accounted for the problems encountered in the 1980s. Whatever the aspirations and ideals of the founding fathers of the Community most of the member countries judge the value of membership on a cost-benefit basis and when vital interests appear threatened the European ideal, too, is soon under threat.

The experiences of the UK since becoming a member of the EEC illustrate the fundamental problems facing the Community. When Britain joined most fears centred on the unrealistic prospect of a diminution of national sovereignty – unrealistic in the sense that Britain chooses to subject itself to EEC regulations and like Greenland in 1983 it can withdraw from the Community whenever it pleases. At the same time it was realised that there would be a price to pay for membership in terms of a deficit on the balance of payments – both as a result of the net contribution to the Community budget and in the form of higher food prices than would have been paid to traditional suppliers. However it was anticipated that there would be changes in the structure of the Community's finances in the future which would reduce this burden. In addition Britain was expected to benefit directly from industrial and other EEC grants, from access to a larger 'home' market and from greater technological co-operation between member states, particularly in pooling development resources. Indirectly membership was expected to

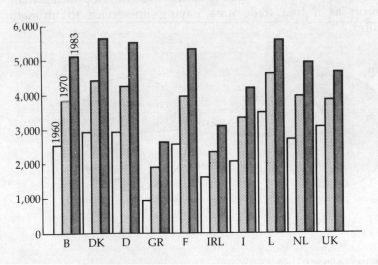

Source: *Eurostat*

Fig. 22.2 Gross domestic product at market prices per inhabitant, in real terms

provide a stimulus to both export growth and economic growth. That the reality has been less than expected stems partly from the failure of the British economy to withstand unrestricted European competition and partly from the failure of the Community to transcend its inter-nation disputes and rivalries and go on to develop as expected.

The world recession of the 1970s inevitably made all countries more defensive of their economies and as the EEC continued to be bogged down with an overemphasis on agriculture Britain was cast as the 'anti-European' always seeking to fight the rest for narrow self-interest, particularly over the budget. In reality the problem facing Britain throughout the late 1970s and early 1980s was that as the seventh richest member of the EEC in terms of *per capita* income she was expected to pay sometimes a larger net contribution to the budget than all the others put together. While no country should be obsessed with always getting out what it puts in, nor should any country consistently be a net contributor if not one of the richer members. In 1980 the net budget contribution was reduced but by 1984 it had once again reached extreme proportions. With other minor squabbles between members on matters affecting the vital interests of one or other country the position has been reached where the EEC could face a real threat of bankruptcy and even if this threat does not materialise the Community needs a major rethink in attitudes if it is to continue to develop rather than stagger on as a free trade area paying lip-service to ultimate integration.

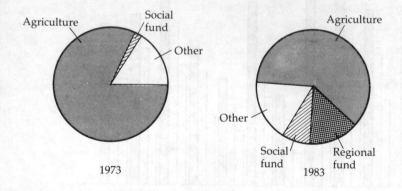

Source: *Eurostat*

Fig. 22.3 Distribution of the expenditure of the general budget of the European Communities

Multinational companies

Just as countries benefit from uniting into larger units for the purposes of trade and international specialisation the multinational companies enjoy the advantages of international economies of scale and being regarded as a 'home industry' in more than one country. By the late nineteenth century many European and American companies were establishing overseas subsidiaries to avoid tariff barriers or to benefit from ample supplies of cheap labour. However, the greatest period of multinational growth came after the last war. In the process of reconstruction in Europe, American companies avoided European tariff barriers by establishing European subsidiaries, a move welcomed by European governments who saw improvements in employment opportunities and capital investment levels without a continued drain on foreign currency reserves. Earlier in the chapter reference was made to the encouragement given to European multinationals by the EEC and in the 1960s and 1970s there was a rapid growth in European multinational companies alongside those of America and Britain, and European companies increasingly began to establish their own subsidiaries in America, especially during the period of the weak dollar in the late 1970s. However, with European labour now as expensive as American, the emphasis in the 1970s shifted to the establishment of subsidiaries in the more stable Asian countries where American and European multinationals were joined by Japanese companies to make use of unskilled labour at cheap rates of pay as mass-production techniques were applied to more and more industries. The growing prosperity of the Asian economies enabled the development, by 1980, of Hong Kong, Korean and Taiwanese multinationals – themselves able to use local or neighbouring supplies of cheap labour.

Multinational operations may take many forms. The commonest form originally was the vertically integrated company with the parent company producing goods in the home country using raw materials supplied by the overseas subsidiary – Brooke Bond and Unilever are examples of this form. In the present century the horizontally integrated company, such as General Motors or IBM, has become more common with the parent company having a number of overseas subsidiaries all producing the same or similar products in different countries. Of increasing importance in recent years is the reverse vertical operation where the parent company produces its goods in less developed countries to benefit from cheap labour or other cost advantages and then exports them back to the home market or other sales area.

ECONOMIC IMPACT OF MULTINATIONALS

The size of the multinational companies in terms of sales and assets is such that they rival the national incomes of smaller developed countries and often completely overshadow those of the under-developed countries within which they operate. Their existence and methods of operations raise questions both for the parent country from which they originate and the host country to which they spread their operations.

The parent country.   Traditionally countries benefited from overseas expansion by companies domiciled in them because for a prosperous country with full employment and a healthy balance of payments foreign investment provided a means of utilising surplus funds to increase the company's productive capacity and perhaps increase the flow of goods available to the home market, in particular vital supplies of raw materials. Despite the fact that foreign investment represented a deficit on the balance of payments capital account this would be compensated, in the long run, by the flow of dividends and interest repatriated by the parent company's subsidiaries. Of increasing concern, however, has been the extent to which the multinational is directing resources from the development of domestic productive capacity and the creation of employment so that in pursuit of higher profits the company may increasingly neglect the country in which it began – British shipping lines using foreign-registered ships or seamen is one example; closing down British factories to open in a poor country would be another.

The host country.   Firstly it must be stated that when a multinational company opens a subsidiary company it brings several advantages to the host country. Firstly it contributes to the balance of payments in the export of raw materials or finished goods to the multinational's other markets and in the saving on foreign currency brought about by the replacement of imports by domestically-produced goods. Secondly the country gains from the new technology introduced by the multinational provided that the technology is of use to the host country and is passed on to the workforce in training and the imparting of expertise – there is little gain if the local workforce are not recruited for skilled work. Thirdly their employment opportunities will be stimulated by the presence of the multinational corporation either directly through the employment by the company of a substantial local workforce or indirectly through the multinational's own spending on local goods and services creating work opportunities. However, the multinational may also pose a threat to the host country because decisions are taken outside the country which may do harm to its economic policies and the activities of the company may aim to minimise the effect of controls to which it is subject in both the parent and host country.

The first problem arises over taxation. Clearly the multinational will wish to minimise its tax burden and it will therefore be attracted to those locales where taxation is lowest or it will seek to ensure that profits if not output are concentrated in that base of operations. If tax rates are lower in the host country there will be an incentive to reinvest profits made in the host country back into the local economy and to move the parent company's profits to the subsidiary. The opposite will be true if tax rates are lower in the parent country. This movement of profits cannot be accomplished openly without the risk of one government or the other taking action so a system of transfer pricing is used. Transfer pricing is the practice of selling goods between parent company and subsidiary at artificial prices higher or lower than would be the case if the two companies were independent concerns. Thus if tax rates are lower in the host country the parent company will sell goods to its subsidiary at low prices, thus reducing the profits of the parent company and raising those of the subsidiary. The only limit on transfer pricing is the fear of provoking all governments to clamp down collectively on this form of tax avoidance.

The second question concerns the movement of capital. By having subsidiaries in different countries and thus access to several financial markets the multinational has the opportunity to reduce its borrowing costs for the whole corporation by borrowing where the cost is lowest and transferring the funds where they are needed, if necessary through transfer pricing to avoid government restrictions on the movement of capital. Related to this question is that of currency movements. The multinational is concerned not only with the interest rates offered in different financial centres but also with the strength of particular currencies – it may well be worth borrowing in a depreciating currency even if interest rates are high since the principal will be falling in value against other currencies. The desire to hold assets in hard currencies and liabilities in weak ones leads the multinationals to be very active both in the foreign exchange and the eurocurrency markets and they can do great damage to particular currencies by their activities – in particular they may weaken further an already weak currency by pulling all their funds out of it.

Thirdly the multinational poses problems for the host country's control over its own economy – and potentially even over its sovereignty. While the multinational shares a common interest with the government in promoting a healthy economy the government will at times wish to pursue economic objectives contrary to the short-term advantage of particular industries and in such circumstances the government is less likely to receive understanding for its policies from a multinational than from a national company. The host government may even be forced to moderate its policies to obtain the co-operation of a multinational, particularly as the multinational is less susceptible to government pressure because of its world-wide interests, and because it might threaten to shift planned new investment to other countries or even close down altogether.

THE MULTINATIONAL VERSUS THE NATIONAL COMPANY

Apart from the problems caused for the host nation's government the multinational also enjoys a number of advantages over the purely national company and this may hamper the development in newly emergent countries of their own competitive domestic industry. Furthermore the multinational possesses considerable advantages over the well-established national company in the developed economies. These advantages are:

1. They can make greater use of such international economies of scale as the use of cheap labour, internationally based marketing strategies, financial and taxation economies.
2. The ability of the multinational to offer higher rates of pay may attract skilled workers from local firms and disrupt the labour market.
3. To attract the investment of a multinational the host government may be prepared to offer tax and location concessions and subsidies not normally available to a local company.
4. They enjoy stronger bargaining power in their dealings with trade unions since they can threaten to move their operations elsewhere and they can use this threat to play the workers of one country off against those of another.
5. The multinational can exert a degree of market dominance in a number of countries. In each national market the multinational differs from its rivals in that by exploiting its scale advantages it can undercut its rivals' prices. Their impact on the industry will

be to reduce competition by taking over weak firms or forcing them out of the market, though once dominant the multinational may force up prices, reduce choice and impose products suitable to their international scale of operations but not necessarily appropriate to local needs.

CONTROL OVER MULTINATIONALS

The activities of the multinationals and their impact on the economies within which they operate led to increasing hostility towards them in the 1970s to the extent of greater efforts being made to control their activities. The regulations imposed by some states have become sufficiently rigorous as to deter some multinationals from further expansion in those countries and include price controls, taxation or limitation of repatriated profits, insistence on part-ownership by the host government or a local company, quotas on the use of foreign labour and insistence on the use of local supplies or components. In the ultimate case of such controls being ineffective the host government may even consider nationalisation or expulsion.

The greatest hopes for successful regulation of the multinationals lie, however, with international organisations. In 1976 the Organisation for Economic Co-operation and Development drew up a voluntary code of conduct for multinational companies to ensure that they behave with propriety in the movement of capital to and from member countries where conflict with national governments or other organisations such as trade unions might occur. In 1979 the EEC supplemented the code as far as activities within its borders are concerned by legislation to ensure that trade unions are consulted by companies on any decision to move production or close plants. Multinational expansion within the EEC is likely to be made more difficult in any case with the emergence of stricter controls on merger activity. Similar controls exist in other parts of the world and various attempts have been made to bring these controls under the umbrella of the United Nations. Though, as so often, little progress has been made along these lines it is likely that the late 1980s will witness an extension of multinational regulation – at least on a regional, if not a global, basis.

Cases for discussion

1. Your company has for many years operated both as a manufacturer and distributor of toys, many of your products being im-

ported from Third World countries for resale. The EEC has introduced new tighter regulations to ensure that the standards of toys available within the EEC are harmonised.

(a) What problem areas are likely to result from such harmonisation of standards by the EEC?

(b) Consider the steps which will need to be taken to deal with such problems.

(c) Assess the impact of your decisions on the company's costing, pricing and sales policies.

2. Your company is a leading multinational manufacturer of medicines and drugs operating in the UK. One of your products has been accused of causing personality changes and mental instability in some of its users and this has resulted in a campaign to have the product banned by a pressure group composed of members of the medical profession and consumers' associations. Their activities have led to adverse publicity for your company in the press and on television and aroused concern at the Department of Health and in Parliament. Despite the publication by your firm of extensive research papers and reports supporting your case that the product cannot be held responsible for the alleged mishaps sales have dropped substantially and the threat of a ban on sales of the product has become very real.

Discuss the political and economic options open to your company to convince the government and other interested parties to change their position.

FURTHER READING

General economic texts

P. Hardwick, B. Khan and J. Langmead, *Introduction to Modern Economics*, Longman, 1982

D. Begg, S. Fischer and R. Dornbusch, *Economics*, McGraw-Hill, 1984

A. Griffiths & S. Wall, *Applied Economics*, Longman, 1984

Micro-economic theory

P. J. Curwen, *The Theory of the Firm*, Macmillan, 1976

S. J. Prais, *The Evolution of Giant Firms in Britain*, CUP, 1976

R. Turvey, *Demand and Supply*, Allen & Unwin, 1980

A. Koutsoyiannis, *Modern Microeconomics*, Macmillan, 1979

Business economics

G. S. Hardern, *Business Organisation and Management*, Philip Allan, 1978

N. Branton & J. M. Livingstone, *Managerial Economics*, Hodder & Stoughton, 1979

J. Dewhurst & P. Burns, *Small Business*, Macmillian, 1983

H. Armstrong & J. Taylor, *Regional Economic Policy and its Analysis*, Philip Allan, 1978

C. Carter (ed.), *Industrial Policy and Innovation*, Heinemann, 1981

Labour economics

C. Mulvey, *The Economic Analysis of Trade Unions*, Martin Robertson, 1978
J. E. King (ed.), *Readings in Labour Economics*, OUP, 1980
F. Blackaby (ed.), *The Future of Pay Bargaining*, Heinemann, 1980

Finance and monetary economics

R. Evans & G. H. Makepeace, *Monetary Theory, Institutions and Practice*, Macmillan, 1979
M. Fleming, *Monetary Theory*, Macmillan, 1972
P. Browning, *Economic Images*, Longman, 1983
E. R. Shaw, *The London Money Market*, Heinemann, 1984

Macro-economic theory

J. Brooks & R. W. Evans, *Macroeconomic Policy in Theory and Practice*, Allen & Unwin, 1978
G. Stanlake, *Macro-Economics. An Inttroduction*, Longman, 1985
R. Bacon & W. Eltis, *Britain's Economic Problem*, Macmillan, 1978
W. Beckerman (ed.), *Slow Growth in Britain: Causes and Consequences*, OUP, 1980
M. H. Peston, *The British Economy*, Philip Allan, 1978

Government economic policy

J. Wright, *Britain in the Age of Economic Management*, OUP, 1979
M. Posner, *Demand Management*, Heinemann, 1979
J. L. Fallick & R. F. Elliot, *Incomes Policies, Inflation and Relative Pay*, Allen & Unwin, 1981
G. A. Renton, *Modelling the Economy*, Heinemann, 1975

International economics

J. Williamson, *The Open Economy and the World Economy*, Harper & Row, 1984

N. Hood & S. Young, *The Economics of Multinational Enterprise*, Longman, 1979

G. Zis, *The Balance of Payments*, Philip Allan, 1978

R. I. McKinnon, *Money in International Exchange: The Convertible Banking System*, OUP, 1980

C. Milner & D. Greenaway, *An Introduction to International Economics*, Longman, 1979

P. Robson, *The Economics of International Integration*, Allen & Unwin, 1984

S. Lall, *The Multinational Corporation*, Macmillan, 1980

INDEX